Bipolar Disorder

Recent Titles in
Q&A Health Guides

Schizophrenia: Your Questions Answered
Romeo Vitelli

Gender Identity and Expression: Your Questions Answered
M. Killian Kinney

Periods: Your Questions Answered
Cristina R. Giambalvo

Bipolar Disorder

Your Questions Answered

Victor B. Stolberg

BLOOMSBURY ACADEMIC
NEW YORK • LONDON • OXFORD • NEW DELHI • SYDNEY

BLOOMSBURY ACADEMIC
Bloomsbury Publishing Inc, 1359 Broadway, New York, NY 10018, USA
Bloomsbury Publishing Plc, 50 Bedford Square, London, WC1B 3DP, UK
Bloomsbury Publishing Ireland, 29 Earlsfort Terrace, Dublin 2, D02 AY28, Ireland

BLOOMSBURY, BLOOMSBURY ACADEMIC and the Diana logo are trademarks of Bloomsbury Publishing Plc

First published in the United States of America 2026

A catalogue record for this book is available from the British Library.

A catalog record for this book is available from the Library of Congress.

ISBN: HB: 979-8-7651-1416-2
ePDF: 979-8-7651-1417-9
eBook: 979-8-7651-1418-6

Series: Q&A Health Guides

Typeset by Integra Software Services Pvt. Ltd.
Printed and bound in the United States of America

For product safety related questions contact productsafety@bloomsbury.com.

To find out more about our authors and books visit www.bloomsbury.com and sign up for our newsletters.

This Book is Dedicated
To the Memory of
Peter L. Myers, Ph.D.
(1942–2020)

Contents

Series Foreword

All of us have questions about our health. Is this normal? Should I be doing something differently? Whom should I talk to about my concerns? And our modern world is full of answers. Thanks to the internet, there's a wealth of information at our fingertips, from forums where people can share their personal experiences to Wikipedia articles to the full text of medical studies. But finding the right information can be an intimidating and difficult task—some sources are written at too high a level, others have been oversimplified, while still others are heavily biased or simply inaccurate. *Q&A Health Guides* address the needs of readers who want accurate, concise answers to their health questions, authored by reputable and objective experts, and written in clear and easy-to-understand language. This series focuses on the topics that matter most to young adult readers, including various aspects of physical and emotional well-being as well as other components of a healthy lifestyle. These guides will also serve as a valuable tool for parents, school counselors, and others who may need to answer teens' health questions. All books in the series follow the same format to make finding information quick and easy. Each volume begins with an essay on health literacy and why it is so important when it comes to gathering and evaluating health information. Next, the top five myths and misconceptions that surround the topic are dispelled. The heart of each guide is a collection of questions and answers, organized thematically. A selection of five case studies provides real-world examples to illuminate key concepts. Rounding out each volume are a directory of resources, glossary, and index. It is our hope that the books in this series will not only provide valuable information but also help guide readers toward a lifetime of healthy decision-making.

Acknowledgments

I would like to take this brief opportunity to acknowledge and thank my family, particularly my wife and two growing sons, for their patience, ongoing support, and forbearance during the time I devoted to this project. I would most wholeheartedly like to thank all of the staff and consultants behind the scenes at Bloomsbury Publishing for helping to bring this work to completion. Chiefly, I thoroughly wish to thank Maxine Taylor, Senior Acquisitions Editor, Reference for ABC-CLIO/Bloomsbury, without whom this journey would not have been taken in the first place and who cheerfully guided me safely through to completion. I have had the pleasure of working for and with Maxine for some time now on several projects and have come to deeply appreciate the many roles she plays with utmost professionalism and, more importantly, with a generous and gracious personality.

Introduction

Bipolar disorder is a mental condition that, to simplify, is characterized by periods of mania and depression. Bipolar disorder can cause unusual shifts in an individual's moods, energy, concentration, and activity levels. It is a major public health concern that can seriously affect daily functioning for millions of individuals. Not long ago, bipolar disorder was considered to be quite rare in children, adolescents, and young adults. Yet we now recognize, and there is a growing body of scientific evidence and scholarly literature to support the recognition that bipolar disorder is more prevalent among younger individuals than previously believed. In fact, bipolar disorder is often first diagnosed during late adolescence, the teen years, or in young adulthood; there are even increasing numbers of very young children now being diagnosed with bipolar disorder and initiating treatment; not that this is not without some controversy.

The book opens with five common misconceptions about bipolar disorder, what it is, and is not, as well as how to assess and respond to it. By answering your questions, it is the intent of this work to grant a better understanding of the nature and course of depression and mania, along with the benefits, complications, and shortcomings of ways designed to address them. Summarizing and explaining current scientific findings of the underlying causes, risk factors, and responses to bipolar disorder not only make this information more accessible to the lay population, but, by not oversimplifying or overstating, also hopefully scaffold a foundation for those who may, in the future, pursue more sophisticated strategies to better understand and address how individuals can cope with recurrent episodes of depression and mania and how those impact persons around them.

Questions are grouped into coherent sections covering general information; causes and risk factors; signs, symptoms, and diagnosis; treating and preventing; and living with bipolar disorder. A few case studies present selected, fictionalized case histories of bipolar disorder in the lives of individuals and in those around them, principally family members. These are written to provide personalized snapshots of how bipolar disorder might play out in the lives and experiences of individuals and their families and close associates. They remind us that without targeted interventions, individuals with bipolar disorder are likely to experience serious difficulties in school and in all life areas. The earlier diagnosis and treatment are initiated, the less adverse impacts bipolar disorder is likely to have in the lives of individuals and in that of those around them. A comprehensive glossary of terms is provided to help with understanding this text, which does cover a considerable amount of scientific research and information, particularly within the fields of psychiatry and neuroscience. An extensive bibliography is also supplied to guide those who may wish to pursue the material introduced here in greater depth; included is a brief listing of various governmental agencies and private organizations, some can offer information and resources, as well as summaries of research and forthcoming initiatives, some can provide guidance, support, lobbying, and advocacy for individuals, families, friends, and professionals concerned with addressing bipolar disorder and associated issues.

Knowledge can be a great leveler, and better-informed individuals can and will be able to more constructively respond to the challenges of mental health issues, including those around bipolar disorder and related conditions. Multiple vicissitudes are associated with their prevention, management, and treatment. However, stigma still abounds with respect to bipolar disorder and mental illness generally. Earlier recognition of the signs and symptoms of such conditions, as presented herein, should reinforce and supplement prior approaches yielding better ways to live with and adapt to them. However, making a diagnosis of bipolar disorder for a younger person in particular, or for anyone of any age for that matter, should be done very carefully.

The label of bipolar disorder carries with it many implications that must not be taken lightly. Many of the signs and symptoms of bipolar disorder are similarly present in myriad other psychiatric and medical conditions. The mainstay for managing and treating, as well as for preventing recurrences of, bipolar disorder has been psychiatric medication. More recently we have come to appreciate, and a growing body of evidence supports, that many young people, as well as others with bipolar disorder, are better served by combination approaches, that may, or may not, include psychopharmacology. The requisite background to better prevent, assess, manage, and treat bipolar disorder is vast; yet, with careful and thoughtful approaches, successes can be achieved. The purpose of this work is to offer readers a research-based platform to engage with the evolving art and science of dealing with bipolar disorder.

Guide to Health Literacy

On her 13th birthday, Samantha was diagnosed with type 2 diabetes. She consulted her mom and her aunt, both of whom also have type 2 diabetes, and decided to go with their strategy of managing diabetes by taking insulin. As a result of participating in an after-school program at her middle school that focused on health literacy, she learned that she can help manage the level of glucose in her bloodstream by counting her carbohydrate intake, following a diabetic diet, and exercising regularly. But, what exactly should she do? How does she keep track of her carbohydrate intake? What is a diabetic diet? How long should she exercise and what type of exercise should she do? Samantha is a visual learner, so she turned to her favorite source of media, YouTube, to answer these questions. She found videos from individuals around the world sharing their experiences and tips, doctors (or at least people who have "Dr." in their YouTube channel names), government agencies such as the National Institutes of Health, and even video clips from cat lovers who have cats with diabetes. With guidance from the librarian and the health and science teachers at her school, she assessed the credibility of the information in these videos and even compared their suggestions to some of the print resources that she was able to find at her school library. Now, she knows exactly how to count her carbohydrate level, how to prepare and follow a diabetic diet, and how much (and what) exercise is needed daily. She intends to share her findings with her mom and her aunt, and now she wants to create a chart that summarizes what she has learned that she can share with her doctor.

Samantha's experience is not unique. She represents a shift in our society; an individual no longer views himself or herself as a passive recipient of medical care but as an active mediator of his or her own health. However, in this era when any individual can post his or her opinions and experiences with a particular health condition online with just a few clicks or publish a memoir, it is vital that people know how to assess the credibility of health information. Gone are the days when "publishing" health information required intense vetting. The health information landscape is highly saturated, and people have innumerable sources where they can find information about practically any health topic. The sources (whether print, online, or a person) that an individual consults for health information are crucial because the accuracy and trustworthiness of the information can potentially affect his or her overall health. The ability to find, select, assess, and use health information constitutes a type of literacy—health literacy—that everyone must possess.

The Definition and Phases of Health Literacy

One of the most popular definitions for health literacy comes from Ratzan and Parker (2000), who describe health literacy as "the degree to which individuals have the capacity to obtain, process, and understand basic health information and services needed to make appropriate health decisions." Recent research has extrapolated health literacy into health literacy bits, further shedding light on the multiple phases and literacy practices that are embedded within the multifaceted concept of health literacy. Although this research has focused primarily on online health information seeking, these health literacy bits are needed to successfully navigate both print and online sources. There are six phases of health information seeking: (1) information need identification and question formulation, (2) information search, (3) information comprehension, (4) information assessment, (5) information management, and (6) information use.

The first phase is the *information need identification and question formulation phase*. In this phase, one needs to be able to develop and refine a range of questions to frame one's search and understand relevant health terms. In the second phase, *information search*, one has to possess appropriate searching skills, such as using proper keywords and correct spelling in search terms, especially when using search engines and databases. It is also crucial to understand how search engines work (i.e., how search results are derived, what the order of the search results means, how to use the snippets that are provided in the search results list to select websites, and how to determine which listings are ads on a search engine results page). One also has to limit reliance on surface characteristics, such as the design of a website or a book (a website or book that appears to have a lot of information or looks aesthetically pleasant does not necessarily mean it has good information) and language used (a website or book that utilizes jargon, the keywords that one used to conduct the search, or the word "information" does not necessarily indicate it will have good information). The next phase is *information comprehension*, whereby one needs to have the ability to read, comprehend, and recall the information (including textual, numerical, and visual content) one has located from the books and/or online resources.

To assess the credibility of health information (*information assessment* phase), one needs to be able to evaluate information for accuracy, evaluate how current the information is (e.g., when a website was last updated or when a book was published), and evaluate the creators of the source—for example, examine site sponsors or type of sites (.com, .gov, .edu, or .org) or the author of a book (practicing doctor, a celebrity doctor, a patient of a specific disease, etc.) to determine the believability of the person/organization providing the information. Such credibility perceptions tend to become generalized, so they must be frequently reexamined (e.g., the belief that a specific news agency always has credible health information needs continuous vetting). One also needs to evaluate the credibility of the medium (e.g., television, Internet, radio, social media, and book) and evaluate—not just accept without questioning—others' claims regarding the validity of a site, book, or other specific source of information. At this stage, one has to "make sense of information gathered from diverse sources by identifying misconceptions, main and supporting ideas, conflicting information, point of view, and biases" (American Association of School Librarians [AASL], 2009, p. 13) and conclude which sources/information are valid and accurate by using conscious strategies rather than simply using intuitive judgments or "rules of thumb." This phase is the most challenging segment of health information seeking and serves as a determinant of success (or lack thereof) in the information-seeking process. The following section on Sources of Health Information further explains this phase.

The fifth phase is *information management*, whereby one has to organize information that has been gathered in some manner to ensure easy retrieval and use in the future. The last phase is *information use*, in which one will synthesize information found across various resources, draw conclusions, and locate the answer to his or her original question and/or the content that fulfills the information need. This phase also often involves implementation, such as using the information to solve a health problem; make health-related decisions; identify and engage in behaviors that will help a person to avoid health risks; share the health information found with family members and friends who may benefit from it; and advocate more broadly for personal, family, or community health.

The Importance of Health Literacy

The conception of health has moved from a passive view (someone is either well or ill) to one that is more active and process-based (someone is working toward preventing or managing disease). Hence, the dominant focus has shifted from doctors and treatments to patients and prevention, resulting in the need to strengthen our ability and confidence (as patients and consumers of health care) to look for, assess, understand, manage, share, adapt, and use health-related information. An individual's health literacy level has been found to predict his or her health status better than age, race, educational attainment, employment status, and income level (National Network of Libraries of Medicine, 2013). Greater health literacy also enables individuals to better communicate with health care providers such as doctors, nutritionists, and therapists, as they can pose more relevant, informed, and useful questions to health care providers. Another added advantage of greater health literacy is better information-seeking skills, not only for health but also in other domains, such as completing assignments for school.

Sources of Health Information: The Good, the Bad, and the In-Between

For generations, doctors, nurses, nutritionists, health coaches, and other health professionals have been the trusted sources of health information. Additionally, researchers have found that young adults, when they have health-related questions, typically turn to a family member who has had firsthand experience with a health condition because of their family member's close proximity and because of their past experience with, and trust in, this individual. Expertise should be a core consideration when consulting a person, website, or book for health information. The credentials and background of the person or author and conflicting interests of the author (and his or her organization) must be checked and validated to ensure the likely credibility of the health information they are conveying. While books often have implied credibility because of the peer-review process involved, self-publishing has challenged this credibility, so qualifications of book authors should also be verified. When it comes to health information, currency of the source must also be examined. When examining health information/studies presented, pay attention to the exhaustiveness of research methods utilized to offer recommendations or conclusions. Small and nondiverse sample size is often—but not always—an indication of reduced credibility. Studies that confuse correlation with causation is another potential issue to watch for. Information seekers must also pay attention to the sponsors of the research studies. For example, if a study is sponsored by manufacturers of drug Y and the study recommends that drug Y is the best treatment to manage or cure a disease, this may indicate a lack of objectivity on the part of the researchers.

The internet is rapidly becoming one of the main sources of health information. Online forums, news agencies, personal blogs, social media sites, pharmacy sites, and celebrity "doctors" are all offering medical and health information targeted to various types of people in regard to all types of diseases and symptoms. There are professional journalists, citizen journalists, hoaxers, and people paid to write fake health news on various sites that may appear to have a legitimate domain name and may even have authors who claim to have professional credentials, such as an MD. All these sites *may* offer useful information or information that appears to be useful and relevant; however, much of the information may be debatable and may fall into gray areas that require readers to discern credibility, reliability, and biases.

While broad recognition and acceptance of certain media, institutions, and people often serve as the most popular determining factors to assess credibility of health information among young people, keep in mind that there are legitimate internet sites, databases, and books that publish health information and serve as sources of health information for doctors, other health sites, and members of the public. For example, MedlinePlus (https://medlineplus.gov) has trusted sources on over 975 diseases and conditions and presents the information in easy-to-understand language.

The chart here presents factors to consider when assessing credibility of health information. However, keep in mind that these factors function only as a guide and require continuous updating to keep abreast with the changes in the landscape of health information, information sources, and technologies.

The chart can serve as a guide; however, approaching a librarian about how one can go about assessing the credibility of both print and online health information is far more effective than using generic checklist-type tools. While librarians are not health experts, they can apply and teach patrons strategies to determine the credibility of health information.

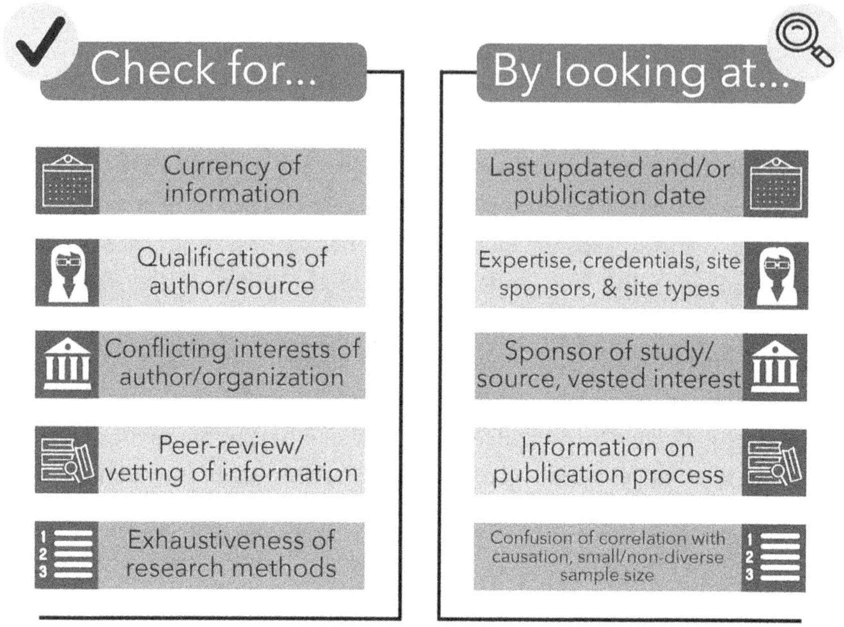

All images from flaticon.com

With the prevalence of fake sites and fake resources that appear to be legitimate, it is important to use the following health information assessment tips to verify health information that one has obtained (St. Jean et al., 2015, p. 151):

- **Don't assume you are right**: Even when you feel very sure about an answer, keep in mind that the answer may not be correct, and it is important to conduct (further) searches to validate the information.
- **Don't assume you are wrong**: You may actually have correct information, even if the information you encounter does not match—that is, you may be right and the resources that you have found may contain false information.
- **Take an open approach**: Maintain a critical stance by not including your preexisting beliefs as keywords (or letting them influence your choice of keywords) in a search, as this may influence what it is possible to find out.
- **Verify, verify, and verify**: Information found, especially on the internet, needs to be validated, no matter how the information appears on the site (i.e., regardless of the appearance of the site or the quantity of information that is included).

Health literacy comes with experience navigating health information. Professional sources of health information, such as doctors, health care providers, and health databases, are still the best, but one also has the power to search for health information and then verify it by consulting with these trusted sources and by using the health information assessment tips and guide shared previously.

Mega Subramaniam, PhD
Associate Professor, College of Information Studies,
University of Maryland

References and Further Reading

American Association of School Librarians (AASL) (2009). *Standards for the 21st-century learner in action.* Chicago, IL: American Association of School Librarians.

Hilligoss, B., & Rieh, S. Y. (2008). Developing a Unifying Framework of Credibility Assessment: Construct, Heuristics, and Interaction in Context. *Information Processing & Management 44*(4), 1467–84.

Kuhlthau, C. C. (1988). Developing a Model of the Library Search Process: Cognitive and Affective Aspects. *Reference Quarterly 28*(2), 232–42.

National Network of Libraries of Medicine (NNLM) (2013). *Health literacy.* Bethesda, MD: National Network of Libraries of Medicine. Retrieved from nnlm.gov/outreach/consumer/hlthlit.html.

Ratzan, S. C., & Parker, R. M. (2000). Introduction. In C. R. Selden, M. Zorn, S. C. Ratzan, & R. M. Parker (Eds.), *National Library of Medicine current bibliographies in medicine: Health literacy.* NLM Pub. No. CBM 2000–1. Bethesda, MD: National Institutes of Health, U.S. Department of Health and Human Services.

St. Jean, B., Subramaniam, M., Taylor, N. G., Follman, R., Kodama, C., & Casciotti, D. (2015). The Influence of Positive Hypothesis Testing on Youths' Online Health-Related Information Seeking. *New Library World 116*(3/4), 136–54.

St. Jean, B., Taylor, N. G., Kodama, C., & Subramaniam, M. (2017). Assessing the Health Information Source Perceptions of Tweens Using Card-Sorting Exercises. *Journal of Information Science*, February. Retrieved from http://journals.sagepub.com/doi/abs/10.1177/0165551516687728.

Subramaniam, M., St. Jean, B., Taylor, N. G., Kodama, C., Follman, R., & Casciotti, D. (2015). Bit by Bit: Using Design-Based Research to Improve the Health Literacy of Adolescents. *JMIR Research Protocols 4*(2), paper e62. Retrieved from http://www.ncbi.nlm.nih.gov/pmc/articles/PMC4464334/.

Valenza, J. (2016). Truth, Truthiness, and Triangulation: A News Literacy Toolkit for a "Post-Truth" World [Web log], November 26. Retrieved from http://blogs.slj.com/neverendingsearch/2016/11/26/truth-truthiness-triangulation-and-the-librarian-way-a-news-literacy-toolkit-for-a-post-truth-world/.

Common Misconceptions about Bipolar Disorder

1. Bipolar disorder doesn't really exist and is something that people just need to get over

Many believe bipolar disorder is essentially made up as an excuse for "weak" individuals. It is speculated if people tried hard enough and toughed it thru, they can get over it. Actually, bipolar disorder presents real emotional and physical challenges that sufferers have to deal with, sometimes for the rest of their lives. Telling someone dealing with a legitimate psychiatric disorder what they are experiencing is part of life, that everyone gets a little depressed or happy sometimes, says they are blowing out of proportion an everyday occurrence. This is overly dismissive, inaccurate, and just plain rude. Physical differences have been identified in the brains of individuals with bipolar disorder. Bipolar disorder is more than being slightly sad or elated, it can affect every aspect of life from emotional regulation to ability to productively function. Bipolar disorder is recognized as a neurological disorder as it impairs the ability to function in society without struggling, interpersonally, vocationally, and more. It's a lifelong diagnosis that can, hopefully, be managed with medication, therapy, and other lifestyle practices, perhaps into remission, but can never be fully cured. See, in particular, Questions 2, 14, 15, 19, and 39 for more information.

2. Individuals with bipolar disorder frequently alternate between manic and depressed moods

All individuals with bipolar disorder don't necessarily alternate frequently between manic and depressed moods. The extent and severity of the mood swings differentiate mere mood swings from bipolar disorder. Those with bipolar disorder can experience periods with balanced and stable moods. However, these individuals will, if they have bipolar disorder, sometimes experience extremely stressful mood changes that can become frequent and/or persistent. They may go for days without sleeping when manic, or sleep excessively, perhaps not leaving home for extended periods, maybe engaging in self-harm, including suicide. Others with bipolar disorder, particularly children, can experience mixed episodes, where they may exhibit symptoms of both depression and mania simultaneously. There is also a type of rapid cycling disorder where individuals experience at least four distinct episodes in a year switching between manic and depressive episodes, but not necessarily alternating within a single day or week. For more information, see Questions 1, 4, 20, 22, and 41.

3. Mood swings are always indicative of bipolar disorder

Mood swings are sometimes, but not always, indicative of bipolar disorder. Mood swings, by themselves, are usually a response to life challenges. They are a normal way to deal with stress; the extreme lows and highs of bipolar disorder are different. Bipolar disorder exists along a spectrum. Individuals with bipolar disorder experience extreme lows and highs, but these are different from mood fluctuations all experience. Those with bipolar disorder often experience very extreme changes in activity, energy, and sleep, which are more pronounced, frequent, and persistent than mood swings. They can engage in outrageous activities, like shopping sprees, spending beyond their means, and racking up debts. Others may be very anxious or irritable; some get upset by small things and start snapping at family and friends. Someone manic might lose the ability to control their thoughts and actions, maybe even losing touch with reality. However, another might have a psychotic break. Thus, although mood swings can be a sign of bipolar disorder, they can also be caused by other things. See Questions 4, 5, 16, 18, 22, 23, and 39.

4. There is a simple test to determine if someone has bipolar disorder

For many conditions, there is a simple test to determine presence. However, there is no definitive test to determine if someone has bipolar disorder; professionals must talk to individuals and family members, about symptoms and behaviors. This is necessary for diagnosing and differentiating between various subtypes, and to rule out other conditions. Diagnosing can be challenging requiring a clinical assessment based primarily on a diagnostic interview. Health care professionals gather reports of the individual's symptoms, family history, and behavioral and health history to make a diagnosis. As other medical conditions can mimic symptoms of bipolar disorder, blood and other tests are often conducted. There are brief instruments that can screen for bipolar disorder. See, in particular, Questions 7, 21, 22, 23, 24, and 27.

5. Once the symptoms of bipolar disorder are under control, treatment can be stopped

The first-line treatment for bipolar disorder is typically a medication. Other modalities are used, particularly psychotherapy and with others. Alternative therapies are also available to help prevent, manage, and treat bipolar disorder. Other therapeutic techniques can be called upon, particularly for addressing treatment-resistant bipolar depression. Usually combining pharmacological and other therapies is most effective, both in reducing symptoms and decreasing the likelihood of future episodes. Continuation of treatment after symptom resolution can prevent future depressive and manic episodes. Individuals should never stop, nor begin, any treatment without consultation with a health care provider. See, in particular, Questions 9, 29, 34, 35, 37, and 40.

Questions and Answers

General Information

1. What are mood disorders?

Mood disorders, also called affective disorders, consist of a wide array of psychological conditions characterized by depressive emotional states which sometimes may alternate with elevated mood states. Mood refers to the pervasive, internal feelings, or the emotional state of an individual. Mood disorders markedly influence all aspects of behavior and perception of external events such that they can interfere with daily life functions. Each year, 1-out-of-6 youth aged 6–17 in the United States experience a mental health disorder, most commonly a mood disorder; 50 percent of all lifetime mental illnesses begin by age 14, and 75 percent begin by age 24.

There are twenty-four different depressive disorders and twenty different bipolar and related conditions, a total of forty-four separate mood disorders, classified in the *Diagnostic and Statistical Manual of Mental Disorders, Fifth Edition* (DSM-5). Mood disorders are a broad category of mental illnesses. They can be regarded as being part of a spectrum of mental illnesses. At one end of the mood disorder spectrum is major depressive disorder (MDD), next comes persistent depressive disorder (PDD), then depression with mixed features, depression not otherwise specified, and so on, continuing with bipolar disorder not otherwise specified, bipolar disorder with mixed features, cyclothymia, bipolar II disorder, and at the other extreme end of the mood disorders spectrum would be full bipolar I disorder. This spectrum can be conceptually expanded further, thus advancing out from MDD proceeding through conditions like attention deficit hyperactivity disorder (ADHD), obsessive compulsive disorder (OCD), and so forth, concluding, or beginning depending on your perspective, with, perhaps, schizophrenia. There are varied bodies of evidence to support an ordering of psychiatric conditions along such a spectrum, including research in areas like genetics, molecular biology, neuroscience, neuropharmacology, behavioral sciences, and much more.

Most people have high and low moods from time to time, but individuals with mood disorders can experience prolonged and sometimes severe periods when their moods disrupt the ability to function. Mood disorders are a heterogeneous group of affective conditions; recognition of different subtypes of mood conditions evolved over time; and thus far, we have only been somewhat successful at agreeing upon and identifying respective categories; they will, no doubt, continue to be revised and refined. Nonetheless, mood disorders are widely recognized to be a major cause of disability and mortality.

Mood disorders result in substantial dysfunctions of emotions with extreme lows, or depression, and/or elevated moods, or manic states. Typically, there is the inability to enjoy things previously considered pleasurable, referred to as anhedonia. Mood disorders are frequently accompanied by disturbances in sleeping, eating, and psychomotor activities; these can be exaggerated or diminished. Distorted cognitive functions, like memory impairments, and other executive function problems often occur. Individuals experiencing mood disorders regularly report body complaints, with nearly every organ system involved. Physical complaints reported with mood disorders include things such as headache, muscle cramps, back pain, nausea, vomiting, heartburn, sour mouth, constipation, indigestion, and vision problems. Extensive diagnostic workups are often required to rule out alternative explanations.

Brain images, such as generated by techniques like magnetic resonance imaging (MRI), diffusion tensor imaging (DTI), and positron emission tomography (PET), and other research approaches, like electroencephalography (EEG), confirm abnormalities in parts of the brain responsible for controlling emotions, like the amygdala, caudate nucleus, dorsal anterior cingulate, hippocampus, and prefrontal cortices. Research indicates reduced blood flow and brain volume in dorsal medial and lateral, prefrontal cortex regions, and reduced hippocampal size in individuals with either bipolar disorder or major depression. PET scans indicate decreased activity in left medial prefrontal cortex and increased right and left posterior temporal lobe activity in depressed individuals compared to non-depressed. Neurobiological studies, including those that examine microstructural brain features, like axonal density, complexity, integration, and variability, such as indicated by diffusion of water molecules in brain tissue, as well as macrostructural differences, indicate mood disorders involve altered receptor sensitivity to neurotransmitters like dopamine, norepinephrine, and serotonin.

Mood disorders, including bipolar disorder, as well as MDD, PTSD, and anxiety disorders, are associated with low activity in the brain circuit through the inferior prefrontal cortex, parietal cortex, insula, and putamen, that helps modulate cognitive and emotional control, as well as increased activation in the anterior cingulate cortex, left amygdala, and thalamus network that processes thoughts and feelings. As individuals experience an emotional transition, like a mood swing, there is activation in the insular cortex.

Many reasons have been offered to explain why mood disorders seem to have greater prevalence in females than males. Biologic explanations, like those focused indirectly or directly on female anatomy and physiology, such as roles hormones have on human behavior, have long been considered. It is recognized loss of traditional psychosocial support systems, especially those more supportive of traditional female roles, like those associated with extended families, cohesive neighborhoods, and religious institutions, added to stress women must deal with. Criteria for diagnosis have improved recently yielding more attention to conditions commonly reported by women with mood disorders. There is a consistent female to male 2:1 ratio of mood disorder prevalence reported, including higher hospitalization rates, annual incidence, and lifetime rates. Mood disorders tend to run in families; they occur in 25 percent of first-degree relatives of individuals with bipolar disorder. Among individuals in the United States aged 18–44, mood disorders and psychosis spectrum disorders account for almost 600,000 hospitalizations each year. Mood disorders are essentially sustained emotional states out of proportion, in the extreme, to the context and impairing major life areas.

2. What is bipolar disorder, and are there different types?

Bipolar disorder, also referred to as bipolar affective disorder, and as bipolar spectrum disorder, is a mental condition characterized by periods of mania and depression. It is a major public health concern that can seriously affect daily functioning and which refers to a group of mental health conditions characterized by unusual and extreme fluctuations in mood. The term "bipolar" refers to the two opposite ends, or poles, of the emotional spectrum. In bipolar disorder, emotions range along a continuum from the "highs" of mania to the "lows" of depression; as such, it is considered to be a spectrum disorder. As a medical disease, bipolar disorder affects both the brain and body. Bipolar disorder is considered a lifelong medical condition caused by an imbalance of neurotransmitters, the chemical messengers in the brain. There are biological, environmental, genetic, and other factors that can change the functioning and structures of the brain, particularly causing imbalances of the chemicals within the brain and the rest of the central nervous system that result in changes to emotions, thoughts, behaviors, and other functions. Bipolar disorder involves many different alterations, including those of several neurotransmitters. Bipolar disorder appears to be associated, for instance, with a lower glutamate to GABA ratio.

Individuals with bipolar disorder typically alternate between states of mania and depression; these are physiological and psychological states that impact thinking, feeling, and behaving. Between episodes of mania and depression, individuals with bipolar disorder may, or may not, struggle with life's issues; they are often angry, socially anxious, have difficulties with relationships and communication, and routinely experience sleep disturbances. Many individuals with bipolar disorder do not know they have the condition until they are diagnosed by a health care professional.

Individuals with bipolar disorder typically experience distinct mood episodes, which are periods that are substantially different from an individual's usual moods and behaviors. In a mood episode, symptoms generally last every day for most of the day and can persist for several days, weeks, or even months. Approximately 50 percent of bipolar episodes last 2–7 months, with a median of three months. Some individuals experience both manic and depressive symptoms in the same mood episode, which is referred to as a mood episode with mixed features where one can feel very empty, sad, or hopeless while simultaneously feeling highly reenergized. Individuals who are hospitalized for bipolar disorder spend around 20 percent of the rest of their lives in mood episodes.

There may be long periods with no episodes (euthymic) of mania, hypomania, or depression. Around 20 percent of individuals with bipolar disorder have euthymic states that last for about sixty weeks. Year-long euthymic states are most common among older working males, particularly those with lower incidence of alcohol use disorder. There are several subtypes of bipolar disorder. Subtypes vary in symptoms, durations, intensities, and frequencies of mood disturbances. Some of the difficulties in identifying different subtypes might be, at least partly, due to an insufficient demarcation of specific conditions along the bipolar spectrum.

Individuals with bipolar I disorder, also sometimes referred to as classic bipolar, tend to experience depressive episodes and at least one or more manic episodes for at least seven days duration each, with or without psychotic or mixed mood features, or have symptom severity requiring hospitalization. Differential diagnoses, such as substance or toxin-induced mood disorders, mood disorder associated with myriad medical conditions, or other psychiatric conditions, must be excluded. The frequency and pattern with which an individual with bipolar I cycles from depression to mania to hypomania to a normal mood or to a mixed state are highly variable and individualized. Individuals with bipolar I disorder tend to have depressive episodes about 30 percent of the time. Bipolar I disorder is generally considered the most common, with lifetime prevalence reported to be between 0.4–1.6 percent, and also to be the most severe subtype; but, fortunately, it can usually be managed by effective treatment regimes.

Individuals with bipolar II disorder must experience at least one low, depressive episode and at least one excessively happy, hypomanic episode. An individual with bipolar II must have at least one major depressive episode that lasts for at least two weeks, followed by a hypomanic episode that usually lasts around four days. However, the individual cannot ever have a full manic episode and still be classified as bipolar II. In bipolar II disorder, depressive episodes are typically more frequent and less intense than hypomanic episodes, and well-being intervals in between are generally shorter than in bipolar I. However, individuals with bipolar II disorder can be, and usually are, depressed for longer periods than those with other subtypes, which can cause considerable disability, and complicate diagnosis. Individuals with bipolar II disorder tend to have depressive episodes about 50 percent of the time. Bipolar II disorder is generally considered to be less common, with a lifetime prevalence of roughly 0.5 percent, and somewhat less severe than bipolar I, but typically more severe than cyclothymia.

Cyclothymic disorder, also called cyclothymia, or sometimes bipolar III, is experienced by individuals who have numerous episodes of mild depression and hypomania for at least two years, or for one year if a child or adolescent; but symptoms never fully attain full depressive or hypomanic status but are less severe. Hypomanic episodes can be of extensive durations in which someone can function well and be highly productive. Many experience fatigue and excessive sleepiness, with feelings of indifference, and difficulties in decision making; suicidal ideation is common. They must be symptomatic for more than one year in children or adolescents, and in adults for two years or more, but never experiencing full symptomology of either major depression or mania. Cyclothymia is characterized by milder episodes of both depression and mania. Individuals with cyclothymia tend to cycle through mood fluctuations, but typically in an unpredictable manner. Mood episodes can last for weeks.

During hypomanic episodes, they can feel on top of the world, yet be more irritable than usual and harder to get along with. In depressive episodes, they may have changes in appetite or sleep, perhaps with feelings of worthlessness or guilt. Cyclothymia appears to run in families; if an individual has a family member with cyclothymia, then they are at greater risk for developing it too. Common comorbidities include separation anxiety, fear of rejection, and tendency toward hostility to those perceived to have rejected them. They frequently pursue intense interpersonal relationships when hypomanic, but social isolation when depressed. Estimates are that 0.4–1.0 percent of the general population, with equal prevalence among genders, has cyclothymia at some point in their life; onset typically occurs somewhere in late childhood to early adulthood. However, many individuals initially diagnosed with cyclothymia when younger will eventually transition to bipolar I or bipolar II later. Cyclothymia is typically less severe than bipolar I disorder or bipolar II disorder; and an individual with it will commonly have stable moods for months at a time, but they will experience episodes of both hypomania and depression. This is considered to be the rarest subtype of bipolar disorder and, as symptoms can be intermittent and less severe than other forms, medication is not always prescribed.

Bipolar disorder with mixed features, episodes, or states is another possibility which affects 2.8 percent of the US population, with 83 percent of cases classified as severe. Bipolar disorder with mixed features is defined by the simultaneous occurrence of both depressive and manic episodes for at least one week. For instance, someone might experience features of a depressed episode, yet simultaneously exhibit rapid speech, racing thoughts, and enhanced energetic levels. Individuals in a mixed episode typically do not feel euphoric, but are more commonly very angry, agitated, and miserable. Mixed moods are estimated to occur in 20–40 percent of individuals with bipolar disorder. For example, you can exhibit manic symptoms, but still feel low and be socially withdrawn.

Bipolar disorder not otherwise specified, or bipolar disorder unspecified, is a final subtype used when it is unclear as to what specific variant an individual has; it is sometimes also called subthreshold bipolar disorder, and has a prevalence of 1.4 percent. Individuals who have some symptoms, but do not meet the full diagnostic criteria for the other subtypes, can be categorized under the unspecified subtype. It is generally considered to be a mixture of bipolar I, II, and cyclothymia. They may have periods of unstable moods, yet not to the degree that would warrant a clear diagnosis of any of the other subtypes. Individuals with this subtype of bipolar disorder still experience extreme fluctuations in mood, even if the symptoms are not as severe as in bipolar I or bipolar II; nor do the duration of mood episodes meet full criteria to qualify for any of the other subtypes. Nevertheless, they still typically experience sufficient disruptions in daily functioning, including at school, work, and relationships.

Individuals with bipolar disorder can only have, and be diagnosed with, one respective subtype at a time. Although not common, some individuals can transition from one particular subtype to another over their lifetime, which is consistent with the concept of bipolar spectrum disorder. Increasing recognition of the uniqueness of individuals, and of the spectrum nature of the disorder, has come to influence the diagnostic process around bipolar disorder and its subtypes, as well as, perhaps more importantly, the crafting of personalized treatment plans for those diagnosed. Each individual with bipolar disorder can have a constellation of symptoms unique to them and their dynamic, ever shifting, circumstances; this only complicates diagnosis and treatment.

There is no definitive cure for bipolar disorder, nor any of its subtypes, yet management and prevention are nevertheless possible. Their mood cycles are caused by fluctuations in brain chemistry, such as dopamine, serotonin, GABA, glutamate, glycine, and other neurotransmitter irregularities; they are not random "up" and "down" phases, nor are they the result of a psychotic disorder or resulting from deeply ingrained personality traits. Even on days when one is feeling good, bipolar disorder is still there. It is important to realize that what one is experiencing is real for them, and while the mental health field may not openly use the term "high functioning," it is a condition many have to struggle with. The "up" and "down" episodes may last for weeks or months, not hours or days, as is common in most people. A depressive episode, untreated, lasts on average about eight to ten months. Medications are typically prescribed, particularly in acute cases. Psychotherapy can help individuals learn skills to manage the condition so they can start to feel less like prisoners of their own minds. Other approaches, both more varied traditional medical approaches and those considered to be more complementary, are also available for those with bipolar disorder.

3. What other kinds of depressions are there?

Individuals experiencing depression typically become sad, perhaps feeling hopeless or sometimes indifferent. Depression is a mood disorder that affects millions of individuals around the world. In fact, more than 264 million individuals globally, or about 3.4 percent of all people, 2.7 percent of males and 4.1 percent of females, are estimated to be affected by depression. More than 100 million individuals around the world are estimated to have severe biological depression requiring, but not always getting, medical care. Globally, depression is the leading cause of disability. Depression and anxiety disorders are thought to cost the global economy about $1 trillion in lost productivity each year. Individuals with depression have a 40 percent higher risk of developing cardiovascular and metabolic diseases than the general population. Individuals who are depressed consistently exhibit decreases in metabolic rate in the left prefrontal lobe.

Depression is most often diagnosed in individuals 18–25 years old (10.9 percent) and in those belonging to two or more races (10.5 percent). It is estimated 3.2 percent of children and adolescents aged 3–17 years old in the United States have been diagnosed with depression. About 1-in-5 US adults will be diagnosed with depression in their lifetime. Among young people in the United States under the age of 18, depressive disorders are the most common cause, after excluding hospitalizations relating to pregnancy and birth, of hospitalizations. Hundreds of thousands of additional Americans live with masked depression, when they do not realize their aches and pains are actually symptomatic of depression.

There are, in addition to bipolar disorder, many different kinds of depression. MDD is commonly referred to as clinical depression; it is also referred to as unipolar depression. Our modern term of depression comes from the Late Latin *depressare*, meaning to press down, which is reflected in the affective states associated with depression. If someone experiences many depressive symptoms for more than two weeks, they will often be diagnosed with MDD. Characteristic symptoms of MDD include maintaining a sad, depressed mood; fatigue; lacking interest in activities formerly enjoyed; weight gain or loss; sleep changes; feelings of guilt and worthlessness; difficulties concentrating; and thinking about death and suicide. MDD tends to run in families; it occurs in 14 percent of first-degree relatives of individuals with bipolar disorder. Among US adolescents aged 12–17, 1-in-6 experience a major depressive episode each year. An estimated 21 million American adults, or 8.4 percent of the total population, have at least a single major depressive episode annually; MDD is estimated to cost the United States $210 billion every year. It is believed that 90 percent of individuals who die by suicide had experienced symptoms of a mental health disorder and that 46 percent had a diagnosed mental illness. Among US adolescents aged 12–17, 3 million have serious thoughts of suicide each year; among US young adults aged 18–25, 3.8 million have serious thoughts of suicide each year. More than half of all those who die from suicide had MDD, which represents more than 6 percent of the general population; up to 75 percent were alcoholics. It has been suggested that MDD co-occurs in 32.8 percent of those with alcohol use disorder and in 44.3 percent of those with substance use disorder. Melancholia is also commonly seen in severely ill individuals with both bipolar disorder and MDD.

Persistent depressive disorder (PDD), previously called dysthymia, refers to a chronic form of depression that occurs on more days than not for a period of at least two years, and can be mild, moderate, or severe. PDD affects an estimated 1.5 percent of adults in the United States annually, and it is estimated that about 1.3 percent of American adults will have PDD at some point in their lifetime; it affects more women (1.9 percent) than men (1.0 percent). Children and adolescents with PDD, including autism, commonly present with aggression and self-injury, features often stemming from comorbid bipolar disorder or related conditions. Symptoms of this condition, although not as severe as in MDD, are pervasive and long-lasting, and include sad feelings, lack of interest or pleasure, feelings of irritability and anger, guilt, hopelessness, low self-esteem, problems falling or staying asleep or of sleeping too much, appetite changes, and general fatigue or lack of energy. Treatment for this condition typically consists of both medication and psychotherapy.

Premenstrual dysphoric disorder (PMDD), naturally, only occurs in women. It consists of the common symptoms of premenstrual syndrome, like irritability, bloating, moodiness, food cravings, and breast tenderness, but with more pronounced mood changes, often with bouts of crying and self-criticism.

Postpartum depression (PPD) also occurs only in women and must have peripartum onset; however, fathers are at increased risk for depression and anxiety during the postpartum period. PPD is more severe and long-lasting than the typical anxiety and mood changes that can occur during pregnancy or after giving birth; a PPD episode must last at least two weeks. It is estimated that 15 percent of mothers experience depression after birth and that PPD occurs among 3–6 percent of the general female population; but the risk is up to three times greater among women with bipolar disorder, and 25–30 percent of women with bipolar disorder experience manic or depressive episodes during pregnancy or after delivery. Furthermore, a woman with bipolar disorder who has a relative who experienced PPD has twice the risk of getting it herself. Symptoms include those of other depressive disorders, but also sometimes include difficulty bonding with their baby, thoughts of hurting their baby or themselves, feelings of anxiety or panic attacks, as well as social withdrawal. In more severe cases, it can manifest as postpartum psychosis, which may consist of general confusion, hallucinations, or delusions. If untreated, PPD can persist for up to a year. Effective treatments include antidepressant medication, psychotherapy, and hormone therapy. Women with a previous diagnosis of bipolar disorder are at higher risk for not only PPD, but also postpartum psychosis; it is estimated that between 20–30 percent of them will experience psychosis during the postpartum period.

Seasonal affective disorder (SAD) is characterized by symptoms of depression, as well as commonly weight gain and sleepiness, typically occurring during the fall and winter months, when the sun sets earlier; however, SAD is also recognized to occur during the spring and summer months, often along with more manic-like symptoms, but also with depressive symptoms like insomnia and loss of appetite. The classic SAD condition is thought to be caused by disruption of the normal circadian rhythms resulting from seasonal loss of daylight. Interestingly, individuals with bipolar disorder appear to be light sensitive. Individuals with SAD or with bipolar disorder have low plasma baseline levels of melatonin and diminished nocturnal melatonin suppression compared to individuals with MDD and those without any mood disorders. SAD appears to be more common among children than older individuals; further, women with SAD are about 60 percent more likely to have PMS during the winter. The prevalence of SAD is geographically dependent as seasonal daylight variation is greater the further from the equator one is; while the condition only affects 1 percent of the population in Florida, it affects 9 percent of those in Alaska. Light therapy is often a sufficient treatment modality for treating SAD.

Depressive disorder with atypical features is characterized by symptoms similar to other types of depression, but they rapidly resolve with the occurrence of a positive life event. This form of depression generally responds well to treatment with a monoamine oxidase inhibitor. There are other, less common, kinds of depression, some of which are culturally specific, but any of these can be comorbid with bipolar disorder. Reactive depression is triggered by experiencing stressful life events, like being assaulted or loss of a loved one. Circadian depression consists of disrupted 24-hour, sleep-wake cycles, reduced physical activity, weight gain, and low energy. Catatonic depression is characterized by an inability to function physically or verbally for extended periods of time, sometimes accompanied by abnormal movements.

Many individuals with bipolar disorder are initially misdiagnosed with other kinds of depression, most usually MDD, particularly among women, as well as other types of mental illnesses, such as schizophrenia or anxiety disorders, that is until they experience a profound episode of mania. As depression often manifests with many physical ailments, such as chronic pain, constipation or diarrhea, and varied forms of inflammation, it is also commonly misdiagnosed as myriad physical illnesses. Depression, like bipolar disorder, is known to run in families; however, familial expression of depression is reduced with better lifestyle choices, such as increased physical activity and better dietary choices.

4. What are mania and hypomania?

Mania and hypomania are both symptoms of bipolar disorder characterized by elevated moods, emotions, and levels of energy. Our term "mania" comes directly from the Greek *mania*, meaning madness or raging; it was used to refer to a state of divine madness, whether a curse, more typically, or a blessing, from the ancient gods. Mania is more severe and is typically associated with bipolar I, while hypomania is milder and more associated with bipolar II or cyclothymia. It is important to differentiate between mania and hypomania as it influences diagnosis and treatment. Both conditions are characterized by episodes of unusually high levels of mental and physical energy, but they tend to be less intense and shorter lasting in hypomania than in mania. The probability of having a manic or hypomanic episode has been found to be associated with heightened impulsivity, reward sensitivity, reward neural circuitry activity, and sleep-circadian rhythm disturbances. Furthermore, imaging studies of brain activation during reward activation, specifically in the ventrolateral prefrontal cortex, has also been found to be highly predictive of mania and hypomania.

Mania consists of abnormally elated, enthusiastic, excited, expansive, and/or agitated mood and is often accompanied by excessive activity, rapid speech, racing thoughts, and irritability. It is estimated that about 10 percent of individuals will have only one manic episode during their life, but most will have more. To be diagnosed with a manic episode, the individual must have been overly elated, euphoric, or irritable for one week or more, almost every day, for most of the day, unless manic for less than a week but requiring hospitalization. An individual in a manic mood may feel energetic, euphoric, or excited and is prone to flights of fancy such that they may commit to unrealistically ambitious endeavors. They frequently find themselves unable to sit still or to sleep. An individual in a manic state may have a high degree of distractibility, feel overly joyful, experience rapid flows of disjointed thoughts, and engage in acts of sexual hyperactivity or promiscuity. They frequently will engage in risky and even self-destructive activities, like compulsive gambling or binge buying sprees.

About half of individuals with mania will experience psychosis; most typically delusions. They may believe that certain fantasies are actually true and real, often exhibiting delusions of grandeur. Thoughts of grandiosity can become extremely pronounced and delusional. The extent of activation in the ventrolateral prefrontal cortex during decision-making in reward contexts is predictive of symptom severity during a subsequent manic episode. Individuals who experience more manic episodes tend to have more cortical thinning, particularly in the prefrontal cortex, along with progressive abnormal enlargement in the brain's ventricles; this may help explain why some individuals experience worsening bipolar symptoms with the greater number of episodes of mania experienced.

There are different subtypes of mania; dysphoric mania, for instance, is characterized by angered irritability. Mania can be euphoric, characterized by energized and elated mood, or dysphoric, characterized by energized but low mood, typified by not sleeping and not being tired the next day and by angered irritability. About 50 percent of individuals with bipolar disorder experience seasonal mood shifts; this seasonality includes those with depressive episodes or even full-blown SAD in the fall and winter, but also includes individuals who tend to experience manic or, more commonly, hypomanic episodes in the spring or summer; perhaps attributable to an underlying biological sensitivity to the length of daylight which disrupts circadian rhythms. Around 90 percent of those who experience manic episodes will also experience severe depression; actually, mania without depression is relatively rare. A manic episode can be misconstrued as agitated delirium, but the consistency of the elated state in bipolar disorder contrasts sharply with the less consistent elated mood of someone who is delirious. Someone with bipolar disorder experiencing mania commonly has a desire to engage in unrealistic goal-oriented objectives, generally they feel elated, self-important, are often excessively talkative and sociable, while exhibiting aspects of impatience, impulsiveness, irritability, and hyperactivity, frequently having less need for sleep; manic episodes are often followed by depressed episodes. Manic episodes typically last for a week or more and may require hospitalization. A manic episode, untreated, lasts on average about six months. Mania, in some cases, may trigger a psychotic break from reality. When mania progresses to a psychotic episode, it is often accompanied by auditory or visual hallucinations, delusions, and/or paranoia. A possible mechanism behind psychosis may involve the stimulation of cognitive maps stored in the hippocampus, which can be simulated in the prefrontal cortex; this process normally functions as part of decision-making.

Part of the mechanism behind mania involves amygdala activation that includes release of epinephrine and cortisol, which increase perception and reactivity to stimuli, making emotional regulation more difficult and potentially resulting in a manic episode. Other mechanisms are, of course, also involved; for instance, synaptic bioactive phospholipids, such as PRG-1 and lysophosphatidic acid (LPA), and enzymes, like autotaxin, regulate the balance between excitation and inhibition of brain signaling; accordingly, low levels of autotaxin and elevated levels of synaptic lipids may be implicated in mania.

There is evidence suggesting that manic episodes result in some damage to the brain. For instance, with increasing successive bipolar manic episodes there is a correlation with increased lateral ventricular volume, suggesting a progression of pathological consequences. A shrinkage in the size of the corpus callosum, the hippocampus, and other brain regions is associated with more manic episodes experienced.

Hypomania essentially means a little manic, literally low mania. An individual with hypomania may exhibit a slightly elevated or cheerful mood and may be overly confident or grandiose. They typically engage in tangential, or non-goal-directed, thinking that may seem muddled and unlikely to lead to any clear conclusions. Risk taking is common, such as gambling, sex, or spending, and they may be easily distracted, sometimes they are even slightly delusional. Episodes of hypomania may only last a few days (at least four consecutive days required for diagnosis), while those of mania are typically longer-lasting (at least one week or longer). To be diagnosed with hypomania, an individual must have at least four consecutive symptomatic days of elevated mood with three diagnostic symptoms or irritable mood with diagnostic symptoms. An individual in a hypomanic state may be able to maintain their regular daily activities and others may not even notice the changes; if anything, they are often more productive during hypomanic episodes. While hypomania can sometimes be managed by lifestyle changes, mania typically requires combinations of medication, psychotherapy, and support.

Recent emotional traumas, sleep deprivation, and significant life events, like loss of a loved one, divorce, or moving, can trigger mania or hypomania. Certain diseases can produce mania and hypomania, including hyperparathyroidism, hyperthyroidism, lupus, multiple sclerosis, dementia, encephalitis, seizure disorders, and schizoaffective disorder, as can a brain tumor. Certain medications, including steroids, some ADHD medications, antidepressants, cannabis, cocaine, LSD, PCP, and mescaline (peyote), can cause drug-induced mania. Annual incidence of first-episode of bipolar mania is about 5/100,000 population; with peak onset between 21–25 years old; most (87.5 percent) of these individuals will no longer meet criteria for diagnosis within the first year. Up to 35 percent of individuals who develop mild mania in their teens will later in life develop full bipolar disorder or MDD. Furthermore, about 75 percent of those with bipolar disorder will experience one or more episodes of mania before experiencing their first episode of depression. For individuals with bipolar I or bipolar II disorder, the duration of episodes of depression is typically much longer than those of mania or hypomania.

5. How can bipolar disorder affect someone over the course of their life?

Bipolar disorder is characterized by distinct cyclical periods of extreme disturbances of moods, behaviors, and/or thoughts. It is a lifelong, chronic condition consisting of dramatic episodes of elated, expansive, or irritable moods, often alternating with depressive mood periods, including feelings of worthlessness, fatigue, and lack of concentration. Bipolar disorder symptoms, once diagnosed, can usually be managed with an array of proper treatment approaches. Unfortunately, bipolar disorder is perhaps one of the most commonly misdiagnosed mental health disorders. Consequently, it is important to seek professional help from a qualified mental health provider if someone thinks they have symptoms of bipolar disorder. Without treatment, the recurrence of disruptive episodes, compounded by increased frequency and severity, is all the more likely to occur.

The first stage of the life of an individual who will eventually develop bipolar disorder can be thought of as that of being at risk. It consists of the host of factors that predispose one to increased vulnerability to bipolar disorder, including things like low birth weight, various maternal infections during pregnancy, and of the amount and quality of prenatal and perinatal care that can predispose one to later in life transition to bipolar disorder. Family history of bipolar disorder is highly predictive of later onset, as are multiple psychiatric diagnoses in parents and/or grandparents. Adherence to a proper maternal diet, perhaps including nutritional supplements including folate or Vitamin D, may be a helpful intervention at this stage.

The second stage could be considered the wellness interval. This stage is the lifespan up until that of either the first appearance of symptoms or full-blown bipolar disorder. This stage, which can vary from a few years to decades, would include the array of environmental risk factors that could occur in childhood and adolescence, and even into adulthood in some cases. These might be traumas, like physical, sexual, or emotional abuse, or the loss of a parent or other close family member, as well as myriad health assaults, such as numerous infections or other medical conditions. Acquisition of healthy lifestyle habits, particularly proper sleep hygiene and stress management, is highly advantageous; as is treatment of maternal PPD and of other familial psychiatric conditions, all of which may be helpful interventions at this stage.

The third stage of a possible model of a lifespan of someone with bipolar disorder can be considered as a prodromal one. In this stage an individual would usually first experience mild symptoms similar to those of the disorder, but with less intensity; perhaps, something like mood instability. A large cluster of potential comorbidities might precede the onset of bipolar disorder; these could include diverse conditions such as ADHD, anxiety disorders, conduct disorders, oppositional defiant disorder (ODD), even MDD, or varied substance use disorders, from that of alcohol or cannabis to substances like hallucinogens, stimulants, or opiates. Psychotherapy and/or early pharmacological interventions, including addressing potential medication non-adherence, may be helpful at this stage.

The fourth stage could be that of disorder onset. It could consist of clear episodes of mania and/or depression. There could, rather too frequently, be one or more misdiagnoses at this stage. The earlier the age of onset, the more likely it is that the initial episodes will be depressive rather than manic. Treatment trials, most often pharmacological, are almost universally instituted after diagnosis, sometimes, not surprisingly, with adverse results. However, treatment delays are exceedingly normative at this stage, and frequently of considerable duration. Seeking early assessment from a qualified and experienced mental health professional may be a helpful intervention at this stage.

Sleep problems can develop at several stages as a result of bipolar disorder, such as lack of sleep from manic episodes or excessive sleep from depressive episodes. In addition, sleep abnormalities can be a cause of mood swings and trigger bipolar disorder. Sleep deprivation is actually the most frequently reported cause of mood episodes, while proper sleep hygiene can both prevent and help treat bipolar disorder. Behaviors that can disrupt sleep schedules, such as excessive consumption of caffeine or alcohol or use of cell phones and other electronic devices in bed, should be avoided.

Some individuals with bipolar disorder may attempt to self-medicate themselves, which can result in substance abuse and even in addiction. Substance use can trigger manic, hypomanic, or depressive episodes as they can change the delicate balance of neurochemicals, as well as reduce the effectiveness of bipolar medications if taken. Substance use disorders have a higher comorbidity with bipolar II disorder than with other subtypes.

Subsequent stages could vary with the alternate courses of the disorder in the lives of different individuals. For some, there might well be a regression to wellness episodes, but these would typically be followed by periods of disorder recurrence. These often, in retrospect, can be mapped out from a personal history as a stage of disorder progression. Regularly, there could be phases of treatment resistance, usually alternating with brief or longer disorder episode free periods. Concluding, one way or another, with a late or end stage of bipolar disorder or, unfortunately, with death.

6. How prevalent is bipolar disorder and is the condition becoming more common?

Bipolar disorder is a common, complex, severe, potentially disabling, and highly recurrent mood disorder associated with high morbidity and greater mortality. It is characterized by recurring episodes of elated and depressed moods, often associated with profound alterations in behavioral activities; five years after initial diagnosis, relapse rates of over 70 percent are reported. Bipolar disorder affects at least 1-in-every-50 individuals, and, by some estimates, up to 1-in-every-25, putting them at risk for the many adverse consequences associated with the condition. For example, the mortality rate of those with bipolar disorder is 2–3 times greater than that of the general population.

Bipolar disorder prevalence is roughly equivalent across races, ethnicities, social classes, and genders, but with some notable exceptions, particularly with respect to a difficult-to-treat variant known as rapid cycling. Past year prevalence of bipolar disorder is reported at, respectively, 2.8 percent for females and 2.9 percent for males. The average age of onset for bipolar disorder among both males and females is at 17.2 years of age; earlier age of onset is associated with worse prognosis. Females are generally diagnosed with bipolar disorder later in life than males, and they typically have less intense episodes of mania, but longer episodes of depression, and are more prone to rapid cycling. Research also suggests that women with bipolar disorder experience more depressive episodes and more mixed episodes than men with bipolar disorder. Males generally have longer periods of mania and are more likely to act out, like spending all of their money, and are also more likely to experience extreme delusions, but are less likely to seek help, more likely to have a comorbid substance use disorder, and more likely to commit suicide. Women are at greater risk of experiencing bipolar episodes during the postpartum period, immediately following childbirth. Furthermore, lifetime prevalence rates among first-degree relatives in individuals with bipolar disorder are much higher than among those without neuropsychiatric disorders.

Estimates of lifetime prevalence of bipolar disorder are between 1.3–1.6 percent, affecting about 40–50 million individuals worldwide. Globally, bipolar disorder is the sixth leading cause of disability. It is associated with a loss of between 10–20 years of potential life; globally, risk of death for those with bipolar disorder from natural causes, like coronary heart disease, is twice that of the general population. It is estimated that nearly 1-in-5 US adults (20 percent) experiences a mental illness sometime in their life. In the United States alone, bipolar disorder afflicts about 5 percent of the general population, which is around 15 million people. It affects about 5.7 million adult Americans every year, or about 2.6 percent of the US population aged 18 years and older. One recent study reported that 1 percent of adolescents aged 14–18 years old met diagnostic criteria for bipolar disorder. Between 2–7 percent of Americans will develop bipolar disorder at some point in their life; but only about half will ever be properly diagnosed or appropriately treated. The median age of bipolar disorder onset in the United States is at the age of twenty-five years; although, the condition can start in early childhood or later in life, including the forties and fifties. People 18–29 years old have the highest bipolar disorder rates reported at 4.7 percent, with the lowest among those sixty and older at 0.7 percent; adolescents are reported at 2.9 percent. Everyone with bipolar disorder affects the lives of others around them, including their parents, brothers, sisters, grandparents, spouses, children, friends, teachers, and health care professionals. It can be estimated that at least approximately 20 million individuals' lives in the United States alone are impacted by bipolar disorder.

Bipolar disorder is frequently a highly disabling condition. About 25 percent of those with bipolar disorder are unable to go to school, work, or otherwise function. More than 50 percent of those diagnosed with bipolar disorder have at least four or more serious episodes each year. A few persons with untreated bipolar disorder experience symptoms of mania and depression almost continuously throughout their lives. Bipolar disorder costs the US workforce up to $14 billion annually. Each worker with bipolar disorder loses, on average, 65.5 workdays each year. The total estimated annual cost of bipolar disorder in the United States is $219.1 billion, or $88,443 per person every year. New onset bipolar disorder in later life affects about 1 percent of the elderly, being more frequently reported among older men than women.

Bipolar disorder can create serious health problems. Heart problems are more common in those with bipolar disorder than in those without. Headaches, especially migraines, are more frequent and more disabling. Accidents, especially automobile accidents, injuries, and death, are more prevalent among those with bipolar disorder. Life expectancy is lower in those with bipolar disorder, particularly among those insufficiently treated. In fact, bipolar disorder is associated with a reduction of 9.2 years of expected life span; and, up to 1-out-of-5 individuals diagnosed with bipolar disorder will commit suicide. Between 10–20 percent of individuals with bipolar disorder commit suicide, more than 6 percent do so within two decades of their initial diagnosis, with nearly a third admitting to at least one suicide attempt. Suicide rates are twenty times higher among individuals with bipolar disorder compared to the general population. Fortunately, earlier diagnosis of bipolar disorder is associated with substantially lower rates of suicide and of lower incidences of other adverse consequences.

With respect to subtypes, bipolar II is more prevalent than bipolar I disorder. Bipolar II disorder has a similar incidence to MDD; further, between 40–50 percent of individuals initially diagnosed with major depression will later be diagnosed with either bipolar I or bipolar II.

While some suggest that bipolar disorder has become more common in recent years, most attribute the slight increase in diagnoses to stem from a combination of factors, including better mental health outreach efforts, increased insurance coverages, and stipulation of clearer diagnostic criteria; as well as less stigma, contributing to greater willingness for individuals to share their diagnoses. Furthermore, revisions to diagnostic criteria can markedly alter prevalence reported as a diagnosis depends upon the number of symptoms and length of time experienced; lowering of any diagnostic criteria can directly result in increased prevalence. Similarly, calls for the recognition of additional subtypes, if accepted, would also add to the numbers of individuals diagnosed. There is no strong evidence that bipolar disorder is actually more prevalent today than in the past.

7. Is bipolar disorder only an issue in the Western, industrialized world?

No, bipolar disorder is a mood disorder that has been observed in most cultures around the globe. Respective cultures mold personal beliefs about health and disease, including bipolar disorder, as well as ideas on disorder recognition, attribution, expression, acceptance, and associated behaviors. In Chinese cultures, for instance, understanding of bipolar disorder is shaped by perspectives on harmony. About 25 percent of the world's population will develop a mental illness at some point in the lives; bipolar disorder being one of the most common. Although first reported in and defined by physicians in countries of the Western, industrialized world, bipolar disorder appears to be an equal opportunity medical condition. However, it is true that higher-income, Westernized nations report somewhat higher rates of bipolar disorder. For example, bipolar I disorder annual prevalence in the United States is reported to be 0.8 percent; while in Germany, 0.6 percent is reported, and 0.1 percent in China, while in sub-Saharan Africa, lifetime prevalence for bipolar I disorder is reported to be 1.06 percent, and 1.57 percent for bipolar II disorder.

The course of bipolar disorder may vary between respective nations. While first bipolar episodes in Western countries tend to be depressive, in India, for instance, first episodes are more frequently manic. In Asian countries, studies suggest tendencies toward mania-dominant trajectories for those with bipolar disorder, while extended depressive episodes, along with comorbid anxiety disorders, more often complicate bipolar II disorder. Among individuals living in tropical regions, such as Hong Kong, India, and Nigeria, who relapse with bipolar episodes, manic episodes are overrepresented.

Lifetime prevalence of bipolar disorder globally is estimated to be about 2.4 percent of population; it is reported to be the highest in the United States at 4.4 percent, and the lowest in China at 0.1 percent, while in sub-Saharan Africa it is reported to be between 0.1–1.83 percent. Reports on the prevalence of bipolar disorder in Asian and African countries are generally much lower than in the West. In South Asia, the prevalence of bipolar disorder is reported to be about 0.6 percent. In Japan, lifetime prevalence of bipolar disorder is reported to be about 0.2 percent, with an annual prevalence of 0.1 percent.

Incidence reported varies by demographic contexts and economic resources available for diagnosis and treatment. There are also treatment differences that are culturally based. In the United States, for instance, Black and Hispanic individuals with bipolar disorder are more likely to be misdiagnosed and to receive poorer treatment than non-Hispanic whites; a difference not fully explained by differential rates of health insurance coverage. Asian Americans have a higher reported bipolar I disorder prevalence than others, yet are less likely to receive a bipolar diagnosis.

The annual incidence of bipolar disorder globally is estimated to be 0.7 percent. The lowest annual incidence of bipolar disorder is reported at 0.2 percent for some countries in Asia, such as China, North Korea, and Taiwan. Across South Asia and South-East Asia, as well as in much of Micronesia, 0.3 percent is reported for countries including the Philippines, Indonesia, and Vietnam. Countries including Bulgaria, Pakistan, and Bangladesh report 0.4 percent annual incidence. Across most of Africa and in countries like Japan, Poland, and Russia, 0.5 percent incidence is reported. In the United States, as well as countries including Singapore, Kenya, and Romania, 0.6 percent annual incidence of bipolar disorder is reported. Countries, including Afghanistan, Iraq, Ireland, Germany, and Saudi Arabia, report 0.7 percent annual incidence. Many countries report 0.8 percent, including Antigua and Barbuda, Barbados, Cuba, Dominican Republic, Ecuador, France, Greece, Puerto Rico, Portugal, Sweden, and Switzerland. The UK, Lebanon, and Mexico, as well as much of Latin America and the Caribbean, report 0.9 percent. Israel and Paraguay report 1.0 percent, Australia and Brazil report 1.1 percent, while New Zealand reports the highest annual incidence of bipolar disorder, other than the United States, at 1.4 percent of its population.

Reported comorbidities for bipolar disorder vary by country as well. For example, at least 0.3 percent of adults in India live with bipolar disorder; with 33.3 percent reporting comorbid tobacco use disorder, 14.6 percent reporting other substance use disorders, and 10.4 percent reporting anxiety disorders. Across Asia, depression and suicidal ideation appear more frequently among females with bipolar disorder, while for males with bipolar disorder comorbid substance use disorders are more prevalent. While reported differences in rates of bipolar disorder among varied populations may reflect actual incidence variabilities, it is more likely that it is attributable to other factors, such as amount of resources devoted to bipolar disorder prevention, screening, and diagnosing; levels of societal stress; and, possibly, genetic variation within respective populations.

Since mania has sometimes been associated with recreational substance abuse, or even creativity, artistic expression, or religious fervor, manic traits do not always warrant serious concern in some cultures. Diagnostic criteria for bipolar disorder have consequently changed over time and across cultures. These differences still somewhat persist contemporaneously and, at least partially, explain the disparate prevalence rates reported from different countries.

There is a strong cultural overlay to the social definition and acceptance of bipolar disorder. As culture is a very complex and highly personalized dimension, individuals with bipolar disorder naturally experience it within an individualized framework grounded in a web of cultural beliefs, values, and norms. The course and severity of bipolar disorder are thus profoundly influenced by myriad cultural factors. In addition, the cultural background of mental health professionals directly influences the likelihood of their diagnosing bipolar disorder, as well as what subtype is likely to be indicated. A study of samples of individuals with bipolar disorder matched on gender and illness duration in France and Tunisia, for instance, found that the initial mood episode for 75 percent of the Tunisian sample was a manic episode, while the first mood episode for the majority of French patients was a depressive episode.

In some countries, there is a socially expected masking, or modification, of bipolar symptoms. For example, a study conducted in seven Arab nations found substantial cultural variations. Sudanese individuals exhibited the highest frequency of bipolar symptoms, followed in decreasing order by Palestinians, Egyptians, Yemenis, Qataris, and Jordanians, with Tunisians having the fewest symptoms reported. These sorts of factors can limit the generalizability of the results of respective studies.

Cultural openness to diagnosing and socioeconomic status heavily influences cultural variation. It is accordingly important to consider cultural differences in patient populations. However, beliefs that there are cultural differences in prevalence should not reduce proper diagnosis and treatment of all individuals.

8. Historically, how did individuals conceive of the condition we now recognize as bipolar disorder?

What we today recognize as bipolar disorder has no doubt affected individuals as long as there have been human beings. Moods are part of the human condition. It is speculated that one of the earliest responses to dealing with someone with bipolar disorder was, out of ignorance, misunderstanding, and fear, likely euthanasia. Ancient Egyptians, at least since around 4,000 years ago, believed that the heart, not the brain, was the seat of mental function, both for mental health and mental illness; and that dramatic loss of status or financial ruination could produce depression, which they felt could best be treated by talking it through with prayers for divine, religious intercession and, if unsuccessful, that suicide was an acceptable option. Similarly, in ancient Israel of the Old Testament, despair could erupt as depression, again best resolved by a bulwark of faith.

Ancient Greeks formulated varied explanations as to cause and how to treat or deal with depression and mania. The term "mania" was used by the Greeks to refer to a state of divine madness. In the works of Homer, it was said the Olympian gods took away one's sanity; Aeschylus, more specifically, saw the work of demonic possession, only to be cured by exorcisms; Socrates taught that these maladies were sent down from the heavens, and thus were nothing to be ashamed of, but could only be reversed by a divine blessing; Plato described two types of mania, one of divine origin and the other having a bodily cause; and Aristotle wrote of the curse of melancholia, which he suggested was a by-product of genius and best remediated by music; but he also suggested melancholia contributed to the creative gifts of the minds of artists, poets, and writers. Our term "melancholia" (*melancholia*) meant sadness in ancient Greece and comes from the Greek *melas* (black) and *khole* (bile). Hippocrates looked for natural, medical causes, which were curable by abstaining from excesses, bolstered by a vegetarian diet, and moderate physical exercise. Accordingly, an individual with too much black bile purportedly had a melancholic disposition characterized by despondencies and fears; it was believed fluxes of the blood involving an imbalance of the humors could transform melancholy into mania. This concept of disease as an imbalance of the four humors prevailed from at least the fifth and fourth centuries BC, through Roman and Medieval eras, to early modern times.

Aretaeus of Cappadocia (in modern Turkey) was a first century AD Greek physician credited with being the first to describe the alternating patterns of depression and mania for what we now understand as a mood spectrum with opposite extremes of mood, which he suggested were related to problems in the brain. Celsus, a second century AD Greek philosopher, understood melancholia as a type of madness which could be diverted with assorted techniques like listening to entertaining stories and varied forms of persuasion. Galen, another prominent second century Roman-era Greek physician, speculated on psychic functions of affected brains that might be swayed by direct confrontations, perhaps with some touches of humor aided by healthy exercises. Medieval and Early Modern convictions tended to blame the victims, often for moral lapses that opened portals for evil spiritual possession. Bipolar disorder then probably generally interpreted to be possession by the devil or by demons. That spawned the establishment of asylums to seclude and lock sufferers away from society.

Medieval Arabic physicians, such as al-Kindi and Avicenna, wrote about *huzn*, a melancholic condition. By the Late Middle Ages, European poets and chroniclers wrote about a pervasive state of suffering and gloom characterized as melancholia. Sir Robert Burton, an English scholar and Anglican clergyman, in 1621, wrote *The Anatomy of Melancholy* from both a medical and literary perspective suggesting music and dance as the core for treating melancholia and mental illness in general. In 1686, Theophile Bonet, a Swiss physician, coined the term *manico-melancolicus* linking mania and melancholia. By the late eighteenth century, English physicians asserted that the English, in particular, were liable to *morbus anglicus*, a state of despair stemming from the damp, chilled British climate, exacerbated by a beef-rich diet, and working in the fast-paced commercialism of the emerging Industrial Age. In 1801, the term "hysteria" was coined in a medical text written in Latin and used to describe a neurotic condition in women thought to result from a dysfunctional uterus. It served as an attempt to control women by means of a mental health fallacy, implying females were unable to control their emotions.

In the mid-nineteenth century, French psychiatrists linked cycles of mania and depression to the same disorder; Jean-Pierre Falret called it *folie circulaire* (circular insanity), which had cycles of varying intervals; he urged physicians to try different medications hoping one might prove effective; Jules Baillanger referred to it as *foile a double forme*, which held individuals directly cycled between periods of mania and depression, which many referred to as manic-melancholic. At that time, symptoms of mania and depression that occurred simultaneously were referred to as mixtures or middle forms; for instance, German psychiatrists at the beginning of the nineteenth century referred to mixed states as *mischungen* or *mittleformen*; while it was Jules Falret, Jean-Pierre's son and also a French psychiatrist, who coined the term "mixed states."

By the turn of the twentieth century, a German psychiatrist Emil Kraepelin in 1902 coined the notion of manic-depressive insanity; he outlined its characteristics and distinguished it from what is now recognized as schizophrenia. In 1917, Sigmund Freud wrote "Mourning and Melancholia," which he identified as stemming from losing a loved object creating lack of interest in daily life and a pervasive sense of dejection. Freud suggested this was a perilous condition threatening destruction of the ego, while emphasizing the violent, even at times sadistic, impulses melancholia could generate. Freud argued the superego of one who is melancholic was driven by the death drive (Thanatos) refusing to let go, but maintaining a libidinal desire for a lost object, whether a person, thing, or idea, internalizing it into their own ego and so could be treated, rather than resorting to mourning. This purportedly manifests in European societies as a cultural malaise. Freud essentially implicated childhood trauma and unresolved developmental conflicts as the cause of bipolar disorder. Several subtypes of melancholia were created. Affective melancholia occurs primarily during what we now recognize as depressed episodes of bipolar disorder. Suicidal melancholia manifests as an impulse to commit suicide, typically associated with profound feelings of melancholia. It is sometimes accompanied with hypochondrial thinking and a pronounced reduction in psychomotor activities, frequently including a sense of the inability to love self or others.

In the early 1950s, Karl Leonhard, a German psychiatrist, introduced the term "bipolar" to differentiate between unipolar depression, now typically called major depressive disorder, from bipolar depression. The early DSMs (*DSM-I* and *DSM-II*), listed various types of manic-depressive illnesses, like manic type, depressed type, and circular type. Accordingly, prior to 1980 with the release of *DSM-III*, which was led largely by Robert L. Spitzer, bipolar disorder was generally known as manic-depressive disorder to emphasize its predominant emotional symptoms, but this largely ignored the presence of its cognitive and/or physical symptoms. With *DSM-III* and several subsequent editions and revisions, the condition was referred to as bipolar disorder and listed under the mood disorders category; but, with release in 2013 of *DSM-5*, bipolar disorder was separated from the chapter on mood disorders, and an emphasis was made focusing on shifts of energy level and on goal-directed behavior. More recently, many have come to regard bipolar disorder as existing along a spectrum of mood disorders, which, in turn, is part of a broader spectrum of psychiatric conditions.

9. Historically, what were some of the methods used to treat what we now recognize as bipolar disorder?

Methods to treat what we now identify as bipolar disorder have substantially differed historically. Just as notions of what bipolar disorder is, and what it is caused by have varied in different historical contexts, so have approaches to dealing with and treating it. In many ancient societies, if someone was behaving manic, or otherwise irrationally, they were likely to be banished, if not killed outright, or otherwise removed from social interaction. Two of the oldest methods used for treating bipolar disorder and other mental health conditions, perhaps, are mechanical restraints and hydrotherapy.

Mechanical restraints consist of physical devices to restrain an individual, sometimes, but not always, with minimal discomfort and pain. Mental health patients are still mechanically restrained to prevent harming themselves, others, or property. However, restraint is the treatment of last resort and generally reserved for those whose behaviors cannot be otherwise managed.

Since ancient times and into the modern era, the mentally ill with bipolar disorder and related conditions were physically restrained with chains, ropes, and other devices, such as shackles or pillories. During the Enlightenment, it was believed that restraining mentally ill individuals could help restore a sense of reason. Use of mechanical restraints became widespread during the eighteenth century, with the intention of effective social control; this resulted in substantial increases in use of involuntary mental health hospitalizations and more individuals being restrained.

During the nineteenth century, insane asylums became numerous across Europe and in the United States, but these soon became overcrowded and staffed with poorly trained staff who resorted to use of restraints to attempt to maintain order and calm. Actual causes of bipolar disorder and other mental illnesses were poorly understood; many believed the mentally ill had lost control of their morals, and that discipline and order imposed by restraints could help them regain self-control. In Great Britain, Robert Gardner Hill, in 1838, abolished the use of mechanical restraints at Lincoln Asylum; soon thereafter, John Connolly did the same at the Lunatic Asylum in Hanwell, England. These efforts were part of reformist movements, which led to developments of modern psychiatric care.

Hydrotherapy is treatment of disease, including bipolar disorder, with water. It is purportedly built around scientific application of water as medicinal treatment. Hydrotherapy was particularly popular for treating mental illness during the late nineteenth and early twentieth centuries. The term "hydrotherapy" is derived from the ancient Greek *hydor*, meaning water, and *therapeia*, meaning treatment. Hydrotherapy has a long history including in ancient Egypt, Israel, Iran, China, Japan, Greece, and Rome. Bathing in hot springs, as prescribed by the ancient Greeks and Romans, may be partially vindicated by findings that many such springs actually contain natural lithium salts, now understood to sometimes be an effective treatment for bipolar disorder. During the Middle Ages, mentally ill individuals in Europe were routinely immersed in consecrated waters, like wells dedicated to the Virgin Mary or various saints, to cure them, a custom called "bowssened."

In the seventeenth century, J. B. van Helmont advocated ducking treatment for those with "mad ideas," where persons were suspended head first under water until loss of consciousness; after being revived, if they could, they were considered cured. This led to a treatment called the "bath of surprise," where they were immersed into water without a warning. In the eighteenth century, assorted hydrotherapeutic approaches were developed to treat those in the emerging asylums. This was considered useful to lessen the heat of madness, as well as to rouse the melancholic.

By the nineteenth century, elaborate hydrotherapeutic apparatuses were constructed in asylums, such as in Paris. In Austria, Vincenz Priessnitz developed his *wasserkur* (water cure), which was said could treat melancholy and other ailments of the time, including gout, indigestion, rheumatism, and tuberculosis; this led to a water cure craze as an alternative medical treatment popular throughout the Western world. Early proponents of hydrotherapy included Sir John Floyer (1649–1734), Dr. J. S. Hahn (1696–1773), Prof. E. F. C. Oertel (1764–1850), James Currie (1756–1805), and J. H. Rausse (1805–48). In Europe, particularly in German-speaking nations, spas and sanatoriums specializing in hydrotherapy became highly popular. In the second half of the nineteenth century in Great Britain, the electric bath enjoyed brief popularity. By the late nineteenth and early twentieth centuries, hydrotherapy was used punitively for treating the mentally ill as it was coercively used. This *douche* approach was pioneered somewhat earlier by Philippe Pinel (1745–1826), a French physician, and thereafter many European and American doctors utilized punitive hydrotherapy as a moral treatment for the insane, including those we would now consider to have bipolar disorder. Wet packs and prolonged baths were used instead of mechanical restraints for agitated patients, such as those who were manic.

During the early twentieth century, in developed nations and elsewhere, hydrotherapy was used for treating mental illnesses, including bipolar disorder. It was observed that when patients were exposed to warm applications, like warm wraps, warm water baths, and stream baths, for extended periods of time, they tended to become calm. Patients, therefore, considered suicidal or assaultive, regularly got these treatments. The London Asylum for the Insane, for example, operated a continuous bathroom throughout the early to middle twentieth century, where continuous supplies of fresh, hot water were poured into tubs, while existing water was drained, to maintain consistent temperatures for the time of treatment. Patients were laid in hammocks resting in a canvas covered tub, with heads poking through a hole in the canvas. The room was lowly lit and quiet, helping patients relax, and often go to sleep. Continuous baths, not surprisingly, were used to treat those with insomnia. Prior to World War II, various forms of hydrotherapy were used to treat alcoholism and other illnesses, including bipolar disorder. Similarly, prior to the 1950s, psychiatric hospitals had varied hydrotherapeutic installations, like special tubs, foementation stations, sitz baths, and steam baths. Use of hydrotherapy for treatment of mental illnesses during the first half of the twentieth century, was consistent with emerging ideas of mental problems coming from the brain, rather than from an immaterial mind, and that therapeutic approaches treating the body, such as hydrotherapy, could therefore be effective.

Electroshock, or electroconvulsive therapy (ECT), is another psychiatric treatment technique that has been, and under certain circumstances, still is used to treat certain cases of bipolar disorder and related conditions. Since the early sixth century in Europe, physicians used various techniques to induce seizures in attempts to treat psychiatric conditions, including bipolar disorder. At least by the late eighteenth century, British physicians were using electricity for varied medical treatments. Benjamin Franklin suggested the use of an electrostatic machine to cure female "hysterical fits." In 1801, James Lind and Giovanni Aldini, independently, used galvanism to treat mental illnesses. In the middle of the nineteenth century, G. B. C. Duchenne was integrating electrotherapy into his medical practice. During the second half of the nineteenth century, asylums in Great Britain were routinely employing electrotherapy.

In 1934, Ladislas J. Meduna, a Hungarian neuropsychiatrist, introduced convulsive therapy using cardiazol (metrazol) to treat epilepsy and schizophrenia. In 1937, Swiss psychiatrist Max Muller organized an international conference on convulsive therapy for schizophrenia. In 1938, Ugo Cerletti, an Italian neuropsychiatrist, began using electric shocks, instead of cardiazol, to induce seizures. By 1940, Friedrich Meggendorfer was advocating the use of electroconvulsive therapy in Germany and Austria; it was also introduced to the United States and Great Britain, and became widespread through the 1940s–50s for treating severe depression, among other conditions then regarded as intractable. However, these early applications of ECT were severe and induced full-scale convulsions without anesthesia. Similarly, prefrontal lobotomies were increasingly performed from the 1930s to the 1950s for manic individuals, along with those who had other conditions thought to be intractable, in the mistaken belief that neural circuits were fixed in the brain and that cutting the connections between hemispheres could change the undesirable behaviors.

Beginning in the 1970s, modern electroconvulsive therapy was administered as brief pulses with patients under anesthesia, but public opinion about the earlier, overused and inhumane applications of intense electroconvulsive therapy led to a decline in use. However, by the mid-1980s, researchers were again demonstrating the efficacy of modern electroconvulsive therapy for selected, but severe, psychiatric conditions, including selected cases of bipolar disorder. Contemporary electroconvulsive therapy is given in very short durations, at low intensities, and has been shown to effectively disrupt neural circuitry leading to improved brain rewiring and greater degrees of neuroplasticity; it has been particularly useful in treating severe or prolonged mania.

10. Who are some famous (or infamous) individuals who had or may have had bipolar disorder?

Many individuals with bipolar disorder, or at least for historical figures who are generally thought to have had bipolar disorder, long before the condition was recognized and defined, whether treated or not, have been successful in diverse areas. Many persons with bipolar disorder have contributed to making a better world in disparate fields, including explorers; scientists, mathematicians, philosophers; politicians; artists, animators, graphic artists, manga artists; actors, actresses, comedians; television personalities, film directors, and producers; singers, musicians, rappers, hip-hop artists, composers, conductors; dancers, models; authors, poets, journalists, publishers; business leaders, financiers, and entrepreneurs; athletes; and physicians and mental health advocates. It is difficult to absolutely say that a particular person in the past, before the condition was even recognized, actually had bipolar disorder or not. Nevertheless, reviewing biographical or autobiographical details about specific historical individuals allows reasonable consideration of whether they exhibited characteristics now recognized as indicative of bipolar disorder; the following persons are generally regarded in mainstream, academic sources, as having had or they themselves divulged, that they were, in fact, bipolar.

Some noted explorers exhibited qualities consistent with bipolar disorder, and this condition, particularly its manic aspect, may have even contributed to their visionary searching for the unknown. For example, Rene-Robert Cavelier, Sieur de La Salle, the seventeenth-century French explorer and fur trader, ventured into the Great Lakes regions of Canada and opened up North America for further explorers and then settlers.

Prominent scholars in many fields are considered to have had bipolar disorder, including leading scientists, mathematicians, and philosophers. Among scientists with bipolar disorder were individuals like Julian Huxley, Emily Martin, Dimitri Mihalas, Isaac Newton, and Gabriele Rabel. Mathematicians, such as Ada Lovelace, Emil Post, and Norbert Wiener, the originator of cybernetics, have been identified as being bipolar. Philosophers who were bipolar include Louis Althusser, Robert S. Corrington, and Kannadasan, who was from Tamil Nadu, India.

Former and current politicians from many countries, and at different times, are thought or acknowledged to have bipolar disorder. The famous British statesman William Pitt, 1st Earl of Chatham, is recognized in this group, as are Winston Churchill, Benito Mussolini, Henry VIII, and Julius Caesar. Australian political figures in this category include Eoin Cameron, Neil Cole, and Michael Costa. US politicians with bipolar disorder include people like Jesse Jackson, Jr., Patrick J. Kennedy, Karen McCarthy, Lynn N. Rivers, and Ron Thompson. The Canadian politician Svend Robinson was diagnosed with cyclothymia.

Creative pursuits have been speculated to sometimes be enabled by manic, as well as depressed, episodes. Artists who probably, or definitively, had bipolar disorder include the likes of Frida Kahlo, Michelangelo, Jackson Pollock, Gilbert Stuart, and Vincent Van Gough; as well as others such as Marcel Barbeau, Elbridge Ayer Burbank, Cosmo Campoli, Isa Genzken, Helmi Juvonen Arthur McIntyre, H. V. Meyerowitz, Kate Millegan, Valdemar Schonheyder Moller, Francesco Scavullo, and Paul Sharitis. Animators, graphic artists, and manga artists who are, or were, bipolar include Paul Boyd, Barney Bubbles, Akio Chiba, and Ellen Forney. Artists who almost certainly had bipolar disorder and who successfully committed suicide include Ralph Barton, Francesco Bassano, Francesco Borromini, Edward Dayes, Arshile Gorky, Benjamin Haydon, Ernst Ludwig Kirchner, Jules Pascin, Mark Rothko, Nicolas de Stael, and Henry Tilson.

Many entertainers probably had or have bipolar disorder. Actors, in this category, include Robert Downey, Jr., Richard Dreyfuss, Mel Gibson, Burgess Meredith, Charlie Sheen, and Jean-Claude Van Damme, as well as many others like Maurice Benard, Jonathan Brandis, Jeremy Brett, Jeff Garlin, David Harbour, Drewe Henley, Jang Keun Suk, Antoine Kamerling, David Strickland, David Walliams, and Lee Thompson Young. Actresses who have acknowledged that they are bipolar, many of whom authored revealing memoirs, include Patty Duke, Carrie Fisher, Linda Hamilton, Margot Kidder, Kim Novak, Kristy McNichol, and Catherine Zeta-Jones, as well as others including Amanda Bynes, Keisha Castle-Hughes, Mariette Hartley, Cassia Kis, Mary Lambert, Vivien Leigh,

Jennifer Lewis, Jessica Marais, Nicola Pagett, Lynn Perrie, Aubrey Peeples, Gene Tierney, and Ruby Wax. Comedians who were, or are, bipolar include the likes of Maria Bamford, Kemah Bob, Russel Brand, Stephen Fry, Spike Milligan, Benoit Poelvoorde, Tony Slattery, Brody Stevens, Taylor Tomlinson, and, the legendary, Jonathan Winters. Television personalities who shared their bipolar diagnosis include Tyler Baltierra, Dick Cavett, Caroline Flack, Kerry Katonia, Bill Oddie, Jane Pauley, Gail Porter, Amber Portwood, Katja Schuurman, and Michael Tunn. Film directors and producers who are bipolar include Maria Bello, Francis Ford Coppola, Paul Dalio, Adam Deacon, David LaChapelle, and Arthur Lipsett.

Numerous figures in the music industry had or have bipolar disorder and might have benefited from the creativity and the "blues" that characterize it. Paul Robeson, for example, experienced alternating episodes of mania and depression throughout his life; diagnosed at different times as manic-depressive (as bipolar disorder was formerly called) and also as cyclothymic, he was admitted to hospitals more than fifty times in the United States, the Soviet Union, UK, and Germany receiving various medications and ECT treatments. Other singers, both male, like Aaron Carter, Chris Brown, Mike Doughty, Tom Fletcher, Justin Furstenfeld, Daniel Johnson, Lee Joon, Petr Muk, Steven Page, Charlie Pride, Frank Sinatra, Peter Steele, Matthew Sweet, Nick Traina, Townes Van Zandt, and Will Wood; and female singers like Mariah Carey, Rosemary Clooney, Connie Francis, Selena Gomez, Beth Hart, Meg Hutchinson, Phyllis Hyman, Sarah Joyce, Demi Lovato, Allison Moyet, Sinead O'Connor, Nina Simone, and Amy Winehouse, have largely been open about being bipolar. Many musicians have likely been bipolar, individuals like Michael Angelakos, Adam Ant, Sean Costello, Vincent Crane, Matthew Good, Boon Gould, Glen Gould, Kristin Hersh, Randy Meisner, Dolores O'Riordan, Jaco Pastorius, Odean Pope, Lou Reed, Charlene Soraia, Devin Townsend, Scott Weiland, Pete Wentz, and Brian Wilson. Rappers who are bipolar include Adam Deacon, DMX, The Game, Yung Lean, YoYo Honey Singh, and XXXTentacion. Hip-Hop artists who are bipolar include Charles Hamilton, Krizz Kaliko, and Oxxxymiron. Composers, such as Hector Berlioz, Ray Davies, Gaetano Donizetti, George Frederic Handel, Gustav Holst, Charles Ives, Otto Klemperer, Gustav Mahler, Sergey Rachmaninoff, Giocchino Rossini, Robert Schumann, and Peter Tchaikovsky, and conductors like Ronald Braunstein and Otto Klemperer, were likely bipolar as well.

Some noted dancers and models are known to be bipolar. Dancers in this group include the famed Alvin Ailey and Britney Spears, while noted models include Sophie Anderton, Helen Flanagan, Rene Russo, and Naomi Sims.

Writers in many genres are represented among successful individuals who probably, or certainly, had bipolar disorder. Authors who were likely, or clearly, bipolar include Hans Christian Anderson, Honore de Balzac, Samuel Clemens (Mark Twain), Joseph Conrad, Patricia Cornwell, Swadesh Deepak, Charles Dickens, Ralph Waldo Emerson, Willian Faulkner, F. Scott Fitzgerald, Zelda Fitzgerald, Alan Garner, Graham Greene, Ernest Hemingway, Hermann Hesse, Marya Hornbacher, Henry James, Linea Johnson, Margarita Karapanou, Yoon Ha Lee, Thomas Ligotti, Herman Melville, Robert Munsch, Edgar Allan Poe, Heleen van Royen, Mary Shelley, Robert Louis Stevenson, Leo Tolstoy, Ayelet Waldman, Dorothy Wall, Mary Wollstonecraft, and the incomparable Virginia Woolf. Noted poets who were likely bipolar include Sherman Alexie, A. C. Benson, William Blake, Robert Burns, Lord Byron, Samuel Taylor Coleridge, Emily Dickinson, T. S. Eliot, Victor Hugo, Samuel Johnson, John Keats, Robert Lowell, Boris Pasternak, Ezra Pound, Alexander Pushkin, Theodore Roethke, Michael Strunge, Lord Tennyson, Dylan Thomas, and Walt Whitman. Poets with bipolar disorder who committed suicide include Thomas Lovell Beddoes, John Berryman, Thomas Chatterton, Hart Crane, John Davidson, Sergei Esenin, Randal Jarrell, Heinrich Von Kleist, Vachel Lindsay, Vladimir Mayakovsky, Gerard de Nerval, Cesare Pavese, Sylvia Plath, Anne Sexton, George Trakl, and Marina Tsvetayeva. Journalists with bipolar disorder include Jayson Blair, Jennifer Frey, Bernard Levin, Bill Lichtenstein, and Otto Pavel. Publishers, such as Larry Flynt and Philip Graham, were also bipolar.

Business and industry leaders who likely had bipolar disorder include individuals such as Andy Dunn, Paul M. English, Ted Turner, and Mark Whitacre. Financiers and entrepreneurs who rose and fell with cycles of bipolar disorder include those like John A. Mulheren, Robert Campeau, Heinz Prechter, Rene Rivkin, and Steven Thomas.

Myriad athletes from diverse sporting fields are known, or suspected, to have bipolar disorder. American football players are well recognized in this group, such as Davone Bess, Quincey Carter, Everson Griffen, Charles Haley, Johnny Manziel, Alonzo Spellman, Dimitrius Underwood; as is Australian rules footballer Jonathan Hay. Rugby players include the likes of Angus Crichton, Greg Inglis, Andrew Johns, and Tim Smith. Basketball players are represented by individuals like Penina Davidson, Ben Gordon, Byron Houston, "Fast" Eddie Johnson, Jimmy Piersall, and Delonte West. Professional wrestlers in this category include Teddy Hart, Chris Kanyon, and A. J. Lee. Boxers who are bipolar include Frank Bruno and Mike Tyson. Other types of athletes with bipolar disorder include cricketer Michael Slater, figure skater Debi Thomas, golfer David Feherty, ice hockey player Doug Harvey, runner Suzzy Favor Hamilton, soccer player Paul Gascoigne, and swimmer John Konrads.

Health care professionals are also among the ranks of individual with bipolar disorder. This category includes physicians, such as Devika Bhushan, Liz Miller, and Mark Vonnegut. Not surprising, perhaps, many prominent figures in the mental health field have publicly discussed their bipolar diagnosis and how they have coped with it; such individuals include psychiatrists, psychologists, and mental health advocates, such as author and educator Mary Ellen Copeland, psychiatric professor and writer Kay Redfield Jamison, Japanese psychiatrist and writer Morio Kita, and British psychologist and writer Stuart Sutherland. Bipolar disorder, as we can see, can affect almost anyone of any background and this puts them at high risk for the types of problems with family, school, work, and social lives typically reported by those so afflicted.

Causes and Risk Factors

11. Who is most likely to experience bipolar disorder?

Many factors have been suggested as predisposing one for bipolar disorder, including experiencing varied causes and behaving in certain ways that can increase the risks for bipolar disorder. For example, bipolar disorder is strongly associated with traits like mood instability, higher educational attainment, sleep disturbances, use of alcohol, and use of tobacco. In order to establish a causative relationship between traits and risk factors for developing bipolar disorder, several conditions must be met. These factors include variables such as biological plausibility, consistency, dose-response associations, specificity, and temporal relationships. Statistical correlations alone are clearly insufficient to assert clear associations, particularly when it comes to associations between risk factors and specific outcomes that have not been demonstrated in randomized clinical trials, but are only based on observational findings. Unfortunately, such is the case with long-standing debates on the relationships between bipolar disorder and related mental health conditions, and a plethora of risk factors. Accordingly, the available scientific evidence presently available is largely based on generally well-conducted observational studies that have assessed both the protective factors and the potentially harmful effects of selected factors. To better illuminate the relationships between bipolar disorder and the underlying mechanisms, specifically those of possible biological plausibility, that determine how examined factors may, or may not, affect our brains and associated mental health, it is critical to shed light on the underlying mechanisms. Currently, our understanding does not seem to be entirely convincing or exhaustive. The actual pathogenesis of bipolar disorder is not yet fully understood, but some of the processes currently being considered include inflammatory homeostasis, mitochondrial functioning, monoaminergic signaling, and neuronal-glial plasticity. Many risk factors, particularly childhood trauma, have been implicated.

There are many habitual behaviors some people have that can erode their mental health and predispose them to bipolar disorder and related conditions. Those who constantly berate themselves and engage in negative self-talk can weaken their self-esteem and potentially lead to feelings of worthlessness. Excessive worrying about the future, or about things beyond their control, can become overwhelming and lead to anxiety. Overworking can lead to burnout and adversely impact overall wellness, including mental health. It is unrealistic to demand perfection in all life activities, such expectations can foster undue stress. Unhealthy coping strategies, like avoidance behaviors or binge eating, can threaten mental health. A pattern of procrastination can become a stressor as guilt overtakes one for incompletions. Being in a toxic relationship, or surrounding yourself with negative individuals, can be draining and erode self-esteem. Consistently comparing yourself to others, whether in real life or more commonly on social media, can foster feelings of inadequacy and threaten self-esteem. Withdrawal and social isolation can exacerbate loneliness and generate depressing thoughts. Blowing things out of proportion or catastrophizing may foster anxiety and generate irrational fears. Constantly people-pleasing others, or seeking external validations, may foster a loss of sense of self and result in insecurities. Not seeking help when struggling with mental health issues, whether letting pride or stigma prevent such, can prolong suffering and inflame symptoms. Focusing on past regrets or mistakes can foster feelings of shame and guilt, preventing moving on. Suppressing or avoiding difficult emotions, such as anger, grief, or sadness, can foster emotional numbness and damage mental health. Ignoring your own boundaries, or allowing others to violate them, can foster emotional exhaustion and breed resentment. Individuals displaying these sorts of behaviors may unknowingly be undermining their mental resilience and stability; thus making them more likely to transition to bipolar disorder. Resilient individuals typically exhibit enhanced whole-body health, including more active brain function, healthier gastrointestinal tract microbiomes, less inflammation, and, consequently, better emotional regulation, including less depression and anxiety, as well as increased connectivity between reward circuits and sensorimotor networks. Less resilient individuals, like those with bipolar disorder, tend to be on the opposite side of the spectrum.

Gender appears to only somewhat influence the prevalence of bipolar disorder. Slightly more women than men are diagnosed as bipolar. Fluctuations in reproductive hormones, such as that occur during pregnancy and in menopause, when estrogen levels decline, have been speculated to trigger onset. Incidence of bipolar disorder in women is greatest during reproductive years. Women with bipolar disorder who are pregnant, or new mothers, have a sevenfold increase for hospitalization related to a significant mood episode, compared to pregnant women who are not bipolar. Males with bipolar disorder have a greater likelihood than females to have a history of violence and to have had legal problems, while females are more likely than males to attempt suicide.

It is widely recognized that early life experiences can have profoundly deep and lasting effects on mental health, including probability for bipolar disorder. Intense early experiences have long been understood to have the potential to affect brain plasticity and alter neurodevelopmental pathways related to mental health, such as corticolimbic circuitry involved in emotional regulation and hypothalamic pituitary-adrenal axis function. Emotional maltreatment at young ages has been demonstrated to increase amygdala activation and volume, and to decrease volume and functionality of a frontoparietal network associated with complex social and cognitive processing, as well as dysregulation of reward circuitry, including response to reward in the prefrontal cortex and striatum, that can lead to mood disorders, including bipolar disorder. These early impacts can become biologically embedded, that is epigenetically, directing the formation of stress response systems, including neural pathways between the limbic and prefrontal regions. Whereas the latter typically undergoes protracted development, the former and other critical regions, particularly the amygdala, tend to mature relatively earlier, making them more sensitive to earlier social environmental forces. While these phenomena can produce adverse psychopathologies, they can also enhance potential for resilience and better well-being. More support for promoting positive influences, such as caregiver behaviors that can assist in dampening cortisol reactivity, can thereby help in prevention of bipolar disorder and related conditions, such as posttraumatic stress disorder (PTSD), anxiety, and other forms of depression.

Sexual orientation can play a role in the prevalence of bipolar disorder. Members of the LGBTQIA+ communities are at increased risk for mental health conditions generally, including bipolar disorder. While the lifelong prevalence rate for bipolar disorder among US adults is 4.4 percent, that for males and females who identified as bisexual appear to have the disorder at a rate of about 7 percent.

One of the most salient predictors of who is most likely to experience bipolar disorder is being diagnosed with some other psychiatric condition. About 20 percent of adolescents with major depressive disorder will within five years of the onset of depression, develop bipolar disorder. In fact, up to a third of the 3.4 million children and adolescents in the United States, thought to have depression, may actually be experiencing early onset of bipolar disorder. Individuals who have psychotic-like experiences, such as auditory hallucinations, delusions, and paranoia, which are associated with mania, are at higher risk for suicidal ideation; similarly, risk of suicidal ideation goes up if one experiences insomnia, also sometimes a feature of bipolar disorder. Between 40–50 percent of individuals with bipolar disorder experience paranoia. Interestingly, even association with someone else who has a psychiatric condition may increase one's own risk. For instance, a study of 700,000 9th grades in Finland who had a classmate who experienced a mental illness found that one year after such exposure, 13 percent had a mood disorder, like bipolar disorder, anxiety, or an eating disorder.

Experiencing features of sleep disturbance, such as nightmares, sleep latency, and sleep quality, appears to be associated with increased risk of bipolar disorder, as well as of suicidal ideation. Just getting insufficient sleep for one night can make your body's cells age faster, especially those of your largest body organ, your skin, and increase disease susceptibility, including for bipolar disorder and related conditions; our brains are severely impacted as well by not getting enough sleep. Individuals with insomnia are ten times more likely to develop some depression; on the other hand, around 75 percent of individuals who are depressed have difficulty falling asleep. Sleep disturbance is fortunately a potentially modifiable factor.

Having a history of substance use and abuse is an area of increased risk for many adverse health outcomes, including bipolar disorder. Heavy alcoholic beverage consumption damages virtually all body systems, including the brain, not only increasing chances of bipolar disorder, but also premature death from cancers, liver and heart diseases, and many other causes, including accidents. It is estimated that there are over 380 deaths every day in the United States from excessive drinking. Tobacco smoking is commonly resorted to, in unsuccessfully attempting to get relief via temporary happiness and excitement. Smoking also damages our skin by damaging the collagen and elastic fibers in the skin, leading to sagging and premature wrinkles. It also makes our body more acidic and less alkaline, which accelerates aging, and increases disease susceptibility, including for bipolar disorder. Among adolescents and young adults, regular marijuana use and cannabis use disorder are associated with greatest risk for psychosis, as sometimes experienced when one is having a manic episode. Psychoactive substances, by definition, affect how the brain works. They impair the brain's communication pathways, causing impairments in moods, cognitive functions, coordination, and memory. They can impair the immune system and metabolic regulation, as well as damage most body organs and systems, particularly the liver and cardiovascular system. When consumed over long term adverse impacts can change both the function and structure of the brain, creating symptoms that mimic bipolar disorder and even facilitate transitions to bipolar disorder. Substance use and abuse is, again, a highly modifiable factor fortunately.

Lack of regular physical activity is a pervasive factor impacting nearly all aspects of health and well-being. Sitting for prolonged periods of time can seriously impair health and wellness and escalate risks for becoming bipolar. It has been suggested that excessive sitting is the new smoking with respect to its adverse public health consequences.

Inappropriate nutritional history also plays a role in the possible occurrence of bipolar disorder. It is recognized that dehydration can result in an array of mild to severe symptoms affecting emotional and cognitive function, which could increase risks for bipolar disorder. On the other hand, a recent study suggests that higher levels of arachidonic acid, a type of omega-6 polyunsaturated fatty acid, may help prevent risk of bipolar disorder. Genes that encode enzymes in the liver which metabolize arachidonic acid from linoleic acid, another omega-6 fatty acid, are associated with lower risk of bipolar disorder, while higher levels of linoleic are associated with higher risk. The physiological pathway of metabolizing linoleic acid appears to modulate the risk of developing bipolar disorder; higher levels of arachidonic acid actually contribute to cell membrane health and are crucial to infant brain development. Dietary and other lifestyle interventions that target ways to increase arachidonic acid levels could therefore be highly beneficial.

Metabolic dysfunction, which can alter brain pH and lactase levels making the brain more acidic, has been implicated in bipolar disorder and related neurological conditions. Poor dietary habits are another, closely related, but often underestimated area, of possible risk. For instance, unhealthy dietary habits which lower levels of GABA and raise those of glutamate have been correlated with corresponding neurotransmitter imbalances in the brain and reductions of gray matter in frontal brain regions, both associated with symptoms of depression and anxiety. Chronic high sugar intake may simulate hyperactive foraging by stimulating by stimulating an evolutionary-based metabolic pathway producing pleasure desensitization, with associated craving, impulsivity, risk taking, and aggression and, ultimately, inducing depressive episodes. Consumption of highly ultra-processed foods, such as frozen pizzas and microwavable meals, and associated dietary substances, including artificial sweeteners, affects the vast garden of microbes in the gastrointestinal tract that play a large role in metabolism and in producing proteins that function as building blocks for many neurotransmitters throughout the body, including the brain. Gut microbiome changes due to dietary habits high in saturated fats and sugars have been demonstrated to reduce numbers of parvalbumin interneurons essential for GABA delivery. Increased consumption of ultra-processed foods appears to be associated with greater risk for brain damage, like cognitive impairment and stroke. High fat and cholesterol diets also change cell membranes such that a neurotransmitter imbalance can result. Poor diets may contribute to at least 10 percent of all causes of preventable deaths. Obesity, resulting primarily from overeating and inactivity, creates a cascade of health problems not only including bipolar disorder and other mental illnesses, but even leading to a shorter lifespan. Again, however, diet and nutritional habits are readily modifiable risk factors.

Exposure to excessive screen time, particularly with social media platforms, has repeatedly been shown to be associated with an array of mental health issues, including bipolar disorder. In fact, excessive use of social media has been associated with feelings of anxiety, depression, and loneliness. Those who get an average of six hours per day of screen time may lower their lifespan by an average of 4.8 years, as well as increasing likelihood of bipolar disorder. In order to be pre-emptive, we need initiatives and strategies to create safe and secure digital spaces where young people, in particular, can explore their feelings without compromising their privacy or their wellbeing. To better ensure more supportive online systems, we need to create online environments free from stigma and judgment, that foster inclusivity and compassion by allowing for healthy online engagement.

Individuals who experience inflammation of the brain are known to be more likely to progress to bipolar disorder and related mental health conditions. For example, migraine headaches are 3.5 times more common among individuals with bipolar disorder than those without, so might be used as a predictor; as could, perhaps, many other causes of inflammation of brain tissue, which can result from a plethora of causes, including head injuries that can result in traumatic brain injury. Inflammation in the brain can be indicated by elevated levels of proinflammatory biomarkers, which have often been reported in individuals with bipolar disorder.

Many other risk factors have been suggested; accordingly, more research is clearly needed in order to gain a better understanding of which specific risk factors are most impactful for bipolar disorder outcomes. While the direct causes of bipolar disorder are still being figured out, we know that they essentially involve chemical and structural problems in the brain, among, no doubt, other factors. There is very strong evidence for the contributory, but not deterministic, roles of certain risk factors, such as genetics, early trauma, severe stress, certain physical illness, and brain abnormalities.

12. Is bipolar disorder possible in children?

Bipolar disorder was once considered to be quite rare in children and adolescents. Previously, bipolar disorder was thought to arise primarily in midlife; traditionally, considered to rarely appear before individuals were in their thirties. Until the mid-twentieth century, manic-depression, as bipolar disorder was then called, was generally thought to affect people beginning in the early twenties and up. It was not regarded as a condition that occurred among adolescents, let alone children. Psychoanalytical theory at the time asserted that prepubertal children could not experience classic depressive symptoms. In the 1980s, there was an emerging understanding that bipolar disorder could be diagnosed in adolescents and, sometimes, even if rarer, in children. In the 1990s and early 2000s, there was a general tendency for health care professionals in the United States to overdiagnose bipolar disorder in children and adolescents, while at the same time in Europe it tended to be underdiagnosed. Today, health care professionals are careful about diagnosing children with bipolar disorder.

There is considerable evidence indicating bipolar disorder is more prevalent at younger ages than was previously thought. One national survey reported a 40 percent increase from 1994 to 2003 in the number of children and adolescents treated for bipolar disorder. Bipolar disorder is most often diagnosed in young adults, but it can appear in adolescents, and, although less commonly, in younger children as well. Many individuals develop mental illness early in their life; about 50 percent of mental illnesses begin by age 14, with 75 percent occurring by age 24. More specifically, 12 percent of children with bipolar disorder show symptoms between the ages 5–9 years; 30 percent do so before the age of 14; and about 50 percent of people are diagnosed before the age of 25 years. The average age of the onset of symptoms for bipolar disorder is around 18–20 years old. It is estimated that bipolar disorder accounts for 5 percent of disability in adolescents aged 15–19 around the world, making it the fourth leading cause of disability in that age group. At any rate, bipolar disorder is sometimes underdiagnosed in children and adolescents; it is estimated that there are 1.1 million children and adolescents diagnosed with depression who may, in fact, have early onset bipolar disorder.

Emotional ups and downs are normal in children and adolescents and do not typically require treatment. However, there certainly are cases where emotional issues and behaviors in children and adolescents can become more severe and/or persistent, even sometimes progressing to a point that they can disrupt daily functioning, particularly in school or family settings. Unfortunately, many children and adolescents with bipolar disorder go undiagnosed and poorly treated, which can have devastating consequences, including substance abuse and suicide. Also troubling is that many of the children and adolescents now being diagnosed and treated for bipolar disorder are typically being prescribed psychiatric medications; many tending to exhibit behaviors parents and/or teachers find disturbing, with medication being an effective tool for pacification.

Identification of mental health conditions, like bipolar disorder in children and adolescents, presents additional challenges. Diagnosing bipolar disorder at any age can be complicated; it generally takes several assessment sessions and evaluation by means of multiple techniques. However, there are no definitive psychosocial, biological, laboratory, genetic, or brain imaging tests that independently can conclusively confirm a diagnosis of bipolar disorder in children, adolescents, or anyone of any age for that matter; accordingly, multiple measures are routinely utilized by health care providers to comprehensively evaluate someone. A diagnosis of bipolar disorder, particularly in children and adolescents, is essentially one of exclusion of other possibilities, such as attention deficit hyperactivity disorder (ADHD), conduct disorders, oppositional defiant disorder, anxiety disorder, other depressive disorders, autism spectrum, substance use disorders, or early traumatic experiences. Many conditions, particularly those in children and adolescents, can present with symptomologies similar to bipolar disorder; furthermore, comorbidities are rather common as well, in which one may have more than one, and also more than two, conditions simultaneously.

Symptoms of bipolar disorder in children are not so different from those in older individuals, but they tend to present differentially. When these sorts of symptoms cluster, we refer to it as an episode, but at other times, they may demonstrate more usual moods and behaviors. Episodes of mania in children and adolescents, for instance, generally are characterized by more psychiatric features than in adults, often leading to a misdiagnosis of schizophrenia. Children and adolescent when manic typically tend more toward states of aggressiveness and irritability, and so are more prone to destructive outbursts, than adults who when manic typically exhibit states of elation or euphoria. Children and adolescents when depressed may present with more physical complaints, like headaches or stomachaches, claim to be tired and fatigued; they are also more likely to exhibit poorer academic performance and social isolation, be more irritable, and be more sensitive to rejection or failure than adults. In addition, symptoms are often more ongoing, or chronic, in children and adolescents as opposed to the more often episodic, or acute, presentations in adulthood. Children with bipolar disorder are frequently impulsive, easily distracted, and hyperactive, which can easily lead to a misdiagnosis of ADHD. The aggression expressed by children can often lead to violent outbursts, which can be misdiagnosed as conduct disorder. Ultimately, again, bipolar diagnosis is essentially one of exclusion of alternatives.

A major symptomatic characteristic of bipolar disorder in children and adolescents is intense swings in mood that differ from usual mood swings, particularly with respect to duration. Episodes of mania and depression in children and adolescents can be rather brief, at least sometimes of shorter durations than episodes typically are in adults, which can make them harder to identify. Children and adolescents with early onset bipolar disorder are likely to have more extensive family histories of bipolar disorder and more likely than adults to experience rapid cycling. However, periods of anger, sadness, or joy have been found to typically be longer and more intense in preschoolers and toddlers with bipolar disorder compared to non-bipolar preschoolers and toddlers. Behaviors that tend to be more impulsive, aggressive, or even hyperactive, to an extent that they affect social interaction, are of utmost concern and are indicative of emotional reactivity. Children and adolescents who appear to have racing thoughts, usually evidenced by talking rapidly and frequently, and quickly changing subjects while talking are a major tell. Some children or adolescents with bipolar disorder may engage in risky and reckless behaviors, particularly those that are of a sexual nature, or use alcohol or other substances. Adolescents with bipolar disorder often exhibit abrupt or extreme changes in interests, affiliations, or appearance. Sleep disturbances are common. Some may have inflated estimates of their capabilities and possibilities. Older children and teenagers may exhibit suicidal or self-harming thoughts or behaviors, as well as acting out sexually. Paranoia may sometimes be expressed.

While "classic" bipolar disorder clearly exists in children and adolescents, there is also a broad spectrum of less severe, subsyndromal bipolar conditions. Preventing and remediating bipolar disorder, and its symptoms, in children and adolescents can be a major public health initiative with benefits not only to individuals concerned, but to larger societies as well. Early identification and interventions can help prevent the development of more serious issues and can substantially reduce the effects of mental illness later as individuals grow older. In this regard, about 25 percent of depressed adults started having symptoms before they were seventeen years old, yet half were not diagnosed until around thirty years old.

13. Are there biological or behavioral traits that can help predict who may develop bipolar disorder?

There are many biological or behavioral traits that are predictive of who may likely come to experience bipolar disorder. While most of the research in this area has focused on behavioral predictors, the promise of identifying clear biological indicators could provide immense advancements in developing more effective prevention and early interventional strategies, particularly as bipolar disorder is now considered a medical condition resulting, at least in part, from particular anomalies in the brain and its neurotransmission systems. There is research which indicates that stem cells in individuals with genetic predisposition for bipolar disorder develop differently than in those who do not. This suggests that from the very beginning of their life, these individuals are different biologically.

Neuroscience clarifies that there are clear differences in the brains of individuals who later transition to bipolar disorder long before the condition fully emerges. These differences include less connectivity in neural networks in specific regions of the brain, particularly in the left inferior and mid-frontal brain areas, as well as more extensive thinning of cortical tissue and more pronounced volume reduction of right lateral frontal areas, and a general loss of gray matter. Neurodevelopmental changes from adolescence to young adulthood, the primary time for emergence and diagnosis of bipolar disorder, involve considerable reorganization of multiple structural brain networks. Connectivity weakening has been found in individuals with bipolar disorder in a neural network linking the left inferior and middle frontal brain region, the left striatal and thalamic structures, the left fusiform, and the right parietal and occipital brain regions. This network weakening is even more pronounced in individuals who already had their initial manic or hypomanic episode. However, while these sorts of brain changes produce considerable reorganization of structural brain networks, these are not absolutely necessary, nor sufficient by themselves, to always result in the disorder. Yet they do, nonetheless, substantially elevate the risk.

Blood testing for specific biomarkers could potentially help differentiate between bipolar depression and other psychiatric conditions, particularly other types of depression. There is a biomarker blood test using a targeted mass spectrometry-based platform, which, along with an online assessment, can correctly diagnose about 30 percent of bipolar disorder cases. Specific RNA sequences, eight different ones in fact, have recently been identified by a French company, Aistiag, using artificial intelligence (AI), to identify bipolar biomarkers.

Individuals experiencing euphoric mania tend to report seeing vivid colors, their vision flirts about broadly, and their eyes widen and sparkle; while individuals experiencing dysphoric mania tend to squint with a narrowing of the visual field, things appear less colorful, and the pupils of their eyes are enlarged. Ophthalmological studies have reported reduced pupil response in individuals in depressive episodes, which is supported by brain imaging indicating lack of activation of the locus coeruleus, both of which are physiological consequences influenced by low responsiveness of noradrenergic neurons to norepinephrine, which is responsible for upregulation of arousal in the nervous system, and thereby manifesting as listlessness and low affect. Reduced pupil response could be a diagnostic aid suggesting that antidepressants could be more effective than other medications in those individuals; furthermore, the degree of pupil reactivity could be utilized to optimize medication dosage.

There are far more behavioral traits that have been suggested to serve as early predictors of bipolar disorder. These behavioral predictors include varied domains such as poor mental health, commonly identified by obvious lack of self-care, hypersexuality, hyper-religiosity, and many others.

There's a good chance that someone who is neglecting their mental health is about to rocket down the trajectory of developing bipolar disorder, or some related mental illness. If they continue not to take care of themselves, they may later exhibit some of the characteristic traits of someone with bipolar disorder.

Hypersexuality, for instance, is a profoundly alarming sign in which individuals are typically unable to control their sexual behaviors. They usually exhibit various sexual indiscretions, like having intercourse with individuals who are married or otherwise have partners, with strangers, or with slight acquaintances, circumstances which can not only destroy their own relationship, but likely expose them to potentially fatal sexually transmitted diseases (STDs), unwanted pregnancies, and otherwise socially isolate them from family, friends, and peers.

Other individuals may become hyper-religious; someone in a manic phase with grandiosity may even believe they are the next messiah or great prophet. Wild outbursts can appear out of nowhere, usually in response to a combination of irritability, racing thoughts, and intense energy levels. Outrageously high self-esteem, usually unfounded in reality, can erupt in bouts of grandiosity, an individual with no technological background may think they have designed the greatest invention ever that will save the planet and humankind. High risk-taking activities may proliferate, such as excessive shopping sprees, quitting their jobs with no new replacement, or investing all the family savings in some hair-brained venture. Talking incessantly, jumping from one topic to another and another, vocalizations that seem more like stream of consciousness than a reasonable conversational modality are not uncommon. They might engage in overly intense, hyper-focused apparently goal-directed activity that is ultimately aimless, and which no one else seems to regard as important, like taking the washing machine literally apart to get out every last bit of lint. Often the individual may be entirely unable to experience any real sense of pleasure or joy, but rather feel excessive, inappropriate guilt. Excessive guilt can commonly move into suicidal ideations.

Individuals with a wide array of medical conditions have been reported to have higher incidences of bipolar disorder. For example, the prevalence of bipolar disorder in adults with mood disorders is about 35 percent; with approximately 6.2 percent of those having seizure disorder, or epilepsy, with the greatest risk is for those with temporal lobe epilepsy. More seizure-like brain activity appears to be correlated to more episodes of hypomania. It has been suggested that seizure-like activity in the brain, or actual seizures, might contribute to manic symptoms and of full-blown manic episodes in those with comorbid bipolar disorder. Unfortunately, some antiseizure medications, such as levetiracetam, topiramate, and perampanel, may increase risks for aggression, depression, and psychosis. On the other hand, some medications effective at treating symptoms of bipolar disorder, such as bupropion and certain tricyclic antidepressant medications, like clozapine and maprotiline, may increase seizure risk.

The emerging consensus is that bipolar disorder should be understood as a chronic disease with an underlying biology, rather than as a consequence of negative psychological influences. Mental processes are seen as occurring in a biological brain, part of, not separate from, the rest of the body. There actually appear to be multiple biological mechanisms that interact with many external factors and, thus, there is no one cause of bipolar disorder.

14. What do we know about genetic and familial risks for bipolar disorders?

Genetics and familial risks play a larger role in some conditions, including bipolar disorder, than in others, but are always influential rather than deterministic in nature; as attested by twin studies and related research; and, as with all risk factors, are only ever expressed under certain environmental conditions. Nevertheless, familial and genetic studies both suggest that bipolar disorder is a multifactorial condition resulting from combinations of genetic and environmental factors. At any rate, concordance rates for bipolar disorder in monozygotic, identical twins are roughly 65–75 percent, and about 14 percent for dizygotic, fraternal twins. Children of parents with bipolar disorder have a 4–15 percent risk of also having the condition, while children of parents without bipolar disorder have a 0–2 percent risk. Research findings strongly suggest a polygenic risk such that many alleles likely each contribute a small effect that combine to affect susceptibility; this is supported by phenotypic complexity as evidenced by multiple subtypes of bipolar disorder and their associated comorbidities. For instance, bipolar I disorder has a higher genetic correlation with schizophrenia, while bipolar II disorder is more associated with major depressive disorder. Genes implicated in bipolar disorder are primarily those involved with brain processes such as synaptic signaling pathways, particularly those associated with high degrees of specificity of expression with neurons of the hippocampus and the prefrontal cortex, those associated with neurotransmitter receptors and transporters, and those encoding plasma membrane proteins regulating ion channeling.

Familial studies strongly support the notion that bipolar disorder has a heritable component. For instance, more than two-thirds of individuals with bipolar disorder have at least one close relative either with the same condition or with major depressive disorder. Similarly, bipolar disorder is much more likely to affect children whose parents have the disorder; when one parent has bipolar disorder, the risk for each of their offspring is 15–30 percent greater; when both parents are bipolar, the risk rises to 50–75 percent higher. If a brother or sister has bipolar disorder, the likelihood of their sibling having it increases 5 percent. Likewise, if an aunt, uncle, or grandparent has bipolar disorder, the risk also increases 5 percent. Twin studies confirm a contributory role of genetics in bipolar disorder as the risk of a non-identical twin being bipolar when the other is increases by 20 percent, while in identical twins the risk is increased 40–70 percent. Adolescents with bipolar disorder are significantly less likely to be living with both biological parents than adolescents with no history of psychiatric illness, which, by itself, elevates their risk. However, expression of familial risk for bipolar disorder is reduced with increased levels of physical activity and other healthy behaviors.

The brains of relatives of individuals with bipolar disorder and related conditions appear to differ from those without such family history. Brain scans of first-degree relatives of individuals indicate they tend to have larger intracranial volumes, an indicator of early brain development. This suggests the notion that familial risk for bipolar disorder influences brain development early in life.

It is important to understand that genetics is not predestination. Lifestyle factors can substantially influence how strongly or weakly genes are, or are not, expressed. Epigenetics, which will be discussed further, explains how environmental factors play a major role in cause or treatment of conditions like bipolar disorder. Individuals and their families can profoundly impact bipolar symptoms and their phenotypic expression by modifying their environments in positive, neutral, or negative ways, such as through changes in factors such as exercise, sleep, and diet.

Evidence indicates that regular physical activity, for instance, can not only heavily decrease, it can even completely reverse the adverse epigenetic consequences of trauma, distress, and myriad life events. Healthy exercise habits can promote brain health, facilitate brain cell growth, enhance efficacy of brain functioning, increase neuronal and synaptic plasticity, and reinforce learning and mood regulation, such as by improving executive function, memory, and attention.

This is not to imply that bipolar disorder has not been found to be frequently inherited and that it, in fact, is one of the most heritable mental health conditions, with the place of family history as a major risk factor. Evidence suggests that you are highly likely to inherit your corticolimbic system more from your mother than father, as it is the region of the brain most responsible for emotions, feelings, and even depressive episodes, and it is closely associated with your risk for bipolar disorder. This risk appears stronger for daughters than sons; in fact, the genetics behind the corticolimbic system, which plays a major role in control of emotional regulation, indicates that it is more likely transmitted from mothers to daughters, than from mothers to sons or from fathers to children of either gender. We understand that an individual has a 9 percent greater probability of developing the condition if they have a first-degree relative, like a parent, sibling, or child who has bipolar disorder. Genetic factors, overall, are thought to account for somewhere between 60–80 percent of cases of bipolar disorder. Certain genes have been identified as being involved in bipolar disorder. Actually, four different chromosomes, numbers 6, 13, 18, and 22 specifically, have been indicated as carrying genes that produce proteins which confer susceptibility to bipolar disorder. For instance, a gene, known as AKAP-11, has been identified as being a high-risk factor for bipolar disorder; it makes a protein, also called AKAP-11, that interacts with the metabolic pathway modified by lithium, the main pharmacological treatment for bipolar disorder. The protein AKAP-11 interacts with another protein, GSK3B, a molecular target of lithium and similar medications. Researchers are exploring whether variants of the AKAP-11 protein can serve as a biomarker for the disorder. Some of the strongest evidence indicates that chromosomal region 6 is associated with bipolar I; this is partly due to this chromosome harboring the melanin concentrating hormone receptor 2 gene (MCHR2), which is implicated in intracellular calcium release, the phosphoinositol pathway, and the kynurenine pathway, all suspected to be involved in the ability of lithium to stabilize mood; another gene on chromosome 6, that for the organic cation/carnitine transporter gene (SLC22A16), is also implicated.

Many other candidate genes are being studied for their possible association with bipolar disorder, including two that are known to be associated with circadian patterns; respectively, aryl hydrocarbon receptor nuclear translocator-like gene (ARNTL) and the circadian locomotor output cycles kaput gene (CLOCK); as disrupted circadian rhythms are thought to play a role in bipolar disorder. The nesprin-1 gene (SYNE-1) seems to be associated with mediating the internalization of glutamate receptors in postsynaptic neurons. The alpha-1 subunit of the L-type voltage-gated calcium channel gene (CACNA1C) is thought to inhibit the inositol 2,3,4-triphosphate receptor, which suggests the role of calcium signaling in bipolar pathophysiology. The ankyrin G node of Ranvier gene (ANK3) also appears to contribute to calcium regulation. The brain-derived neurotrophic factor gene (BDNF) appears to be associated with rapid mood cycling, and it is recognized that BDNF also helps neurons survive and grow, which are essential for neuroplasticity.

A recent genome-wide association study (https://doi.org/10.1038/s41588-021-00857-4) of a total combined sample of 41,917 persons with bipolar disorder and 371,549 persons without bipolar disorder identified sixty-four genomic locations, consisting of at least 161 individual genes, associated as risk loci for bipolar disorder, after accounting for all variations studied across the human genome. These genomic loci included thirty-three that had not been previously reported in bipolar disorder studies; among these newly identified genes associated with bipolar disorder are several involved in immune functioning through a major histocompatibility complex. Several of the genes identified as risk loci for bipolar disorder are known to be involved in how brain neurons signal each other. A significant, but incomplete, genetic overlap, as expected, was found between bipolar I and bipolar II. In addition, an association was found between bipolar disorder and other mental illnesses, including major depressive disorder, schizophrenia, and some childhood onset psychiatric disorders, like ADHD. Schizophrenia and ADHD, in this regard, were found to have stronger genetic correlations with bipolar disorder I, while major depressive disorder had a greater correlation with bipolar disorder II. Genetic markers for bipolar disorder appear to heavily overlap with those for other psychiatric disorders, such as schizophrenia and major depressive disorder. Genetic correlations, or overlaps, have also been identified with selected traits including alcohol and tobacco use, daytime sleepiness, insomnia, and sleep duration. Polygenic risks have been identified, for example, linking full bipolar disorder and ADHD to insomnia via the NRF-2-KEAP1 neural pathway.

It is speculated that ancient viral DNA known as human endogenous retroviruses (Hervs), some of which may even predate the emergence of *Homo sapiens*, and that now make up about 8 percent of the human genome, play a role in susceptibility to bipolar disorder and related psychiatric conditions like schizophrenia and major depressive disorder. If these retroviral infections occurred in sperm or egg cells that successfully produced offspring who survived to reproduce, then some of their genetic material could have been incorporated into the human genome transmitted to subsequent generations. These RNA molecules could facilitate production of proteins and/or other regulatory mechanisms, such as synaptic modification, that could potentially result in expression of bipolar disorder.

Epigenetics, which literally means "above genetics," refers to acquired changes to the functioning of genes that become heritable. The term "epigenetics" was coined in 1942 by Conrad Waddington, an embryologist who observed developmental processes in which phenotypes in different environments interacted with and modified genotypes. These processes involve structural regulatory changes to proteins which bind to DNA and are heritable. Epigenetics explains how chemical modifications by means of factors like regulatory enzymes, histones, and methylation either amplify or silence the actions of particular genes, which, in turn, modulate their ultimate expression. Epigenetic changes that alter controlled release of dopamine at specific locations may be able to modify gene activity even without the genetic mutations associated with bipolar disorder. Excesses in dopamine signaling have been indicated to trigger bipolar disorder.

It is recognized that genetics alone does not fully account for occurrence of psychiatric conditions, including mood disorders. Mood disorders, in fact, develop through a complex interaction of genetic predispositions, metabolic processes, neurochemical factors, and life experiences, including environmental conditions, particularly excessive distress. For example, genetics and age-specific processes interact to forge the neurobiological underpinnings on early onset and late onset bipolar disorder. Environmental conditions are clearly involved in gene expression. Exposure to poor air quality during the first then years of life, for instance, is associated with higher prevalence rates of bipolar disorder and major depressive disorder. This research reminds us that the better understandings of bipolar disorder are not to be found by asking only genetic or environmental questions, but rather by more deeply exploring the complex interactions that are possible between genetics and environment. This is because genes and environments interact in complex ways; most cases result from a mixture of genetics, biology, and stressors.

15. What brain chemicals and structures are involved in bipolar disorder?

In order to better understand bipolar disorder, it is important to understand how the human brain functions. Bipolar disorder is now recognized as a brain-based disease; accordingly, a review of brain chemicals and structures offers a better understanding of the condition. The average adult human brain weighs about 3.09 lbs. (1.4 kg) and has an average volume of 97.6 cubic in. (1600 cubic cm). Interestingly, brain volume and surface area, particularly in brain regions associated with memory and learning, appear to be increasing in recent generations. These larger brain structures may be related to improved brain development and improved brain health, which may yield larger brain reserves that could buffer risks of Alzheimer's and related dementias.

The brain is a highly structured sack of fluid containing a complex mixture of specific chemicals. Every thought, emotion, and sensation we have is created by the actions of chemicals in these structures. Many of these chemical molecules that have been identified so far, over sixty (it is speculated there are up to 2,000), are the neurotransmitters. Each neurotransmitter has a distinct chemical structure and shape that fit into the shape of other specific protein molecules, known as receptors, like a key fitting into a lock. There are different classes of neurotransmitters, including the amines, like acetylcholine, dopamine, norepinephrine, and serotonin; neuropeptides, like dynorphins, beta-endorphin, and substance P; amino acids, like aspartate, glutamate, glycine, and gamma-aminobutyric acid (GABA); enkephalins, like leucine and merhionine; and so forth.

The human brain consists of over 100 billion differentiated cells; thousands (*c.* 3,000) of different types of brain cells have been identified. The primary nerve cells of our brain and nervous system are called neurons. The brain is composed of approximately 100 billion neurons grouped into numerous clusters, sub-clusters, super-clusters, and interneurons; and billions of glial cells, like astrocytes and oligodendrocytes, and microglia. Neuronal diversity is consistent with functional diversity; some neurons are excitatory and some inhibitory; some dopaminergic, some glutamatergic, others serotonergic, along with many other kinds. The nucleus of the neuron regulates cellular metabolism and many, but not all, other dynamic internal activities. Combinatorially, these neurons express themselves via myriad neurotransmitters and neuropeptides.

Each neuron has its own structure; many consist of a few major components. Dendrites may be considered the beginning of each neuron as they extend outward, like branches, from the cell body (soma). One dendrite can have up to 30,000 branching extensions, each of which typically contains sensory receptor sites where chemical messages from neighboring neurons can be received as released neurotransmitters. Dendrites are not passive structures as dendritic excitability shapes neuronal response variability. Connections between dendrites of neurons, or neural pathways, are formed as learning takes place, including with regard to emotional regulation. Dendrites continuously establish new links and break old links with other neurons; this process of forming connections, or neural pathways, is how learning and memory occur. However, dendrites do not completely touch other neurons; there is a space, called a synapse, between neurons. Charles Sherrington, in 1892, was the first person to refer to the space between nerve cells as a synapse. The dendrite receives a chemical message which it converts to an electrical impulse if sufficiently stimulated; this electrical and chemical messaging is referred to as neurotransmission. The electrical impulse is transmitted down the body of the neuron, known as the soma, to the other end of the neuron.

As each of the roughly 100 billion brain neurons can potentially form about 10,000 connections to other neurons, complex networks can be established to transmit information to and to receive information from these pathways. However, when these neuronal communication circuits malfunction, assorted disorders, including bipolar disorder, can develop. Synaptogenesis, the formation and maintenance of synapses, is partially facilitated by adhesion protein molecules; a better understanding of these processes might enable formulation of molecular manipulations to intervene in the prevention and treatment of bipolar disorder and related conditions, like autism, epilepsy, and schizophrenia. Repeated signaling of messages, or lack thereof, makes synaptic linkages stronger, or weaker, larger, or smaller, respectively, which is referred to as synaptic plasticity. The size of synapses directly determines signal transmission. Smaller, weaker synapses are less likely to transmit messages, which could be more associated with depressive episodes. Larger synapses can generate stronger electrochemical impulses as they have the potential to simultaneously release greater amounts of neurotransmitters.

While the neurons actively involved in emotions and cognition constitute about 10 percent of the brain, the other 90 percent of the brain is still very active and essential, including other neurons, white matter, blood vessels, cerebrospinal fluid, and so forth, all required for healthy brain functioning. More than neurons are involved in neurotransmission. For example, astrocytes, non-neural glial cells in the brain, appear to help regulate synaptic strength, which, in turn, modulates the degree of response in neurotransmission. In bipolar disorder the activity, numbers, and sizes of glia, not just neurons, are reduced in several brain regions, including the frontal cortex, anterior cingulate, and other brain areas. There is a substantial thinning of gray matter in the frontal and temporal regions that control motivation and inhibition. The pathophysiology of bipolar disorder includes a downregulation of mitochondrial fusion-related proteins, as well as a significant decrease in citrate synthase activity, both of which contribute to the observed brain volume loss, cellular dysfunction, and cognitive declines observed in those with the disorder. Thus, many diverse neurological factors are at play in the development and maintenance of bipolar disorder.

The lengthwise extension of the neuron consists of the axon, which can range from 0.05 in. (0.127 cm), to up to 3 ft (almost 1 m) or more in length and that provides the electrical pathway along which messages are transmitted as action potentials within the neuron. These electrical messages, also called nerve signals, travel down the length of a neuron at a speed of up to 410 ft (125 m)/s. Axons in the peripheral nervous system are bundled into nerves, while those in the spinal cord and brain form neural tracts. Neurons are arranged in complex neural tracts in order to receive and transmit electrochemical signals. These signals are how messages get to the brain, how they get processed, and how responses are sent out. The brain sends out messages at a speed of about 268 m/h which directs us how to respond to stimuli. Axons terminate at synaptic terminals.

Synaptic terminals, or buttons, are situated at the opposite end of the neuron from the dendrites. Synaptic terminals consist of specialized protuberances that store specialized chemicals, neurotransmitters, or at least their precursors, in specialized sacks called vesicles. As the electrical impulse races down the length of the axon, it stimulates synaptic knobs to open, which allows a release of positively charged sodium ions. An action potential lasts less the one-thousandth of a second. Some neurons transmit action potentials continuously, while others only do so occasionally. An action potential translates the electrical signal inside the neuron into a chemical signal to be transmitted (exocytosis) from the synaptic terminal by opening calcium channels.

The neurotransmitters are stored in vesicles located at the terminal ends of neurons. The vesicles storing the neurotransmitters are signaled to release their contents into the synapse, the space between neurons, if sufficient electrical impulses achieve an action potential. To accomplish its mission, the vesicle moves closer to a neuronal membrane and fuses with it so that the neurotransmitter inside it can be released into the synapse. The action potential results in the electrical message being translated into a chemical one as respective neurotransmitter substances are released into the synapse. The synaptic cleft, the space between adjacent neurons, is only about an 18-millionth of an in. (*c.* 20 millionths of a millimeter, or 50 nm) wide, and it takes less than one-five-thousandth of a second for the neurotransmitter to cross the synapse, if it ever does find its way to an appropriate receptor. Myriad neurotransmitters are released to flow across the synaptic cleft to possibly connect onto the surfaces of receptor regions of adjacent neurons. One neuron may be exposed to perhaps thousands of synapses via varied dendrites. A healthy human brain contains more than 100 trillion synapses, each a potential connection across which neural messages can be transmitted.

Neurotransmitters are continuously produced, stored, released, and either broken down or recaptured as neurotransmission occurs. There are both excitatory and inhibitory neurotransmitters, the former stimulate receiving neurons to fire, while the latter prevent, or inhibit, firing. Neurons can fire up to a rate of about 1,000 times a second and many neurons can release multiple types of neurotransmitters. There are enzymes and other substances or mechanisms in the synaptic cleft that can prevent neurotransmitters from transmitting their messages, as well as other mechanisms that either prevent or increase the production of neurotransmitters in the first place. For instance, levels of enzymes, like ankyrin-G (ANK3) and diagylglycerol lipase a (DAGLa), that regulate synaptic transmission, either too little or too much, have been associated with bipolar disorder, as well as related conditions, such as schizophrenia and autism. After traveling across a synapse, a neurotransmitter attempts to bind to a receptor located on the membrane of a postsynaptic neuron. It takes about 1 ms for a neurotransmitter signal to be released and to bind to a receptor. Receptor sites are made of proteins shaped for specifically shaped chemically structured neurotransmitters to fit into. Neurotransmitters that fail to bind to receptors must be eliminated one way or another. Some are broken down, or metabolized, by specially crafted enzymes, the end products of which can be recycled to produce new neurotransmitters, others are simply captured by reuptake mechanisms and directly recycled. Neurons monitor neurotransmitter levels and dynamically adjust production levels if too high or too low.

In 1921, Otto Loewi realized that a chemical signal was being transmitted across a synapse; he called the chemical substance a neurotransmitter, which he specifically identified as acetylcholine. Acetylcholine is considered one of the classic neurotransmitters along with other catecholamines, like dopamine; these have relatively short circulating half-lives ranging between 10 s and 1.7 min and typically are recycled. Catecholamines are mainly metabolized in the cytoplasm of certain neurons, where their by-products are re-synthesized to produce new neurotransmitter molecules.

Respective neurotransmitter systems like the dopaminergic or the serotonergic interact with each other in complex interactions that if they become imbalanced in the brain can result in various neuropsychiatric disorders, including bipolar disorder. Catecholamines, such as dopamine and norepinephrine, are, under genetic direction, synthesized from varied amino acids, such as phenylamine and tyrosine, to function within both the sympathetic and central nervous systems. Stimulant drugs, like amphetamines and cocaine, function basically as catecholamine analogues, which is why their abuse can sometimes trigger bipolar disorder by forging imbalances.

The two major neurotransmitters implicated in bipolar disorder are norepinephrine and serotonin. Neurotransmitters are produced under genetically controlled directives. However, a plethora of risk factors can impact transcriptional regulatory mechanisms that modulate gene expression in different types of cells, some of which alter the production of proteins and other structural elements and thus eventually can result in neuropsychiatric disorders, including bipolar disorder. Norepinephrine is an excitatory neurotransmitter and its imbalances can produce manic symptoms, like agitation, anxiety, distractibility, hyperactivity, inattention, and insomnia, when released in large quantities; and, when levels are too low, depressive symptoms, like fatigue, lack of motivation, and oversleeping, are the result.

There is a noradrenergic system of neurons beginning in the locus coeruleus (lit., blue place), located in the brainstem and extending through the midbrain up throughout the cerebral cortex. Similarly, the serotoninergic system originates in the raphe nuclei located in the brainstem and midbrain and extends through neural pathways to the thalamus and gray matter in the cerebral cortex and includes much of the limbic system and the hypothalamus. Both systems are responsible for many different dysfunctions involved in bipolar disorder, such as those of moods, appetite, sexual activity, and sleep.

Imaging studies also support the importance of dopamine in the pathophysiology of bipolar disorder, indicating elevations in D2/3 receptor availability, a hyperactive reward processing network, and increased dopamine transporter levels. Failure to maintain homoeostasis between dopamine receptor and transporter levels is suggested to be the neurobiological underpinning of bipolar disorder, for both manic and depressive episodes. Acetylcholine is another neurotransmitter implicated in bipolar disorder. When it is at high levels, symptoms of depression are observed; with low levels, we see an association with manic symptoms. Several other neurotransmitters have been implicated in bipolar disorder, including GABA, glutamate, and glycine.

There are structural, and thereby functional, differences in the brains of those with bipolar disorder. Structural abnormalities, such as those in the prefrontal cortex and subcortical limbic brain regions, as well as cortical thinning and volume reduction, appear to result in impaired neural network connectivity that can manifest as cognitive deficits and emotional dysregulation (e.g., impairments to memory, processing speed, and sustained attention). One of the most pronounced structural deficits associated with bipolar disorder is the loss of tissue volume in many brain structures. Such neurodegenerative effects in the prefrontal cortex are greater in those with bipolar disorder, even surpassing the shrinkage observed in those with major depression. Similarly, the generally reduced volume found in the dopamine reward system of those with bipolar disorder tends to exceed that of those with unipolar depression, such that the anhedonia of bipolar disorder typically is more intense than that in major depressive disorder. Not surprisingly is the dramatic loss of tissue volume in the brain's emotional memory center. On the other hand, as the controller region of the prefrontal cortex tends to be less active in depressive episodes of bipolar disorder, the amygdala, which is normally restrained by the controller, becomes hyperactive and even enlarged. Conversely, in manic episodes the controller region of the prefrontal cortex increases activity, consequently inhibiting effects of the amygdala, particularly the fear mediating that normally restrains inappropriate behavior so typical in mania, and, this in turn, contributes to the intense seeking for pleasurable stimuli which manifests as the excessiveness exhibited in mania, like hypersexuality.

The smaller prefrontal cortex regions, which are responsible for supporting emotional regulation and inhibition, are generally much less active in those with bipolar disorder, even compared to those with major depression. In particular, as the area of the prefrontal cortex identified as assessing that aspect of excessive function comparing relative values of optional decisions is less active in bipolar disorder, more reckless behavior is demonstrated, typically to the detriment of the individual who is manic. Another area of the prefrontal cortex reduced in size and activity in mania is that which exerts cognitive control over emotional responsiveness, which typically sends regulatory feedback to the amygdala, essentially functioning as a braking mechanism. This can result in increased impulsivity and other inappropriate behaviors. Accordingly, when the brakes are not working properly, mania typically can result. The extent of the duration of the last manic episode is directly correlated to the degree of reduction in activity of the regions of the prefrontal cortex responsible for response inhibition and selection of goal-appropriate behaviors; this loss is most extensive in those with rapid cycling bipolar disorder, which explains why it is so difficult to treat.

Many, but not all, neurons are insulated and protected by a fatty layer known as myelin. The myelin sheath helps the neuron transmit electrical signals faster and more efficiently. In fact, neurons covered with myelin can transmit messages over a thousand times faster than neurons without it. There are two major types of proteins along the sheath; one kind works as signal proteins to transmit signals inside the neuron after specific molecules from outside the neuron bind to them, while the other kind functions as channel proteins letting certain molecule readily pass through them. Empty spaces between lengths of the myelin sheath are known as nodes of Ranvier. Neurolimma, also called Schwann cells, perform myelination of axons along nerves of the peripheral nervous system outside the brain; this again accelerates rates at which messages can be transmitted to organs, muscles, and other destinations. The shrinkage of brain structures as observed in bipolar disorder often includes a substantial reduction in myelin. This shrinkage and its effects are exacerbated by a roughly 30 percent loss of myelin coating of neurons, which impairs overall neurotransmission rates. Neurons without myelin fire 20–90 times slower than neurons with myelin coating.

Synapses in the amygdala and the subgenual anterior cingulate cortex are two major brain regions that regulate emotions, behaviors, and memories, and also play a principal role in the pathophysiology underlying bipolar disorder. Genes regulating these areas, as well as those influencing immune and inflammatory synaptic function appear to cause structural and chemical changes that impair communication between brain cells; this miscommunication results in the severe mood swings that characterize bipolar disorder.

Collectively, these structural and functional differences in the brain manifest as the features characteristic of those with bipolar disorder. Functional neuroimaging of individuals with bipolar disorder indicates, for example, decreased glucose metabolism in the amygdala and caudate. When individuals with bipolar disorder engage in tasks requiring regulation of emotions, they tend to exhibit excessive activation of the amygdala and inhibition of activity in the prefrontal cortex, where much executive functioning is performed, like planning, predicting, and decision-making. Due to demonstrable brain deficits, individuals with bipolar disorder lack the ability to show appropriate emotional responses, are more irritable, reckless, pleasure seekers; have impaired cognition and attention; and may have difficulty clearly expressing themselves. Areas in the right prefrontal cortex are less active during manic episodes, while those on the left side are less active during depressive episodes. There are also changes in activity in respective neural networks. In depressive episodes, the default mode network, which negatively assesses self-esteem, dominates activity over that of central executive and salience networks; while in mania, the salience mode network tends to suppress these other networks. The transition from a depressive episode to a manic one involves a switch in the insula from the default mode network to the salience mode network and attention is moved from a predominantly internal focus on self to an external one. However, it is important to understand that cognitive impairments associated with bipolar disorder are not necessarily permanent, particularly if appropriate treatments are utilized, nor do they automatically prevent individuals from performing above average at school or work.

Brain alterations associated with bipolar disorder are also evident at the neuronal level. In bipolar disorder, neurons are less able to avoid inflammation, to remove toxins, to engage neuroplasticity, and to promote neurogenesis. Neurons in those who are bipolar are, accordingly, less able to repair themselves, to maintain high levels of activity, to form new connections, and to engender the creation of new neurons to help cope with stressors. Neural pathways, as a consequence, tend to be dysfunctional and to atrophy. These consequences culminate in loss of brain structure and function, which can eventually result in a cascade of adverse health impacts, including coronary heart disease, diabetes, osteoporosis, stroke, suicide, and premature death, as well as, of course, bipolar disorder.

Neurotransmitter signaling appears altered and impaired in individuals with bipolar disorder. Neurotransmission, the translation of electrical impulses into chemical messages and of chemical messages back into electrical signals, employing neurotransmitter substances and other chemical molecules, that is repeated billions of times per second in order to enable the brain to convert clusters of neurotransmitters into all of our integrated emotions, actions, thoughts, and memories. It is an abnormal balance, an imbalance, of these chemical substances, either too little or too much, as they are coordinated for release and reabsorption, that can ultimately manifest as symptoms of bipolar disorder. Better understandings of this phenomenon not only can enhance our knowledge of the condition itself, but may also suggest novel and more effective prevention and treatment approaches.

16. What is the relationship between stress and bipolar disorder?

Chronic stress can wear one out, making you not only feel miserable, but cause excessive wear and tear to body organs, including the brain, and may even cumulatively result in depressive episodes, as well as premature aging and death. Acute stress has also been identified as a trigger for bipolar disorder. Rhythm disruptions, both to psychosocial rhythms and to biological rhythms (e.g., circadian rhythms), which are highly interrelated, are thought, along with acute stressful life events, to engender instabilities that seem to commonly trigger the onset of bipolar episodes in vulnerable individuals.

Traumatic events are major stressors associated with increased risk for bipolar disorder and other mental illnesses, including PTSD, which seems to be related to adverse impacts on the brain. These stress-induced impacts include changes to the amygdala, which helps detect threats and form defensive responses; to the corpus striatum, which serves to translate motivations into behaviors; to the insula, which coordinates internal and external stimuli to establish subjective awareness; and, to the superior temporal gyrus, which allows interpretation of nonverbal sounds. Adversity threats have been demonstrated to be correlated with increased blood-oxygen-level-dependent (BOLD) responses in the superior temporal gyrus and with decreased prefrontal cortex activity. Increased activity was also observed in the anterior cingulate cortex, claustrum, and insula, all involved with inhibitory control tasks, which is a characteristic of bipolar disorder.

Children and adolescents who experience adversities may demonstrate mild, moderate, or severe stress. Individuals under distress may not function as effectively as others in particular environments, such as school or work. Students under mild distress may exhibit excessive tardiness and absences; changes in motivation, social interactions, or attention to tasks; and failing grades. Students under moderate distress may exhibit depressed affect, isolation, or withdrawal; unusual emotional responses; disruptive behaviors; and make repeated requests for extensions on assignments and exams. Students under severe distress may exhibit tiredness or lack of energy; noticeable anxiety or panic; anger, irritability, or increased interpersonal issues; inability to communicate clearly; display highly disruptive behaviors; noticeable changes in hygiene, or excessive weight changes; threats to harm others or self; and suicidal thoughts or behaviors.

Early childhood traumas, in particular, appear to be associated with altered brain function in adults, including exaggerated responses in the amygdala and reduced responsiveness in the prefrontal cortex that helps regulate emotions and related behaviors. Early childhood experiences help not only build the structure of a developing brain but also lay the foundation for later mental health, positively and negatively. Early adverse life experiences can reduce neuroplasticity, possibly resulting in long-term mental health and cognitive challenges. Stress exposure in youth has been shown to alter neural connections between prefrontal and limbic regions, which may be particularly sensitive to such adversity due to both the high density of glucocorticoid receptors along those pathways and to the lack of maturity of those neural circuits. Environmental stress influence on these particular immature phenotypic circuits seems especially profound with respect to subsequent risk for stress-induced psychopathologies. Early stress is associated with factors such as diminished cortisol response to psychosocial stressors, increased inflammation evidenced by higher C-reactive protein levels, lessened hippocampal gray matter volumes, and escalated amygdala response to negative emotions; all correlated with greater psychiatric risks, including for bipolar disorder. Neurodevelopmental pathways altered by stress, particularly during critical stages of early development, including corticolimbic circuitry involved in emotional regulation and learning, significantly influence mental health outcomes associated with bipolar disorder.

There is generally a higher incidence of early adversity in minority communities and structural racism has molded social and other environmental conditions that yield racial inequalities, including inequities in mental health prevention and treatment. In a similar vein, Black, Hispanic, and Native American families are disproportionately exposed to environmental pollutants, experience discriminatory policing and incarceration, attend underperforming schools, have lower incomes, and so forth, all life stressors associated with bipolar disorder. Neural activity and connectivity interact with executive control networks, sometimes stimulating inflammatory responses via sympathetic nervous system signaling and increased activation of the hypothalamic-pituitary-adrenal axis to lead to enhanced production of proinflammatory cytokines in the brain and throughout the rest of the body, which can eventually manifest as chronic physical and mental health issues. These stress-related responses are influenced by myriad factors, including racism and socioeconomic status. For example, Black adolescents who experience acts of blatant racism can react by a reduction of activity in the amygdala, which leads to internalizing of symptoms and thus can make them at higher risk for depression and anxiety.

Although the prevalence of bipolar disorder is the same for Black and white Americans, the mental health consequences are more dangerous for Blacks than whites. In addition, Blacks often are not properly diagnosed as clinicians tend to focus more on the manic, rather than the depressive symptoms in Black patients; this tends to shift diagnoses toward schizophrenia, even when patients present with similar symptoms. This means that Black individuals are less likely to get appropriate treatment for what is actually a very treatable condition. Even if Blacks get treated for bipolar depression, they typically receive less intensive treatment, consequently meaning they will be less likely to be able to lead stable and productive lives.

Twin studies confirm that there is a dose-response relationship between childhood adversity and risks of subsequent psychiatric disorders, including bipolar disorder; as well as other health impairments, such as alcoholism, autoimmune disorders, obesity, diabetes, heart disease, and certain cancers; there is even an association with shortened lifespan. There may be as much as a 30 percent higher risk for suicide among those who experienced negative early life events. On the other hand, having stable, caring, responsive relationships early in life can not only prevent but possibly even reverse the potentially damaging effects of early negative adversities.

Neuroimmunology at least partially explains how stress can manifest as bipolar disorder. Stressful life events elicit the stress response, a nonspecific physiological constellation of reactions that disrupt homeostasis, including triggering the production and release of substances such as antibodies, enzymes, hormones, and, very importantly, cytokines. It is well known that if the immune response to distressful stimuli includes the production and release of cytokines, it causes inflammation. Neurons exposed to cytokines become inflamed and thus are less likely to regenerate via neurogenesis, and are more prone to cease functioning and be destroyed. Inflamed neurons are also less capable of neuroplasticity such that synapses between them are less able to form new neural pathways essential for learning and effective emotional regulation. Inflammation also causes a reduction in levels of serotonin needed for neurotransmission. These sorts of deficiencies, direct consequences of stress, can cumulatively manifest as episodic depression, such as appears in bipolar disorder.

These sorts of changes help explain the observed reduced ability to cope with life stressors that appears to increase susceptibility to bipolar disorder and may serve to help identify biomarkers to better understand the impacts of stress and adversity, as well as of its epigenetic effects that collectively might lead to possible courses of prevention and treatment for bipolar disorder. Cortisol (a stress hormone) levels, for instance, have been studied for some time as an indication of the association between stress and mental health issues. Elevated cortisol levels have been correlated with the onset of mania and with greater severity in mood episodes. We should acknowledge that prenatal cortisol (maternal stress indicator), as well as other prenatal hormonal and other chemical levels, can profoundly impact fetal development, including alterations to later neurodevelopmental parameters in offspring, such as IQ and EQ, both of which influence likelihood of bipolar disorder and similar conditions.

There also appear to be differential impacts by gender. For instance, higher cortisol levels during pregnancy, as an indicator of stress, both maternal and fetal, are associated with lower IQ scores in boys, while higher urine cortisone (a metabolite of cortisol) levels in girls are correlated with improved IQ scores. At any rate, when an individual is in a depressive episode, stressors are known to stimulate increased activity in the hypothalamic-pituitary-adrenal axis, which raises cortisol secretion. Interestingly, biomarkers for mitochondrial dysfunction appear to be correlated with suicidal ideation, a warning sign for bipolar disorder.

Creatine is another substance being considered as a potential biomarker to assess the association between stress and bipolar disorder, specifically creatine levels in a particular brain region, the anterior cingulate cortex, which is associated with response to stress and emotional regulation. Creatine assists with regeneration of adenosine triphosphate (ATP), a primary source of energy within cells; it is essential for maintenance of cellular integrity and functioning. Individuals with higher levels of creatine seem better able to recover from traumatic stress and, thereby, are generally less susceptible to PTSD and related conditions, including bipolar disorder.

It is also important to remember that genes are not actually as deterministic as most people mistakenly believe. Genes are essentially chemicals and, as such, are bound by the same constraints as all chemical reactions. Genomic sequencing, the nucleotide threads, merely functions as information storage, which is passive. It is the phenotype that is active in response to stress. Stressors, accordingly, can profoundly alter phenotypic expression well beyond the effects of genes, including the presence, or lack thereof, of bipolar disorder.

Immediate early genes, in particular, respond rapidly to environmental stimuli, especially to stressors, by activating other genes fostering neuroplasticity. One way they act, for example, is by producing early growth response (EGR) proteins, which encode environmental influences into long-term brain changes, thereby programming responses to things like stressful stimuli and sleep deprivation into, in this instance, the EGR3 gene. These proteins, particularly those produced by the EGR3 gene, along with neurotrophins, particularly brain-derived neurotrophic factor (BDNF) promote neuronal development and survival; reduced levels of BDNF are associated with bipolar disorder episodes of either mania or depression. It appears that EGR3 is repressed in the brains of individuals with bipolar disorder and that in concert with reduced BDNF levels, are interconnected in disrupted regulatory pathways, which results in structural brain changes, impaired neuroplasticity and resilience, and associated cognitive and functional declines potentially increasing vulnerability to stress, and causing more bipolar disorder episodes.

17. Is bipolar disorder related to other psychiatric disorders, such as schizophrenia and eating disorders?

Bipolar disorder is closely related to many other psychiatric disorders, including, among others, schizophrenia and eating disorders. The National Comorbidity Survey reported that 95 percent of individuals with bipolar disorder can meet diagnostic criteria for three or more psychiatric conditions. Relationships between bipolar disorder and related conditions have been found in multiple domains and are supported by diverse kinds of evidence, including strong indications from genetic research and from studies of comorbidities.

Schizophrenia and bipolar disorder have a high comorbidity and are often misdiagnosed interchangeably. Bipolar disorder and schizophrenia together affect more than 3 percent of global population. Symptoms and clinical attributes of bipolar disorder and schizophrenia have considerable overlap, supporting the idea that they are on a spectrum of psychiatric conditions. Synaptic, mitochondrial, and ribosomal molecular evidence from the dorsolateral prefrontal cortex indicates pathway similarities in protein production and energy metabolism between the two disorders; again, supporting the notion both lie on a spectrum. It appears that bipolar disorder, schizophrenia, and schizoaffective disorder have common genetic underpinnings, such as sharing the AKAP11 gene, and together affect about 9 million US adults. Schizophrenia alone affects approximately 3.5 million Americans. It is estimated that about 70 percent of the genetic coding for schizophrenia is shared with that for bipolar disorder. The same gene variants appear to be related to a cluster of related psychiatric conditions which include not only bipolar disorder and schizophrenia, but also major depression. The common genetic risk factors in this cluster appear to be related to immune system functioning and DNA regulation via histone methylation that directs on or off controls for expression of DNA. Another suspected area of the genome is that associated with neural transmission, particularly that for dopamine reception. More specifically, individuals with a particular variant of the GRM3 gene have a three-fold increased risk of developing bipolar disorder. Overactive dopamine signaling might explain why some individuals experience manic episodes. GRM3 also codes for a protein needed for detection of glutamate, another key neurotransmitter implicated in bipolar disorder, as well as for regulation of calcium channels which control brain cell activation. The genetic and biochemical (particularly at the synaptic level) roots of bipolar disorder and schizophrenia are closely related, again, suggesting the conditions may both lie on a spectrum.

Eating disorders, such as anorexia nervosa, bulimia nervosa, and binge eating disorder, have a high comorbidity with bipolar disorder. An estimated 28.8 million Americans will develop an eating disorder during their lifetime. One study suggested almost 15 percent of individuals with bipolar disorder also have an eating disorder. Many individuals with eating disorders frequently have other related psychiatric illnesses besides bipolar disorder; other common comorbid conditions include anxiety disorders, borderline personality disorder, depression, obsessive-compulsive disorder (OCD), alcohol use disorder, and substance use disorders. Individuals with both bipolar disorder and eating disorders, compared to those with only bipolar disorder, tend to be younger and female; have greater mood instability; more rapid cycling; increased prevalence of anxiety disorders, alcohol use disorders, and depressive episodes; more frequent suicide attempts; poorer medication response; and, in general, more severe clinical profiles. Mortality rates double in individuals with anorexia nervosa and another comorbid psychiatric condition, like bipolar disorder. Eating disorders seem to have the highest comorbidity with bipolar II disorder. Furthermore, family studies suggest a genetic link between bipolar disorder and eating disorders as there is a predominance of multigenerational depression in individuals with eating disorders.

Turning to food when feeling uncomfortable emotions is a common response. Some with bipolar disorder report eating helps them to feel more in control during sudden mood changes. For some with bipolar disorder, binge eating may be a maladaptive coping skill resorted to during manic or depressive episodes. Manic episodes actually seem to trigger binge eating more than depressive episodes. It has been observed that brain-derived neurotrophic factor (BDNF) levels plummet during a mood disruption and as one role of BDNF is to suppress consumption of food, and thereby regulate appetite, its decrease could lead to impulsive binge eating. One study of teenagers and young adults with both bipolar disorder and an eating disorder found that 20 percent also had PTSD. Furthermore, variations in a particular gene, PRRS-ARHGAP8, appear to be linked to both bipolar disorder and to binge eating disorder. This is supported by findings that 12–30 percent of individuals with a primary diagnosis of bipolar disorder also have binge eating disorder, and that 7.4 percent also have bulimia nervosa. Bipolar disorder and eating disorders both typically have an onset early in life, usually around late adolescence or early adulthood; both conditions are also cyclical in nature; both produce emotional reactivity and energy level changes; and, accordingly, having either bipolar disorder or an eating disorder seems to predispose one to have the other. In addition, antipsychotic medications, sometimes prescribed for bipolar disorder, affect the brain's reward system, including in the region associated with food rewards; also, weight gain commonly related to use of antipsychotic medications might contribute to cycles of binging and purging.

Many symptoms of bipolar disorder, like anhedonia and amotivation, are held in common with other related psychiatric conditions, specifically major depressive disorder and schizophrenia, suggesting there are likely underlying genetic, neural, and behavioral features shared among them, possibly along a spectrum. These three conditions all involve shared activations of the cingulate gyrus, medial gyrus, and middle frontal gyrus during reward pursuit activities. Supporting this notion, around 20 percent of children and adolescents with major depression transition to experience manic episodes by adulthood. In addition to the shared commonalities, there are some distinctions in brain activation to help differentiate bipolar disorder from other psychiatric conditions. For instance, only individuals with bipolar disorder exhibit increased activation in left precuneus and decreased activation in the dorsolateral prefrontal cortex during reward pursuit.

The three most common psychiatric comorbidities with bipolar disorder among children and adolescents are ADHD, oppositional defiant disorder, and conduct disorder. In fact, more than half of all children with bipolar disorder also have at least one of these other comorbid disorders. Some individuals with bipolar disorder also suffer from seasonal affective disorder (SAD) such that they are more likely to have depressive episodes in the fall and winter, while in the spring and summer they may be in a manic, hypomanic, normal, or mixed state.

There is also a high degree of comorbidity between bipolar disorder and anxiety disorders, certainly with strong genetic overlap. In fact, anxiety is the most common psychiatric comorbidity with bipolar disorder. Individuals with bipolar disorder have a lifetime risk of 51.2 percent for developing an anxiety disorder at some point in their life; this tends to occur more among those with bipolar I or bipolar II than among those with the other bipolar subtypes; more than 30 percent will have multiple disorders. The most common comorbid anxiety disorder among those with bipolar disorder, occurring at a rate of about 20 percent, is panic disorder, followed by generalized anxiety disorder (GAD), social phobia, OCD, and PTSD. Many bipolar symptoms, like irritability, panic, restlessness, and poor sleep, can be difficult to distinguish from those of anxiety. When anxiety symptoms cease after mood stability is achieved, it was likely a bipolar disorder symptom. However, when an individual's mood is stable without a manic or depressive episode underway, but anxiety symptoms persist, then it is likely a comorbid condition. One study found that individuals diagnosed with panic disorders were ten times more likely to have comorbid bipolar disorder and those diagnosed with GAD were twelve times more likely to have comorbid bipolar disorder.

The high degree of comorbidity between bipolar disorder and ADHD is well documented and several reasons have been suggested to explain this. We do know that there appears to be considerable overlap in the genetic factors identified in the predisposition to both conditions, as well as in the neurobiological risk factors for both. There is also considerable overlap in the symptoms of bipolar disorder and those of ADHD. However, it has been suggested that up to 15 percent of children who are diagnosed with ADHD may actually be experiencing early onset bipolar disorder. Furthermore, it is estimated that 10–20 percent of adults with bipolar disorder also have ADHD.

Substance use disorders and related conditions are highly associated with bipolar disorder. Substance abusers have a significantly earlier age of onset of bipolar disorder. Between 60–80 percent of individuals with bipolar disorder will experience alcoholism or other forms of drug addiction in their lives. Bipolar disorder has been recognized to have the highest comorbidity of any psychiatric condition with drug or alcohol abuse. Up to 45 percent of those with bipolar disorder have comorbid alcohol use disorder. Individuals with bipolar I disorder and comorbid alcohol use disorder have poorer recoveries from manic episodes, while those with bipolar II disorder and comorbid alcohol use disorder have more suicidal behaviors, poorer social functioning, and are more likely to transition to bipolar I disorder within five years. One study, for instance, found 60.7 percent of individuals with bipolar I disorder had a comorbid substance use disorder, 46 percent had an alcohol use disorder, and 40.7 percent had a drug abuse/dependence diagnosis. A large-scale study of Danish individuals reported that cannabis use disorder doubled to tripled the chance of having bipolar disorder or major depression. Excessive use of alcohol or other drugs can exacerbate mental health problems and make them more difficult to treat. All substances, from prescriptions to over-the-counter products to illicit drugs, have side effects; when any of these alter brain chemistry, psychiatric symptoms can be presented. Use of stimulant drugs, including amphetamines, cocaine, and methamphetamines, can potentially mimic manic episodes, as can marijuana (cannabis) and PCP (phencyclidine). Marijuana use in young people can result in psychosis. Cannabis use disorder, particularly in young people with its high association with psychosis, may be a precursor to certain cases of bipolar disorder. Use of opiates and opioids, like heroin, fentanyl, and methadone, can produce symptoms that mimic depressive episodes. Use of benzodiazepine tranquilizers, like Librium (chlordiazepoxide), Valium (diazepam), and Xanax (alprazolam), can cause depression, mania, suicidal ideation, and even psychosis. Barbiturates taken by adults can manifest with drowsiness, confusion, and depression; yet when taken by children and adolescents, aggression, excitement, hyperactivity, irritability, or tearfulness may be observed. Individuals with bipolar disorder may misuse substances in attempts to enhance the highs experienced during manic episodes; they may also be attempting to self-medicate. Individuals with bipolar disorder and related conditions like schizophrenia consume all psychoactive substances at higher levels than the general population. There are indications individuals with predispositions to and with bipolar disorder react differently to and experience more adverse consequences from the use of psychoactive substances; for instance, adolescents with higher genetic vulnerability to bipolar disorder or schizophrenia, psychedelic use is significantly associated with more severe manic symptoms than for those adolescents with lower genetic vulnerability. Studies indicate individuals with comorbid bipolar disorder and substance use disorders have a greater number of lifetime psychiatric hospitalizations.

Comorbidities with other psychiatric conditions are higher for those with bipolar disorder than for most other conditions; for instance, about 33 percent of individuals with bipolar disorder also have a personality disorder, such as antisocial, borderline, narcissistic, paranoid, and histrionic personality disorders. Lifetime prevalence rates of OCD among individuals with bipolar disorder are about 21 percent. One study reported that a Danish female with bipolar disorder's risk of being admitted for hospitalization due to schizoaffective disorder by the age of forty-five was about 103 times more than for females in the general population. Obesity has a greater comorbidity with bipolar disorder than with any other psychiatric condition; about 35 percent of those with bipolar disorder are also obese.

Individuals with bipolar disorder have even higher blood levels of inflammation biomarkers than do those with MDD, which is already higher than for the general population; this is a serious concern as inflammation is a major predictor for a plethora of health problems. For example, in a large sample of the Finnish population, researchers found that bipolar disorder increased the risk of premature death six-fold due to a combination of external factors like suicide, accidents, violence, and myriad physical health issues; alcohol-related fatalities in that study were mainly due to liver disease (48 percent), alcohol overdose (28 percent), and alcohol dependence (10 percent), while nearly half (48 percent) of the suicides were from prescribed psychiatric medication overdosing; furthermore, those with persistent symptoms of delusions, hallucinations, and psychosis also had significantly higher risks of death. About one-third (25–50 percent) of those with bipolar disorder will attempt suicide at some point and around 20 percent will be successful, many do so under the influence of alcohol or other drugs.

Individuals with bipolar disorder and other psychiatric conditions generally have serious health problems. Mental health conditions broadly, including bipolar disorder, currently are the leading cause of disease burden globally and in the United States, and they affect about 13 percent of the population around the world. The numbers and proportions of factors such as years lived with a disability, disability adjusted life years lived with bipolar disorder, years of life lost, particularly from suicide, and other related factors underscore the prevalence and burden of bipolar disorder. People with serious mental illnesses, particularly bipolar disorder, schizophrenia, and schizoaffective disorder, have up to double the risk of heart disease, and greater risks for many other health problems including thyroid problems. Research indicates that those with serious mental illnesses die 10–20 years earlier than the general population; heart disease is their leading cause of death. Adults with serious mental illness tend to have more risk factors for heart disease than the general population, including smoking, obesity, diabetes, and high blood pressure. For instance, they are three times more likely to be current smokers, have double the rate of diabetes, and are 50 percent more likely to be obese; about 12 percent of those without mental illness are obese compared to 36 percent who have serious mental illness.

Cognitive deficits are common across many psychiatric conditions, including bipolar disorder and ADHD. In fact, several aspects of cognitive dysfunction are very similar between the two; these include impaired executive functioning, issues with verbal memory and with working memory, problems of attention and vigilance, and delays in processing speed. While it was once thought that we should treat the bipolar disorder before treating the ADHD, we can only consider such with very severe suicidal cases. Concurrently treating both has yielded greater treatment success than treating either independently. The cognitive impairment associated with bipolar disorder in males appears, at least partially, to be attributed to loss of the Akt-mTor neural pathway from dendritic withering. Cognitive impairment is one of the strongest predictors of how an individual with bipolar disorder may function in the community, such as being able to maintain friendships and relationships, as well as being able to perform at school or work.

Many of the causative factors identified for bipolar disorder are equally associated with causing other psychiatric conditions. For example, some of the lasting effects of someone who experienced incidents of sexual misconduct include increased likelihood of developing depression, feelings of blame, posttraumatic stress, eating disorders, substance abuse, and related physical and mental health issues.

When comorbid conditions are conceptualized under a network approach, it is possible to consider the pathways to them arising from the direct relationships between clusters of symptoms of multiple disorders, with overlapping symptoms and overly rigid diagnostic boundaries not typically accommodated for. Under this approach psychopathological symptoms are seen as nodes causally connected by means of feedbacks between biological, chemical, psychological, and societal mechanisms. A disorder state, such as that in bipolar disorder, is, accordingly, regarded as the network becoming stuck in a relative, but by no means absolute, steady constellation state of highly connected symptom networks, which, of course, can change over time.

Signs, Symptoms, and Diagnosis

18. What are some of the signs and symptoms of bipolar disorder and how do they vary among the different types of bipolar disorder?

Several signs and symptoms of bipolar disorder have been recognized and they vary somewhat in presentation among the varied subtypes of bipolar disorder. These common signs and symptoms of bipolar disorder also change over time, both in the lifetime of an individual with bipolar disorder and in the recognition and acceptance of such as indicative of the disorder. When an individual is in a manic episode, they may feel extremely happy and energetic, even unstoppable, or they may be irritable and on edge; feeling overly self-confident individuals may take dangerous risks. When an individual is experiencing a depressive episode, they may feel hopeless, often losing interest in things that they previously enjoyed; they typically will have very low energy, feel completely drained, and may find it difficult to make decisions or to remember things. These episodes, or mood swings, may occur close together, alternating quickly from one to another, commonly described as having a roller-coaster of feelings and emotions; or there may be considerable periods between episodes of mania or depression when they feel themselves.

There are a range of signs along a wide spectrum that individuals with bipolar disorder might feel or display. Sometimes, during depressive episodes individuals feel low and hopeless, lacking energy and/or motivation, often needing extra sleep, even putting on extra weight, and having impaired functioning at school, work, and/or social settings. Sometimes during manic episodes, individuals feel overly energetic, take on many activities simultaneously, perhaps spending money recklessly or being excessively talkative, outgoing, even sexual; their behaviors can appear annoying or strange to others, even putting them into trouble with colleagues or authorities; they may misuse alcohol or other substances.

There are long symptom lists for both mania and depression, the two major mood states characteristic of bipolar disorder; nevertheless, some general characteristics can be noted. Manic symptoms include impulsivity, increased productivity, grandiosity, risk-taking, restlessness, racing thoughts, judgment impairment, and decreased need for sleep. Depressive symptoms include low mood and self-esteem, hopelessness, difficulties concentrating, loss of appetite, interest, and motivation, feelings of sadness and guilt, and sleep impairment.

If some of the signs and symptoms of bipolar disorder occur at younger ages, they are generally considered to be more indicative of greater potential for enhanced intensity and severity of the disorder than if they appear at older ages. Some of these early signs of bipolar disorder include things like extreme mood swings, high levels of energy, being overly euphoric, irritability, impulsivity, engaging in risky behaviors, difficulties concentrating, changes in appetite, dramatic behavioral changes, altered sleep patterns, feelings of worthlessness, episodes of depression, lack of energy, social withdrawal, unexplained ailments, and suicidal thoughts.

Individuals who experienced trauma, such as abuse, neglect, or loss, at a young age typically express self-blame for it. Children commonly assume that if something is wrong, it must be their own fault; due, perhaps, to something that they did, or didn't do properly. Excessive self-blame, not simply accepting responsibility for their own actions, which is healthy, can lead to an overwhelming sense of guilt, which is enhanced by impaired frontal lobe activity characteristic of bipolar disorder. This kind of thinking often grows into intense self-criticism or despair, both of which typically engender depressive episodes.

Some individuals with bipolar disorder may have thoughts of harming themselves, or even wishing that they were dead. When someone is thinking that others would be better off without them, or that there is no way out of the difficulties they are experiencing, it is a serious sign that warrants immediate attention.

To reduce self-blame, it can be helpful to break down a situation and recognize that there are almost always multiple factors at play. When an individual identifies their own contribution to the situation, as well as the external factors beyond their control, they may come to appreciate things from a more balanced perspective, realizing that the issue may not actually be their own fault. This reshaping of thought, as advocated in cognitive behavioral therapy, can significantly reduce the burdens of guilt. Rarely, if ever, is someone solely responsible for a negative outcome, which can halt the escalation of negative thoughts that often erupts in an episode of depression or even of suicidal ideation. Feelings of helplessness and of the inevitability of an adverse outcome can prevent empowerment and progress in crafting a positive coping response to a challenging situation. As an individual becomes depressed, a common response is feelings of incapacity, which can make simple daily activities, like getting out of bed or getting dressed, seem impossible. Self-imposed limitations, particularly of unwarranted and unrealistic, can become severely disabling. Slight modifications of thinking, such as shifting "I can't" to "I have trouble … " can perhaps open possibilities for alternative and effective solutions.

These sorts of warning signs must be present for at least one week in an individual, and cooccur with at least three other signs per episode to indicate full bipolar disorder. Furthermore, the extent of these signs must be extreme enough to possibly necessitate hospitalization so as to prevent harm to self or others. All of these could occur, due possibly to an individual's lack of personal responsibility and not caring about or not taking care of themselves and their needs, or they might not. Perhaps, if they could leave a toxic relationship, exercise more regularly, get more sleep at night, eat better, drink less, talk to a therapist, and so forth, then they might be able to create a better lifestyle that can support and promote healthier brain chemistry and healthier habits, including to break the vicious cycles that can sometimes disrupt their lives, and that of those around them.

19. Why do people with bipolar disorder have bodily symptoms?

While it is true that bipolar disorder is a brain-based condition, to ask why people with bipolar disorder have bodily symptoms is to imply that brain and the body exist independently and are of different domains, which is far from reality. The brain is absolutely a part of the rest of the body and what happens in any part is going to impact all other parts. Ultimately, bipolar disorder arises from changes in the body (which includes the brain) that occurred over time and that may, or may not, manifest as the disorder. All bodily functions influence likelihood of bipolar disorder and related conditions. For example, impaired kidney function, along with an altered immune system, has been shown to be positively associated with bipolar disorder and major depressive disorder.

Bipolar disorder, accordingly, has the potential to affect virtually all parts of the body, not just the brain.

The cardiovascular system, for example, can be directly impacted by bipolar disorder. The intense physiological arousal accompanying a manic episode can severely tax the cardiovascular system; this can include accelerated heart rate, heart palpitations, and an increased pulse; hyperventilation is not uncommon and higher than normal blood pressure may occur.

The skeletal and muscular systems can be affected by bipolar disorder. Depression can manifest with unexplained aches and pain, as well as weakness in muscles. This can make it difficult to engage in normal daily activities, let alone reduce ability to exercise or engage in other physical activities. Injuries are not uncommon with risky behaviors commonly reported during manic episodes.

The gastrointestinal system can be dysregulated, such as by the typical feelings of tiredness and irritability or restlessness associated, respectively, with depressive and manic episodes. Bodily symptoms of this can include appetite changes, abdominal pains, diarrhea, nausea, and vomiting. These can result in substantial changes in body weight, either gains or losses. Obesity is more common in individuals with bipolar disorder.

The endocrine system can be altered by bipolar disorder, with hormone fluctuations commonly experienced. Metabolic signaling, not just in the brain, but throughout the rest of the body, particularly the gastrointestinal tract, which is directly mediated by diet, may influence mood. For instance, higher levels of ghrelin, a hormone produced in the stomach, have recently been demonstrated to play a role in not only regulating energy levels and appetite, but stress response and mood as well, especially after short-term fasting. Thus, short-term fasting interventions may have a mood-enhancing effect, as circulating levels of ghrelin rise, since its production increases when the stomach is empty, thereby eliciting antidepressant effects. Stomach problems can manifest with excessive sweating and rapid breathing and may lead to a prevailing sense of doom, which can progress to a depressed episode, or can erupt as a state of panic. Manic episodes can stimulate libido with significant escalation of sex drive, while depressive episodes might result in decreased libido.

Fatigue is a typical sign associated with bipolar disorder. After experiencing a manic episode, with its accompanying physical intensities, individuals often are physiologically exhausted and routinely feel sleepier than normal. Individuals in depressed episodes may experience a sudden lack of energy, or they may sleep more than normal, or they may have difficulties sleeping.

As bipolar disorder is recognized to be associated with inflammation, it should not be surprising that several medical conditions that typically present with bodily symptoms are more common in individuals with bipolar disorder than in the general population, such as migraine headaches. Children and adolescents with bipolar disorder seem to experience greater incidence of conditions such as asthma, eczema, irritable bowel syndrome, and psoriasis. Women tend to have more physical disorders, like migraine headaches or thyroid disorders, as well as more pain conditions, than men.

20. What is rapid cycling?

Rapid cycling is not a stand-alone diagnosis, but it is sometimes a feature of bipolar disorder. Rapid cycling is characterized by a pattern of frequent, distinct bipolar disorder episodes, at least four or more episodes in a single year, but typically many more; it does not matter whether they be of depressive, manic, or hypomanic nature. However, most episodes last for days, weeks, or even months; these are not typically short-term, temporary changes in mood. Adults with bipolar disorder who experience rapid cycling typically experience durations of 2–8 months.

Between 5–33 percent of those with bipolar disorder will develop rapid cycling in a single year, and approximately 26–43 percent of those with bipolar disorder will experience it at some point in their lives. For most individuals, the rapid cycling is a temporary feature and does not generally typify how they will always experience bipolar disorder, but it can reoccur, particularly if the disorder is not treated appropriately. Some individuals may even experience rapid mood changes within a single day, which is rare and referred to as ultra-rapid cycling if they have four or more distinct episodes within one month. Actually, the most common form of rapid cycling is continuous, or ultradian, cycling. Rapid cycling seems to be most common among younger females with early-onset bipolar disorder, and is generally more frequent among individuals with bipolar II disorder. Among prepubertal children, continuous (ultradian) cycling is the predominant variant. While studies of adults with severe bipolar disorder report around 20 percent experience continuous, rapid cycling, those among prepubertal children and early adolescents with bipolar disorder report about 77.4 percent experience continuous, rapid cycling. Rapid cycling is generally more common in women than in men.

The rapid and dramatic cycling of moods that is a characteristic hallmark of bipolar disorder, the pronounced affective changes, and the quick shifts between highs and lows are all best explained by the dumping and flushing of brain neurotransmitter substances. It is the mechanisms of release and reuptake of neurotransmitters that, accordingly, appear to be the genesis of rapid cycling. Episodes tend to appear unexpectedly and are usually temporary, but not fleeting or transitory. However, it is important to recognize that the processes involved in the release and removal of neurotransmitters, whether by reuptake mechanisms or by enzyme degradation and metabolization, or by other means, are processes that are not instantaneous, but take time.

Research suggests that women with bipolar disorder and people with bipolar II disorder experience more rapid cycling episodes than men with bipolar disorder. Rapid cycling is actually used to differentiate between a diagnosis of bipolar I or bipolar II disorder. A rapid cycler will have at least four, and often many more, distinct episodes that meet full diagnostic criteria for a manic, depressed, hypomanic, or mixed mood episode within a single year. Thus, for bipolar I to be diagnosed with rapid cycling, there must be at least four separate episodes of mania or depression; while for bipolar II, there must be at least four distinct episodes of hypomania or depression with a one-year period, but none fully rising to the level of a manic or mixed episode.

Individuals with rapid cycling experience higher levels of lymphocyte activation and are hospitalized more frequently than those without it and their symptoms are typically more difficult to manage long term. Sleep loss appears to have a stronger correlation to the onset of manic episodes among rapid cyclers; conversely, extended sleep seems to help prevent manic episodes. While rapid cycling, individuals are more prone to relapse to substance misuse or abuse. Rapid cycling may contribute to educational and/or employment difficulties. Rapid cyclers are more often obese and to have diabetes, as well as to be more susceptible to insulin resistance and to hyperthyroidism than those with bipolar disorder without rapid cycling. They are also at higher risk of suicide than individuals with bipolar disorder who are not rapid cyclers, as well as compared to the general population.

21. How is bipolar disorder diagnosed?

The diagnostic process of identifying bipolar disorder, particularly with the specification of which subtype, is determined by means of a comprehensive examination with close scrutiny of symptom presentation. There is no single blood test, brain scan, or questionnaire that can, by itself, determine if an individual does, or doesn't, actually have bipolar disorder; despite research attempting to better utilize these sorts of diagnostic tools for that purpose. Making a diagnosis is a rather subjective process conducted by health care professionals who collect information from the individual and from others, such as family, friends, and teachers. The average age of bipolar diagnosis is around twenty years old, but there is a considerable range of individual variation inherent in this.

A bipolar diagnosis is made through a comprehensive, clinical assessment within guidelines stipulated under recognized medical classification systems, typically the DSM-5 (*Diagnostic and Statistical Manual of Mental Disorders, Fifth Edition*) or the ICD-11 (International Classification of Diseases, Eleventh Edition). The DSMs, the ICDs, and other comparable systems were established to provide common languages with standardized diagnostic symptom criteria for health care professionals to use in identifying definitive lists of mental health conditions.

Our modern term of diagnosis comes from a combination of the Greek prefix *dia-*, meaning between, and the Greek verb *gignoskein*, meaning to know, thus implying that one has distinguished between diseases such as to know the difference; in this case between bipolar disorder and other conditions. A diagnosis for bipolar disorder does not necessarily involve identification of the etiology of the condition, that is, what actually caused it. However, such clarification can sometimes be helpful in treatment optimization and to prevent recurrence of the condition in the future, but it is not necessary to make an initial diagnosis. In fact, it is not uncommon for the initial diagnosis to be of bipolar disorder not otherwise specified, which can subsequently be revised as additional information, such as from a more complete history or from laboratory tests, is collected.

Typically, an individual will present with symptoms of depression and thus it is important to screen, usually beginning with open-ended questions, for mania. There are many screening scales, like the Composite International Diagnostic Interview, and numerous other assessment instruments to either suggest or to rule out a diagnosis of bipolar disorder. Use of such standardized psychosocial tools is more systematic, and enables greater precision and increased sensitivity to change. There are both observer-rated and self-completed psychosocial assessment instruments; most are available in multiple languages. Clinical psychosocial instruments to help diagnose the presence of bipolar disorder include several scales and inventories, such as the Affective Self Rating Scale, the

Internal State Scale (ISS), the Millon Clinical Multiaxial Inventory III (MCMI-III), the Minnesota Multiphasic Personality Inventory (MMPI-2), and the Bipolar Spectrum Diagnostic Scale (BSDS). There are numerous instruments available for specific aspects of bipolar disorder, such as the Hypomania/Mania Symptom Checklist (HCL-32) and the Young Mania Rating Scale (YMRS) for mania and hypomania, and the G. T. MSRS, a rating scale for mixed states. Other psychosocial assessment instruments, such as the Beck Depression Inventory (BDI), the Mood Disorder Questionnaire (MDQ), and the Patient Health Questionnaire-9 (PHQ-9), can be used to screen for depression and to rule out bipolar disorder if there are no indications of mania.

Collateral information needs to be collected and can be very helpful in making a diagnosis. A physical examination is usually conducted to identify any possible medical problems that may be causing the symptoms. A comprehensive patient history is important, including family history as bipolar disorder has a strong genetic component, as well as asking about substance use as such can mimic bipolar symptoms and is frequently a comorbidity. Medical tests can be helpful in making a diagnosis of bipolar disorder, but they are not necessary nor sufficient on their own. A diagnosis can be supported, or ruled out, by respective tests. Routine laboratory testing could include factors like CBC count, creatinine and blood urea nitrogen levels, electrolyte levels, ESR levels, fasting glucose levels, liver and lipid panels, protein levels, substance and alcohol screening, and thyroid hormone levels. Suicidality should be regularly screened. Patterns and durations of symptoms, including acute psychosis and affective lability, with associated features like positive family history, as well as cognitive and sleep changes, along with marked departure from baseline functioning, must all be considered to make a bipolar disorder diagnosis. Regrettably, there is a tremendous amount of overlap in diagnostic symptoms for bipolar disorder and related psychiatric conditions. In addition, most diagnoses do not elucidate the role of adverse and traumatic experiences, nor do they define what the optimal treatments may be.

Diagnoses are sometimes made arbitrarily and uncritically, based on internally inconsistent, if not contradictory, standards from often unclear, or even confused, subjective self-reports. The process assumes all distress is attributable to homogenous disorder categories, rather than the heterogeneity more commonly encountered by clinicians. The variety of individual experiences, the plethora of causal pathways, a more pragmatic assessment approach seems warranted.

A valid bipolar diagnosis may involve evaluation by multiple health care professionals and other specialists. Multiple mental health assessment approaches are typically employed when attempting to diagnose bipolar disorder. Psychosocial instruments may be completed by the individual, as well as by significant others in his or her life, such as family members or close friends. Individuals may also be asked to keep a daily record of their moods, sleep pattern monitoring, eating habits, physical activities, substance use, or other relevant factors to aid in the diagnostic process. All of this information is weighed and evaluated before a definitive diagnosis can be made.

22. Why can it be so difficult to assess someone for bipolar disorder?

Bipolar disorder is a chronic, brain-based psychiatric condition characterized by large episodic fluctuations in mood, energy, and behavior. For example, individuals with bipolar disorder experience significant fluctuations in depression and anxiety over time. The cyclical mood instability of bipolar disorder, as well as of comorbid conditions, makes its diagnosis challenging.

Diagnosing bipolar disorder can often be challenging since, among other things, many of the signs and symptoms are generic to many different psychiatric conditions. As such, there is a sense that the signs and symptoms of bipolar disorder can be considered somewhat nonspecific. Any one specific diagnostic criterion, by itself, can be an indicator for many different psychiatric disorders. Most individuals find it difficult to accurately remember, let alone clearly describe, the extent and duration of their unique experience with particular symptoms, particularly of depressive episodes; such vague presentations are exceedingly hard to tease out into a usable symptom checklist. In addition, cultural background influences how an individual contextualizes, communicates about, and expresses respective symptoms, as well as to whom and how they may share such with in today's multi-ethnic communities. Culture similarly influences what an individual perceives as distressful, acceptable coping mechanisms, and socially possible responses to illness; all of which impact likelihood of bipolar disorder. Furthermore, health care professionals generally evaluate symptoms presented through their respective professional specialty lens, diagnostic preferences, and cultural background. For example, many individuals diagnosed with a schizophrenic spectrum disorder in the United States would more likely be diagnosed with bipolar disorder in the UK. Misalignment between diagnostician and patient, and normative illness presentation within a specific cultural context, is likely to foster misdiagnosis.

A major reason that bipolar disorder is so difficult to diagnose is that it can present with a very broad range of symptoms. The multiple genetic underpinnings of bipolar disorder can mean that with shifting environmental triggers, there can be a vast host of symptoms ultimately expressed, which can vary over time. As bipolar disorder is characterized by shifts in cyclical patterns of mood, often involving both manic episode and depressive episodes, as well as often with extended periods with no obvious symptoms, there are such extremes in presentation, with disparate clustering of symptoms, sometimes at opposite ends of the mood spectrum, that there is no one stable diagnostic state, but a shifting target. Since bipolar disorder is a brain-based condition, there is an array of brain abnormalities that complicate diagnosis. The dysfunction involves substantial alterations in the limbic system, which includes structures like the amygdala, hippocampus, and cingulate gyrus, areas that collectively regulate emotions, memories, fear, and sensory inputs. At different phases of bipolar disorder, different brain impacts are expressed. Even if a health care professional begins to consider a diagnosis, the variations in the severity of symptoms observed in bipolar disorder can influence the different subtypes of the condition diagnosed. A misdiagnosis typically results in delays in getting appropriate treatments, in delivery of less than optimal treatments, and some of these treatments may even cause more harm than help.

Making a diagnosis is essentially one of elimination of other possibilities that could potentially rule out bipolar disorder. For example, symptoms of mania and hypomania common in young people with bipolar disorder, like emotional reactivity sand irritability, are found in many other psychiatric conditions, including disruptive behavior disorders, pervasive developmental disorders (PDD), and PTSD, all of which must be ruled out; this can be a long and challenging process. In this regard, a clinical study of patients with PDD, including autism, reported that 21 percent met diagnostic criteria for mania. While no single psychosocial instrument, laboratory test, brain scan, or other assessment technique can solely be relied on to diagnose bipolar disorder, they can help identify comorbidities that can closely resemble the disorder and, if not comorbid, can exclude a bipolar disorder diagnosis. Failure to utilize any one of these respective diagnostic tools could easily result in a misdiagnosis.

Emotional states are, of course, accompanied by psychophysiological changes; these have been measured by means of various indicators, such as heart rate, blood pressure, skin conductance, electromyographic activity (EMG), eye blinks, and so forth. This approach recognizes that emotions are complex, and have, at least partially, biological correlates that vary in level of arousal and are integral to mood states involved in bipolar disorder and related conditions.

Various other clinical assessments could be conducted by health care professionals to exclude other possible causes of symptoms that can easily be mistaken to be those of bipolar disorder. Syphilis, HIV, and other infectious diseases can be ruled out by blood work, as can a thyroid-stimulating hormone test to eliminate both hyperthyroidism and hypothyroidism. Seizure disorders, like epilepsy, are usually excluded by an EEG. Brain imaging tests, like MRIs and PET scans, can identify lesions and other factors to negate, or support, a diagnosis of bipolar disorder. Electrolyte and serum calcium levels can be measured to exclude some metabolic conditions that mimic bipolar disorder. Urinalysis drug panels can eliminate or confirm substance use.

Studies suggest that bipolar disorder is misdiagnosed or missed about 70 percent of the time. Approximately 40 percent of bipolar disorder cases are misdiagnosed as major depressive disorder; this affects up to 80 million people around the world; and, is generally more common in women than in men. Bipolar disorder and ADHD share many overlapping symptoms, such as hyperactivity in mania, amotivation and lack of focus in depression, and many others; however, ADHD is chronic, while bipolar is episodic; it takes a careful and detailed patient history to differentiate the two. Furthermore, while bipolar disorder principally affects mood, ADHD primarily impacts attention and behavior. Individuals with schizoaffective disorder exhibit psychotic symptoms that can also be part of either a manic episode or a depressive episode. However, in schizoaffective disorder, there are psychotic symptoms presented without a clear mood episode. Research has found that most young people with bipolar disorder received the wrong diagnosis 3–5 times before being correctly identified. Another complication is that individuals may experience different symptoms over time, which can change their diagnosis entirely, or at least their subtype. Without a proper diagnosis, the appropriate treatment cannot be provided. A misdiagnosis generally means getting incorrect treatments that may not help and which may actually harm the individual.

Research has identified numerous structural and functional differences in the brains of individuals with bipolar disorder. In this regard, individuals with bipolar exhibit, for instance, structural disconnections among major brain networks supporting cognitive and affective processes. For example, neural pathways between brain regions responsible for emotional processing and cognition are diminished in those with bipolar disorder, but strengthened in the brains of those with no family history of mental illness, and thus at low risk for developing bipolar disorder. However, the respective technologies able to evaluate brain structure and function, which could potentially be used as diagnostic tools, are somewhat difficult and expensive to use, not readily available, and few health care professionals are specifically trained how to use and interpret them; thus, limiting their current applicability to most diagnostic settings.

23. What psychiatric conditions can look like and be confused as a misdiagnosis for bipolar disorder?

There is a wide array of psychiatric conditions that can mimic and present with signs and symptoms that can easily be mistaken for bipolar disorder and therefore result in misdiagnosing. Of course, any other psychiatric condition other than bipolar disorder can coexist at the same time, in other words, be comorbid. In fact, a majority of individuals with bipolar disorders also experience comorbid psychiatric conditions. Around 65 percent of all individuals with bipolar disorder have a comorbidity; about 67 percent of those with bipolar I disorder and about 76 percent of those with bipolar II disorder have a comorbidity, such as anxiety disorders, ADHD, and substance use disorders. Thinking seriously about attempting suicide, known as suicidal ideations, is relatively common in those misdiagnosed. Comorbidities vary based on gender; females are more prone to have an eating disorder, anxiety disorders, panic attacks, or PTSD as a comorbidity compared to males. Nevertheless, there are several other psychiatric conditions that have symptoms which overlap somewhat with those of bipolar disorder and thus can easily be mistaken and result in a misdiagnosis.

One of the most common misdiagnoses for someone with bipolar disorder is, not surprisingly, major depressive disorder; women, in particular, tend to experience and report more episodes of depression than of mania or hypomania. It is estimated that up to one-third of the 3.4 million US children diagnosed with depression may actually have early-onset bipolar disorder.

Some of the other conditions that can present with symptoms that can lead to a misdiagnosis include ADHD, autism spectrum disorder, anxiety disorders, conduct disorder, oppositional defiant disorder, schizophrenia, schizoaffective disorder, and substance use disorders. For instance, poor self-regulation, a hallmark of ADHD, makes it difficult for individuals to inhibit impulses and emotions, such that they can readily mistakenly be diagnosed with bipolar disorder. Delirium, characterized by visual hallucinations, acute onset, and fluctuating consciousness, must also be ruled out. Disruptive mood dysregulation disorder (DMDD) is characterized by agitated depression or by recurring explosive outbursts in children and is easily mistaken for bipolar disorder. In adolescents, particularly, presenting with mania with psychotic symptoms is typically misdiagnosed as schizophrenia. Black individuals with bipolar disorder are also frequently misdiagnosed with schizophrenia; this may be due to differences in symptoms most commonly reported by Black individuals. Black individuals are more likely to report hallucinations and psychotic symptoms than those of other races, and less likely to report more typical manic symptoms, such as mood elevation and less need for sleep. Schizoaffective disorder is a relatively rare disorder characterized by symptoms of schizophrenia, mania, and depression; consequently, an individual with schizoaffective disorder can easily be misdiagnosed as bipolar, as well as the reverse.

Misuse of alcohol and other drugs, prescribed or non-prescribed, creates changes in brain chemistry that can result in alterations of mood, which can easily be mistaken for signs of bipolar disorder. Roughly one-third of those with mental illness abuse alcohol and/or other drugs. For a few notable examples, ethyl alcohol, a depressant drug, or taking opiates and opioids, narcotic drugs like heroin, pharmacologically makes one depressed; while, cocaine and other stimulant use, like methamphetamines, results in signs of agitation, as well as in chronic fatigue and sleep disorders. Chronic drug abuse often produces apathy, lack of energy and motivation, and myriad functional deficits, sometimes even with cognitive impairments. Long-term drug abuse can damage one to such an extent that irreversible neurological functioning occurs. Side effects of many prescription medications, like antihypertensive drugs and tranquilizers, such as Valium, Librium, and Xanax, commonly include depression and/or mania. There are, in fact, many medications that can produce symptoms appearing to be those of bipolar disorder. Use of some medications, such as interferon and beta-blockers, like metoprolol (Lopressor) and propranol (Inderal), can mimic depression. Other medications, such as antidepressants and stimulants, like amphetamines and methylphenidate (Ritalin), can mimic, and even sometimes induce, mania. Behavioral effects of many drugs are dose or time related, while others vary by user's age or health status to result in signs of either mania or depression, these include, of course, antidepressants, both tricyclics and monoamine oxidase inhibitors; sedative-hypnotics, particularly barbiturates, which may produce manic signs in children or depressive ones in adults; and anticonvulsants like Dilantin (phenytoin). Many over-the-counter medications contain powerful mood-altering ingredients, such as aminophylline, caffeine, ephedrine, phenylpropanolamine, and pseudoephedrine, that can produce symptoms of mania. Illicit drug use can also cause symptoms that look like those of bipolar disorder; this includes drugs such as phencyclidine (PCP), marijuana (cannabis), and many stimulant drugs, such as amphetamines, cocaine, and methamphetamine. In fact, drug misuse is probably one of the more common causes for a misdiagnosis of bipolar disorder. When an individual is under the influence of a mood-altering substance, it is nearly impossible to make a definitive diagnosis as to the actual cause of their aberrant presentation; a drug-free state after detoxing is needed to perform an accurate assessment.

Bipolar disorder and borderline personality disorder are two serious, life-impairing mental disorders that both involve mood swings and impulsivity. They share several characteristic features, including mood instability, extreme emotions, impulsive behaviors, anxiety, and depression. Individuals with either bipolar disorder or borderline personality disorder both tend to initially present with depressive symptoms, which tend to be underrecognized, underdiagnosed, and undertreated. Individuals with borderline personality disorder struggle with extreme emotional sensitivity and trying to control their anger and negative emotions; little things can easily disrupt their peace; and they have a very hard time in calming back down to a stable emotional baseline. They are usually poor at correctly reading other individual's emotions and, on top of that, they typically respond intensely and quickly and entirely out of proportion to the perceived slight. It is the similarities in signs and symptoms like these between bipolar disorder and other psychiatric conditions that make it difficult to make a differential diagnosis.

24. What other types of medical conditions can present with symptoms like those of bipolar disorder?

As if to remind us that the brain and the rest of the body are inseparable and intricately related, many other medical conditions than the sorts of psychiatric conditions discussed above can coexist and they may, or may not, be interrelated. Anyone exhibiting abrupt changes in mood and/or being depressed, without a history of mood disorders, should be diagnostically evaluated, physically examined, and biologically tested. In addition to other psychiatric illnesses, myriad medical conditions can present with symptoms that resemble bipolar disorder. These may be categorized into broad groupings, such as misuse of alcohol or other drugs, endocrine and metabolic disorders, central nervous system disorders, infectious diseases, nutritional and toxic imbalances, and miscellaneous other conditions, like, for instance, cancers. In this vein, many tumors that can develop throughout the body might present with emotional symptoms. Even before a respective type of cancer is diagnosed, many individuals will be fatigued and become depressed. This period of depression can accompany onsets of most cancers, including those of bone, breast, lung, ovarian, pancreatic, parathyroid, pituitary, renal, stomach, testicular, and thyroid cancers. Similarly, individuals with heart diseases and other cardiovascular conditions, as well as numerous other illnesses, including lupus (systemic lupus erythematous), routinely experience depressed moods. Sometimes a flare-up of lupus can result in misattribution of symptoms like those of mania. More commonly, the immunological cascade typical of lupus can induce inflammatory responses that manifest as depressive symptoms, such as poor sleep. There have been numerous cases in which an individual appeared to be having a manic episode, but was, in fact, in several different conditions, such as being in a hypoglycemic state with low blood sugars. A few relatively rare diseases, like acute intermittent porphyria and Wilson's disease, can imitate mania, depression, anxiety, hysteria, conversion disorder, neurosis, schizophrenia, schizoaffective disorder, or school phobia.

Disorders of the endocrine system, whether for underactive or overactive glands, are amongst the most common causes behind misdiagnosis of bipolar disorder and related psychiatric conditions. These include hypothyroidism, hyperthyroidism, Addison's disease, Cushing's syndrome, pheochromocytoma, pituitary disorders, diabetes, hypoglycemia, hyperparathyroidism, hypoparathyroidism, and ovarian and testicular disorders.

There are several central nervous system conditions that can look like bipolar disorder, and if treatment is delayed for these, some of which may be reversible with early interventions, permanent brain and other organ damage can result. Dementias, which can occur as a consequence of disease like AIDS, diabetes, kidney disorders, Parkinson's disease, or Huntington's chorea, as well as from assaults to the brain associated with things such as alcoholism, chronic stimulant drug abuse, myriad infections, or traumatic brain injury, can initially present with highly exaggerated emotional states and rather peculiar associated behaviors, like dramatic mood fluctuations, sleep disruptions, and major changes in appetite, all reminiscent of manic phases of bipolar disorder; while more advanced stages of dementias typically result in flattened affective states akin to depressed phases of bipolar disorder. Similarly, individuals with mid-stage Alzheimer's disease can fluctuate between being loud, restless, embarrassing, chattering incessantly, even making jokes, often inappropriately, to becoming sad, depressed, and possibly even crying; again, alternating between appearing high or low, as typical of bipolar disorder. Other central nervous system conditions that can, if not ruled out, be misdiagnosed as bipolar disorder, including epilepsy, partial complex seizures, Kleine-Levin syndrome, multiple sclerosis (MS), Parkinson's disease, stroke, and post-concussion syndrome.

A few infectious diseases can produce symptoms that can be wrongly interpreted as those of bipolar disorder. Fevers, which by definition accompany infections, can alter brain functioning to an extent sufficient to produce emotional symptoms. Infectious diseases, such as AIDS, infectious hepatitis, influenzas, meningitis, mononucleosis, and viral pneumonia are commonly accompanied by depression. Some infections often directly produce inflammation of the brain, like that accompanying encephalitis, Lyme disease, measles, mumps, and untreated syphilis, which creates behavioral changes that are easily mistaken for bipolar disorder and other psychiatric illnesses. While early stages of tuberculosis (TB) typically produce a state of apathy and depression, later stages frequently result in excited mood and hypomania, characteristic of bipolar II. More dramatically, prior to the discovery of penicillin many syphilitics suffered from general paresis, a condition that looks just like bipolar disorder, and most were then consigned to insane asylums.

There is a plethora of nutritional deficiencies, particularly of the B vitamins and thiamine, but also of other vitamins and essential minerals, as well as of excesses, such as result in toxic imbalances, like from arsenic, copper, lead, manganese, mercury, and thallium exposure, and electrolyte imbalances, particularly of calcium or sodium, that can produce psychiatric symptoms which can overlap with those for bipolar disorder, particularly those associated with depression. Nutritional disorders that can mimic bipolar disorder include pellagra and pernicious anemia. Myriad environmental exposures can also create health problems that can manifest with psychiatric symptoms readily confused with bipolar disorder and related conditions. Tardive dyskinesia, for instance, is characterized by an array of involuntary and repetitive muscle movements in the face, neck, arms, and legs. It is mainly caused by long-term use of antipsychotic medications prescribed to treat psychiatric conditions like bipolar disorder, depression, and schizophrenia, as well as by other medications, particularly by those that block dopamine receptors in the brain. Tardive dyskinesia is estimated to affect at least 500,000 people in the United States; at-risk factors include being older, female gender, Black, and having negative symptoms for schizophrenia, but having a preexisting mood disorder, including bipolar disorder. Tardive dyskinesia negatively affects daily function, emotional wellness, and quality of life. Some nonpharmacological approaches may be helpful.

There are numerous miscellaneous other medical conditions that can mimic bipolar disorder. These include things such as anemia and other blood disorders, including porphyria; dehydration; genetic disorders, like autism and Velo-cardio-facial syndrome; traumatic brain injuries; brain tumors, aneurysms, and cranial bleeds; and many others. For example, some of the features associated with autism spectrum disorders, like aggression, irritability, and moodiness, can easily be mistaken for mania. On the other hand, conditions that may make individuals appear chronically achy, tired, and weak, such as chronic fatigue syndrome and rheumatoid arthritis, are readily attributed to be the causes of depression.

Many physical changes, as well as the plethora of medical ailments and conditions, can cause alterations in brain function. For instance, hormone imbalances, such as occur with puberty and menstruation, can cause substantial neurotransmitter fluctuations. Thorough screening can, hopefully, help to at least reduce, if not entirely eliminate, all of these erroneous diagnoses.

It is important to recognize that identification of any medical condition that can cause mood instability does not necessarily rule out a bipolar disorder diagnosis. An individual can, of course, have bipolar disorder and any other comorbid condition whether psychiatric, other medical, or otherwise. It is also important to remember that human beings are dynamic, not static, creatures always developing, changing, adapting, and metamorphizing. Someone who appears to have another condition and does not meet diagnostic criteria for bipolar disorder today, might tomorrow.

Treating and Preventing Bipolar Disorder

25. What steps can be taken to prevent the development of bipolar disorder?

Bipolar disorder is a complex, chronic condition that comes from a combination of genetics, chemical imbalances, congenital anomalies and conditions, traumatic events, nutritional deficiencies, substance abuse, and other contributing factors; accordingly, prevention of bipolar disorder, or at least decreasing its risk, should involve a multifactorial approach incorporating educational, lifestyle, medical, psychological, and other strategies which in combination are more likely to be successful. Accordingly, there is no simple answer to the question of whether a complex condition like bipolar disorder can be prevented. Unfortunately, while there may be no absolute (100 percent) way to completely prevent the occurrence of manic or depressive episodes of bipolar disorder, there are many practices supportive of mental health that may help lessen the likelihood of their ever developing in the first place, and reduce chances of their ever recurring again, as well as of helping to manage any symptoms.

Individuals who take active steps to avoid, minimize, and/or counter risk factors for bipolar disorder are far less likely to develop the condition later in life or to experience a reoccurrence. In fact, those who seek mental health and related preventative care prior to experiencing many of the identified risk factors are less likely to transition to bipolar disorder or related conditions in the future. Those who get appropriate care and treatment for nonpsychotic major mental health difficulties, including mood, personality, and substance use disorders, benefit from long-term monitoring and support and, consequently, are less likely to ever become bipolar. It stands to reason that getting effective intervention and treatment for the early warning signs of bipolar disorder, such as sleep disturbances, frequent health care visits, escalating self-harm, and previous episodes of anxiety, irritability, and/or depression, could help reduce manifestations of the disorder. At any rate, it is important to recognize how critical it is to create individualized, holistic treatment plans.

We know that those who are undiagnosed for bipolar disorder typically experience a host of adverse health and social outcomes. These include overall poorer health, impaired social adjustment, multiple hospitalizations, interpersonal violence, increased self-harm, and greater suicidality. Averting years of suffering, escalated risks, and other adverse consequences would be more likely if prevented with effective interventions, treatments, and referrals.

The better one can recognize the beginnings of mood swings, the more likely they can, thereby, ultimately prevent the full onset of bipolar disorder. Identification of how one acts, what they say, how their behavior changes, and so forth, at the beginning of a mood swing, is the quickest and most effective way to stop it before it becomes more extreme. Halting this escalation, essentially stopping it in its tracks, is the best way of preventing a mood swing from going too far, such that it manifests as problems in school, relationships, work, and other diverse areas. Stopping mood swings early and learning how to not let them go too far, is perhaps the best way to reduce the likelihood full-blown bipolar disorder and its associated dysfunctions will occur. If it should occur, these steps greatly lessen the chances it will become fully debilitating, less likely it will require heavy doses of medication(s), and much more likely that it will be resolved faster.

Lifestyle changes also contribute profoundly to preventing bipolar disorder as they can significantly reduce the likelihood of initial onset, as well as substantially lessen the severity of mood swings, should they ever actually occur. Blocking the impulsive decisions and poor judgment typically accompanying mania can be life-saving. Appropriately, managing things like diet, exercise, light exposure, healthy relationships, sleep, stress management, and responsible substance use, individuals can not only better manage symptoms of bipolar disorder, but can, hopefully, prevent them from surfacing in the first place.

Awareness of the sorts of things that can trigger bipolar disorder can dramatically reduce the odds that they will and make it more likely that they will more rapidly be recognized and rectified if arising. Making good lifestyle choices and being sensitive to potential triggers is a very positive combination that can go a long way in preventing and managing bipolar disorder.

The brains of those with bipolar disorder are different from those of others without it. Human brains evolved to be adaptable, to recognize salient stimuli, to screen out those things that are not important, and to respond rapidly to physical and emotional challenges. For most individuals, their brains are able to handle these sorts of tasks efficiently; however, for those with bipolar disorder their brains may not always work this way. Someone with bipolar disorder may have a brain that does not function chemically or structurally in the same ways that a non-bipolar brain can, particularly with respect to regulation of emotions, thoughts, and behaviors. The nature and genesis of bipolar disorder and how the brain affects and interacts with this condition is still somewhat enigmatic and abstruse, which only serves to increase the challenges of crafting efficacious prevention strategies.

26. What are the consequences of not having effective early intervention and prevention strategies for bipolar disorder?

Lack of early intervention and prevention efforts directed toward bipolar disorder can produce extended and excessive suffering. Millions of people around the world are affected by bipolar disorder at any one time. Individuals experiencing symptoms of bipolar disorder may not even be aware of what is happening to them, perhaps dismissing such as normal moods. Failure to recognize and thus beginning to address these warning signs is likely to result in worsening conditions, greater disorder prevalence, and an overall lower quality of life.

There appears to be somewhat rigid developmental timing for the formation of some neural circuits. This is because maturation of human neurons appears to take longer than that for most other cells and is modulated by combinations of transcriptional, metabolic, and physiological processes. This process lasts almost two decades for some neurons and allows for an accumulation of epigenetic modifications. However, if bipolar disorder is not prevented but, in fact, occurs, then its adverse alterations to the brain and other body organs can proceed, with all of the typically concomitant negative consequences typically observed, which can be long-lasting and, sometimes, even permanent. Fortunately, high efficacy has been demonstrated for early interventions for those individuals at risk of developing bipolar disorder.

An array of early intervention and prevention strategies for bipolar disorder have been developed and utilized. Psychotherapy, for instance, appears to be effective for prevention of depressive episodes and to be beneficial long term for managing hypomania. For severe hypomania and poor functioning, as occur in both manic and depressive episodes, pharmacotherapy is generally considered an appropriate first-line approach. Many other modalities have also been found to be helpful.

Obviously, if early intervention and prevention strategies are non-existent or ineffective then there would be expected to be a higher incidence of bipolar disorder, but that is not all there is to it. The public health significance of such deficits alone is enormous. Not only would greater prevalence of bipolar disorder be expected, its impacts would likely be more severe. Adverse clinical consequences, such as cognitive dysfunction, longer episodic durations, shorter well intervals, and poorer functional outcomes, such as likelihood of Alzheimer's disease, would no doubt be more profound. Furthermore, we have known for a long time that both psychological and physiological stress can manifest with the same physiological responses. It would also be expected to result in higher rates of the myriad comorbid conditions, including diabetes, obesity, and cardiovascular diseases, consequently, overall poorer physical health individually and societally. As the comorbidity between bipolar disorder and respective substance use disorders is high, untreated bipolar disorder can be expected to result in increased prevalence of conditions like alcohol use disorder, which is estimated to affect 40–70 percent of individuals with bipolar disorder, and nicotine use, recognized as affecting up to 80 percent of individuals with bipolar disorder. Rates of suicide attempts and successful suicides would also be expected to rise, as would overall premature mortality rates. In addition to loss of years of life, bipolar disorder substantially diminishes quality of life of those living with bipolar disorder and of those around them as well. The direct and indirect costs at the societal level could have substantial economic effects and could have devastating impacts on parents and other caregivers. The recognized typical delay between illness onset and treatment initiation would likely be extended, with the increased disease burden associated with treatment delay resulting in even greater costs at the individual, local, regional, national, and global levels.

Earlier identification of the warning signs of bipolar disorder, accompanied by consistent, earlier delivery of evidence-based intervention and prevention strategies, is already associated with less severity of the condition. Amelioration of the negative effects of bipolar disorder earlier in the life-course of an individual provides an increased likelihood of living a better, longer, and healthier life. In sum, the impacts on individuals and society could be rather substantial. This realization supports the need to develop early intervention strategies, particularly those aimed at earlier detection and diagnosis, as well as establishment of evidence-based guidelines for specific treatments for early phases of the condition. Enhanced early detection can be achieved through use of genetic, endophenotypic, and clinical methods. For example, structural MRI studies suggest that individuals at genetic risk for bipolar disorder, hopefully supported by use of reliable biological markers, have larger right inferior frontal gyrus volumes. These sorts of findings can aid us in developing better early intervention and prevention strategies that could seriously alter the trajectories of bipolar disorder and result in improved outcomes for those affected, and lower its prevalence.

27. What kinds of specialists can treat and help prevent future episodes of bipolar disorder?

As bipolar disorder is a complex condition that can manifest differently in different individuals with different symptoms and potentially diverse comorbidities, it is not surprising that a treatment team can be composed of a variable yet also diverse group of specialists. Treatments for bipolar disorder are intended to alleviate symptom frequency and severity and to assist individuals in achieving more disease-free periods. The majority of children and adolescents with bipolar disorder receive much of their medical care from their primary care physician, typically a pediatrician. However, few pediatricians are specially trained to specifically treat bipolar disorder. In fact, the professional treatment team is most often led by a psychiatrist, whether an MD (medical doctor) or a DO (doctor of osteopathy), with specialized training and experience in dealing with the condition; physician assistants (PAs), nurse practitioners (NPs), advanced practice registered nurses (APRNs), and other professionals with specialized training and experience may also serve this role. Psychiatric mental health nurse practitioners (PMHNPs), whose numbers are increasing steadily across the United States, can be an excellent resource for diagnosing and treating individuals with bipolar disorder, particularly in rural and short-staffed locations. In fact, up to 40 percent of individuals with bipolar disorder are treated only by their primary health care provider. Nevertheless, the pediatrician often remains a key member of the treatment team and, not uncommonly, helps select the other professionals who will help treat and prevent the disorder. Pediatricians usually know the health care professionals available in the local area and often help with referrals. An initial consult might be with a neuropsychologist if signs suggest issues with cognition, memory, focus, and other areas that might impinge learning, particularly to possibly rule out alternative diagnoses, such as a traumatic brain injury, neurological illness, or other conditions that can impair learning. Although a pediatrician might be willing to renew prescriptions for psychiatric medications, typically the first-line approach, they rarely would be trained to provide psychotherapy. It is generally a psychiatrist who makes the diagnosis and selects the beginning treatment plan, particularly the specific initial psychiatric medication(s) prescribed.

The remaining members of a bipolar treatment team may come from a very diverse array of professional specialties, including specialists in a host of alternative and complementary approaches. Nevertheless, it is critical that members of the team can communicate openly with each other to ensure a comprehensive, yet integrated treatment plan.

A clinical psychologist (Ph.D, Ed.D., or Psy.D.) usually provides the leading psychotherapeutic approaches, although a licensed clinical social worker (LCSW) or other mental health counselors (e.g., LPC), potentially including marriage and family therapists, addiction counselors, recreation therapists, art or music therapists, and possibly numerous other professionals, such as pharmacists, dieticians, sleep specialists, relaxation therapists, and exercise coaches, may be involved as well. Certified peer specialists are increasingly becoming part of the mental health delivery team.

An array of health specialists can offer more specialized assessment, analysis, and interventions on more narrowly focused areas of health; these could include, for just a few examples, dentists, nutritionists, massage therapists, and personal trainers. Health educators can provide education, support, and resources to help individuals and families improve their overall health and well-being and to better manage any challenges they may have. A wide swath of professionally trained psychotherapists and others may be considered in building a bipolar treatment team.

Many different psychotherapeutic approaches are available to address bipolar disorder, with generally different specialists trained differently in the delivery of respective techniques. Perhaps one of the most common psychotherapeutic modalities used for treating individuals with bipolar disorder is cognitive behavioral therapy (CBT), in which therapists and counselors assist individuals in examining and understanding their thinking patterns as well as in developing more positive coping strategies. Psychoeducational endeavors attempt to improve understanding of the disorder and correct misconceptions. Supportive psychotherapies are drawn upon to assist individuals in talking about their issues, helping them to make more responsible decisions, and encouraging the adoption of ways to better cope with the challenges of daily life. Psychodynamic psychotherapies extend the therapeutic focus into areas such as developmental trajectories, defense mechanisms, and the roles of interpersonal relationships. Interpersonal and social rhythm therapy (IPSRT) attempts to assist individuals in creating routines that can provide balance to counter the ups and downs of mood swings that are characteristic of bipolar disorder; by helping individuals learn how to regulate their daily habits, particularly those of sleeping, eating, and exercising, this approach attempts to help prevent episodic recurrences and to better manage the condition. Pastoral counselors can provide religious and spiritual guidance and support.

Psychotherapy is not an automatic or instant cure and, importantly, it does not always work; nor does any other approach by the way, including medications. The individual with bipolar disorder must be ready and willing to put forth the effort to engage in therapy for it to actually work. This commitment can be particularly difficult when one is depressed. In addition, finding a therapist that the individual can work with is not always easy. The individual and the therapist must develop rapport, which can begin with open-ended questions that allow discussion of an individual's priorities and strengths. Different therapists have been trained differently and they have different styles and various techniques that they employ.

The sad reality is that psychotherapy may not help everyone. Some individuals already know what works for them, such as what coping mechanisms work for them and which do not. Cultural background and beliefs about health and healthcare play a significant role in determining what psychotherapeutic modalities may, or may not, be acceptable. At any rate, a therapist who insists that someone try an approach that they have tried several times before and found unsuccessful, may not be their best match.

Unfortunately, someone cannot just "tell your brain to shut up." Dealing with bipolar disorder is not simply a matter of being rational and one cannot just be talked out of it. The individual with bipolar disorder is not choosing to feel the way they feel. There is, of course, an actual physical component to bipolar disorder and much of this resides in the brain.

Bipolar disorder is a chronic, life-long condition, it's always present. The symptoms may be milder, particularly if they are taking good care of themselves, and the individual may not necessarily ever experience a full-blown mania or depressed episodes. Nonetheless, the possibility is that it is always going to be there and they have to pay attention to it to keep it in check. For some, that may mean initiating and/or continuing to take bipolar medication(s). For others, it may simply be taking care of business as best they can and getting things like cleaning the house or doing laundry, keeping to a healthy routine, and being on top of the simplest things, can sometimes help forestall the sense of impending doom and failure that often precedes a depressed episode.

28. Are different types of bipolar disorder treated differently?

As discussed earlier in this work, there are several different types of bipolar disorder, such as bipolar I disorder, bipolar II disorder, cyclothymia, and so on, each with somewhat different apparent presentations, genetic risks, vulnerable sub-populations, and so forth. Accordingly, it is to be expected that there would be somewhat different treatments for the respective different types of bipolar disorder. Furthermore, as each individual, their genetic predispositions, their physiologies, and their own experience with bipolar disorder is somewhat unique, different combinations of different treatment approaches are routinely utilized. Even for treating individuals with what may be diagnosed as the same respective type of the condition, different combinations of variable treatment options might be necessary.

Treatments for different types of bipolar disorder typically involve some psychiatric medication, usually used in conjunction with myriad forms of psychotherapy and varied counseling techniques, often augmented by complementary health approaches. Different types of bipolar medications work differently, generally to alter the chemical balances in the brain. For example, for individuals with bipolar I disorder with primarily manic symptoms, antipsychotic medications, like aripiprazole, cariprazine, olanzapine, quetiapine, and risperidone, are typically prescribed to manage severe manic episodes; olanzapine has been found to be the most effective. While these five medications are approved for treating bipolar I disorder, only two, quetiapine XR and lumateperone, have FDA approval for treating bipolar II disorder. For individuals with bipolar I disorder with primarily depressive symptoms, antidepressant medications are routinely prescribed to alleviate the depressive symptoms; valproate (valproic acid) has been found to be effective, followed closely by lithium when used in combination with olanzapine. Thus, antidepressant medications and/or antipsychotic medications are the two major types of medicines typically prescribed for individuals with bipolar I disorder. There are several combination-formulated medications, such as the antidepressant-antipsychotic combination of fluoxetine and olanzapine, which serve as both a treatment for depression and as a mood stabilizer and it has been approved by the FDA for treatment of depressive episodes associated with bipolar I disorder. Lumateperone and quetiapine have FDA approval for treating both bipolar I and bipolar II disorder. On April 2, 2024, the FDA approved use of the atypical antipsychotic medication iloperidone for treating acute mania or mixed episodes associated with bipolar I disorder on adults. No FDA medications are approved for bipolar II disorder maintenance. Trial studies are examining use of psychedelic medications, particularly psilocybin used in combination with psychotherapy, for reducing treatment-resistant depression associated with bipolar II disorder.

There are many things individuals can do, with or without taking medications, to help treat, manage, and/or prevent symptoms of bipolar I. Healthy lifestyle practices are a general way to prevent or reduce bipolar I, such as avoiding use of alcohol, tobacco, and other drugs of abuse, including cannabis; staying physically active with regular exercise; getting enough sleep; and eating healthy foods. Individuals with bipolar II disorder can often be depressed for longer periods than those with other types, which may cause considerable life disruption and disability necessitating more intensive treatment. Mania, in some individuals, may trigger a psychotic break from reality, usually requiring a period of hospitalization. For acute manic or mixed episodes, aripiprazole, olanzapine, and valproate have been found to be effective. For rapid cycling bipolar disorder, aripiprazole, olanzapine, quetiapine, valproate, and lamotrigine have been found to be the most effective medications. For prevention of bipolar disorder relapse, lithium and lamotrigine have been found to be the most effective medication approach when used in combination with cognitive behavior therapy (CBT).

As discussed in response to the previous question, there are a plethora of psychotherapeutic approaches that are used to treat different individuals with bipolar disorder. For instance, group psychotherapy and, if appropriate, family therapy are commonly used adjunctive psychotherapeutic modalities for preventing relapse. Family psychoeducation appears to be helpful for many individuals with bipolar disorder and their families.

29. What medications are commonly used to treat bipolar disorder?

An array of medications is commonly used to treat bipolar disorder. Most FDA-approved medications for bipolar disorder are approved mainly to treat mania or mixed episodes. Medications for acute mania include lithium, chlorpromazine, divalproex ER, olanzapine or olanzapine-samidorphian, risperidone, quetiapine

XR, asenapine, and cariprazine. Medications to treat acute depression include olanzapine-fluoxetine, quetiapine XR, lurasidone, cariprazine, and lumateperone. Medications for long-term maintenance include lithium, lamotrigine, olanzapine, olanzapine-samidorphan, ariprazole, quetiapine XR, risperidone, and ziprasidone.

First-line, as well as often long-term, treatment of bipolar disorder is typically built on prescription mood stabilizers, such as lithium, sometimes including anticonvulsant medications, such as carbamazepine, divalproex, gabapentin, lamotrigine, oxcarbazepine, topiramate, and valproate. Atypical antipsychotic medications, such as aripiprazole, asenapine, brexpiprazole, cariprazine, clozapine, lurasidone, olanzapine, quetiapine, risperidone, and ziprasidone, are commonly added, but use of many of these is associated with undesired side effects, particularly weight gain. However, second-generation atypical antipsychotic medications are generally preferred to the first-generation antipsychotics, like chlorpromazine, haloperidol, and fluphenazine, which generally have more extrapyramidal side effects, as well as a high risk for metabolic syndrome. The mechanism of action for second-generation antipsychotic medications that have FDA approval for treating bipolar disorder works by blocking dopamine receptors. Antidepressant medications may be added as well, but they are not usually recommended for mono-therapeutic use with individuals with bipolar disorder.

Antidepressants are prescription medications mainly used to treat depression and other mental health conditions, including bipolar disorder. Antidepressants typically help to reduce depressive symptoms by balancing neurotransmitter levels. There are several different types of antidepressants that act differently on the brain. Tricyclic antidepressants (TCAs), such as amitriptyline, amoxapine, clomipramine, desipramine, doxepin, imipramine, and nortriptyline, are among the first generation of antidepressants. TCAs block the reuptake of serotonin and noradrenaline and also affect the action of acetylcholine; unfortunately, they have large side effect profiles, such as heart arrhythmias and anticholinergic effects including dry mouth, constipation, and sedation. Monoamine oxidase inhibitors (MAOIs), such as isocarboxazid, phenelzine, selegiline, and tranylcypromine, are another type of first-generation antidepressants; MAOIs reduce the activity of monoamine oxidase-A and/or monoamine oxidase-B, two enzymes that help regulate mood and increase motivation by balancing neurotransmitter levels, like those of dopamine, noradrenaline, and serotonin. Selective serotonin reuptake inhibitors (SSRIs), such as citalopram, escitalopram, fluoxetine, fluvoxamine, paroxetine, and sertraline, are the most commonly prescribed antidepressants; SSRIs block the reuptake of serotonin into neurons in the brain, thereby increasing its synaptic levels. This function helps to improve mood and reduce symptoms of anxiety and depression. Serotonin and noradrenaline reuptake inhibitors (SNRIs), such as desvenlafaxine, duloxetine, levomilnacipran, and venlafaxine, help raise brain levels of serotonin and noradrenaline. Noradrenergic and specific serotoninergic antidepressants (NaSSAs), such as mirtazapine and trazodone, are sometimes referred to as atypical antidepressants which tend to be used when other antidepressants are not effective; NaSSAs operate similarly to TCAs by blocking reuptake of serotonin and noradrenaline, but are more focused. *N*-Methyl-D-Aspartate (NMDA) receptor antagonists, such as Auvelity, a combination of dextromethorphan, which increases brain glutamate levels by blocking NMDA receptors, and of bupropion, which inhibits the enzyme that metabolizes dextromethorphan. There are numerous other medications sometimes used for treating individuals with bipolar disorder, such as the benzodiazepines.

Clinical research studies have fairly consistently reported that lithium is the most efficacious treatment for most individuals with bipolar disorder. However, prescribing of lithium for bipolar disorder has declined internationally for decades. Lithium, like any other medication, has side effects and associated long-term risks; for example, a reduction in sodium (e.g., salt) or diuretic (e.g., caffeine) intake can induce lithium toxicity, which can manifest with confusion, nausea, edema, thirst, coma, and weight gain, while an increase in sodium consumption decreases the drug's effectiveness. Nevertheless, evidence supports its pro-cognitive and anti-suicidal attributes. Consequently, lithium is widely recommended as the drug of choice for maintenance, as well as in most cases for first-line administration.

Medications that have Federal Food and Drug Administration (FDA) approval for treating acute bipolar depression associated with bipolar I disorder include carpriprazine, lumateperone, lurasidone, quetiapine, and olanzapine-fluoxetine. Medications that have FDA approval for treating acute mania associated with bipolar disorder are lithium, divalproex, carbamazepine, aripiprazole, asenapine, cariprazine, haloperidol, olanzapine, olanzapine-samidorphan, quetiapine, risperidone, ziprasidone, and combination formulations of aripiprazole, asenapine, clanzapine, or risperidone. Medications that have FDA approval for maintenance treatment for bipolar disorder include lithium, ariprazole (both oral and long-lasting injection), asenapine, lamotrigine (long-lasting injection), olanzapine, olanzapine-samidorphan, and risperidone.

Lurasidone is a first-line pharmacotherapy for treating depressive episodes in bipolar disorder among children and adolescents. Lurasidone is a second-generation atypical antipsychotic medication approved by the FDA for treating both bipolar I and bipolar II disorder. If lurasidone by itself is ineffective, lamotrigine can be added. If depressive symptoms are still problematic after adding lamotrigine, escitalopram, or fluoxetine, SSRIs approved by the FDA for pediatric use can be added. SSRIs generally have a rapid, nearly instantaneous, onset of action at molecular and cellular sites of action. Antidepressants, particularly SSRIs, appear to effectively open up the blood-brain barrier, which could enable not just antidepressant medications, but neurotransmitters and other drugs as well to be delivered faster and at higher dosages. For manic or mixed episodes of bipolar disorder among children and adolescents, ariprazole, asenapine, olanzapine, quetiapine, and risperidone are medications approved by the FDA; if any of these is ineffective, then lithium can be added, which works well for many individuals with bipolar disorder.

Pharmacogenetic factors, such as various polymorphisms in selected genes, like those that encode for serotonin transporters or for serotonin receptors, can result in phenotypic differences in specific pharmacokinetic parameters. This variable can alter the efficacy of respective bipolar medications, particularly among numerous sub-populations of those individuals with the condition, such as those with a first-degree relative with bipolar I disorder. However, this limitation can sometimes be overcome when a respective bipolar disorder medication is administered in combination with another medication. For example, esketamine nasal spray when combined with an oral antidepressant medication has been found to rapidly relieve depressive symptoms for some individuals who were unsuccessfully treated with previous approaches. For other individuals with bipolar disorder, adding a neuro-stimulant medication to other treatments has sometimes been found to be effective. Of course, the decision to prescribe multiple bipolar disorder medications is primarily about risks versus benefits; possible risk increases as more medications are added; these are issues individuals should discuss with their health care providers. However, this limitation can sometimes be overcome when a respective bipolar disorder medication is administered in combination with another medication.

30. Why do some people with bipolar disorder find it difficult to take their medication as prescribed?

There are many reasons why someone with bipolar disorder might find it difficult to take their medication as prescribed. First of all, many individuals with bipolar disorder do not recognize or accept that they have a psychiatric disorder and frequently would refuse to take any psychiatric medication. Even individuals who accept that they have bipolar disorder often find it difficult to take their medication as prescribed. In fact, individuals with bipolar disorder typically consider their episodic emotional experiences, or mood swings, as unwanted and intolerable. They may have a limited behavioral repertoire, often impacted by an unwarranted overestimation of their personal responsibility for having the disorder, which paradoxically can interfere with seeking appropriate treatment. This can surface as a self-fulling tendency to perceive, interpret, and respond to symptoms in negative, or at least maladaptive ways.

Individuals who do not take their medication as prescribed are possibly creating a potentially dangerous situation, they are not only less likely to be successfully treated, they are more likely to experience a worsening of their condition. The risks of increased disorder severity, perhaps including hospitalization and possibly even death are greater by not taking the medication(s) as prescribed. This interferes with the prescribed course of treatment and could easily lead to an unnecessary increase in dosage of the medication prescribed, or perhaps unnecessarily switching to a different bipolar disorder medication. Other common reasons that individuals might not take their bipolar medication as prescribed include things like forgetting if they took what they are supposed to, when they are supposed to; dealing with undesired side effects; fearing that the medication will interfere with their functioning, like their creativity, and/or that they may become dependent upon it; and so forth.

It is usually helpful if the individual has an adequate understanding of their condition and of the role that medication and other treatment and prevention strategies play. Determining the best medication, or combination of medications, as well as psychotherapeutic and other strategies, for treating a particular individual with bipolar disorder can be a complex process as each individual is somewhat unique. Symptoms of bipolar disorder typically present somewhat differently in different individuals. Furthermore, different individuals may vary considerably in their genetic background, enzyme levels, tolerance, drug metabolization rate, allergies, and other pharmacotherapeutic, pharmacodynamic, and pharmacokinetic variables. Frequency and intensity of mood swings can be highly variable as well, which could necessitate different treatment strategies, particularly with respect to medications.

While medications can often be extremely efficacious in helping to stabilize an individual's mood, and often help to minimize the extreme mood swings between the highs and lows, there is frequently a period of trial and error needed with different medications and different dosages prescribed until finding one that works well for a particular individual. The issue of side effects can influence non-compliance with medication adherence and will be discussed further in the next question.

We should recognize that treating bipolar disorder alongside other comorbid conditions can impact effectiveness. Generally, treating both conditions, instead of only one at a time, will usually increase successful treatment rates for both. For instance, simultaneously treating certain comorbidities, particularly ADHD, can decrease non-response to antidepressant medications by approximately 50 percent. Furthermore, taking both a stimulant medication, the most typical initial pharmacotherapeutic treatment for ADHD, and an SSRI, a class of medication commonly prescribed for bipolar disorder, is often well tolerated by someone with bipolar disorder, as it is for ADHD; and this combination approach can usually more successfully address both bipolar disorder and ADHD symptoms.

It is recognized that psychological and cultural factors mediate the effectiveness, or lack thereof, of respective psychiatric medications for bipolar disorder. Myriad factors impact medication outcomes, such as the placebo effect, as well as an array of individual variables like personal attitudes, autonomy, beliefs, character, and temperament, all of which are shaped by specific cultural theories of illness and treatment. These sorts of factors, and others, can clearly make it more difficult for individuals to take bipolar medications as prescribed.

Certainly, finding the right medication and/or other treatment for bipolar disorder can be very challenging. It is recognized that not all bipolar medications work for everyone. For example, antidepressant medication(s) work for only about 50–60 percent of individuals taking them. Nevertheless, research suggests that combination approaches utilizing both medication and other standardized psychotherapeutic approaches, such as psychoeducation, family, cognitive behavioral, and skills-based therapies, may be more effective than when either approach is used alone, both for greater stabilization and for reduction of episodic recurrences.

31. What are the common side effects of medications prescribed to treat bipolar disorder?

All medications, including those for treating bipolar disorder, have side effects. This includes lithium, the longest-established pharmacological treatment for bipolar disorder. Lithium, also known as lithium salts, works as a mood stabilizer by altering the flow of sodium in neurons and other cells. Long-term lithium use has been associated with increased risk of both hypothyroidism, hyperparathyroidism, and hypercalcemia; furthermore, it should be remembered that protein in urine, which is associated with long-term lithium use, typically suggests rapid progression of chronic kidney disease. In fact, long-term lithium use is associated with adverse impacts on both kidney and thyroid function. However, given its demonstrated benefits for treating bipolar disorder, discontinuing lithium is generally a last resort. Nevertheless, there are clinical indicators to consider in making this decision; individuals should be referred to a nephrologist if their eGFR is less than 60 ml/min, but health care providers might even consider stopping lithium if eGFR is less than 45 ml/min, especially if there are comorbid conditions, which commonly include issues such as anxiety, migraines, obesity, substance use disorders, and thyroid disease. However, since each individual can react to medications differently, respective treatment options should be cautiously selected on an individualized basis.

Other types of medications used to treat bipolar disorder have varied adverse side effects as well. For example, two anticonvulsant medications commonly prescribed for bipolar disorder, namely carbamazepine and valproate, are known to be teratogenic and thus should not generally be used for women of childrearing age.

Antidepressant medications have many side effects with unwanted weight gain and changes in appetite being among the most common side effects reported by users. Among the antidepressant medications commonly prescribed, escitalopram has the highest weight gain compared to sertraline. Bupropion is associated with less weight gain; in fact, use of bupropion is associated with a 15 percent reduction in risk of weight gain. Antidepressants can have other side effects including bloating, dry mouth, drowsiness, fatigue, gastrointestinal bleeding, nausea, and vomiting. Older antidepressant medications, particularly the TCAs and MAOIs, have been associated with serious side effects, like arrhythmias, hypertension, liver damage, and seizures, such that they have been largely displaced by use of SSRIs and other newer antidepressant medications. Antidepressants are commonly prescribed in combination with mood stabilizers to treat bipolar disorder, as well as for other psychiatric conditions. It must be remembered that for those individuals with bipolar disorder that the taking of TCAs and MAOIs may induce either a rapid shift to hypomania, or full mania, or increase cycling frequency of bipolar disorder; consequently, they are not generally indicated for long-term use.

Weight gain is one of the most commonly reported side effects of taking bipolar medications. The two most typically prescribed medication classes for treating bipolar disorder are antidepressants and antipsychotics, which also happen to be among the types of medications that cause the most weight gain. In particular, there is strong evidence that second-generation atypical antipsychotic medications can cause rapid increases in body weight during the first few months of taking them, which may not plateau even after a year of use. For instance, use of the combination bipolar disorder medication of olanzapine-fluoxetine has a very high probability of weight gain. Overweight and obesity are major health concerns. In fact, the concern with potential weight gain related to bipolar disorder medications is valid due to the associated metabolic risk factors. Studies indicate that almost 1-in-3 American adults is overweight and that 2-in-5 are obese; the prevalence of being overweight among children and adolescents in the United States is about 15 percent, with nearly 1-in-5 children aged 2–9 years old in the United States being overweight, and 19.7 percent being obese. The prevalence of overweight has increased among both sexes and among all racial, ethnic, and socioeconomic groups. Concerns over the side effect of unwanted weight gain are one of the leading reported reasons individuals refuse to take bipolar medications.

Tardive dyskinesia is a condition typically, but not exclusively, resulting from long-term use of certain psychiatric medications, including those prescribed to treat bipolar disorder. It is characterized by an array of involuntary and repetitive muscle movements in the face, neck, arms, and legs. It is primarily caused by long-term use of antipsychotic (as well as other) medications, particularly those that block dopamine receptors in the brain and that are used to treat psychiatric conditions such as bipolar disorder, MDD, and schizophrenia. Tardive dyskinesia negatively affects daily functioning, emotional stability, and overall quality of life. It is estimated to affect at least 500,000 individuals in the United States; at-risk factors include older age, being female, Black, and having negative symptoms of schizophrenia, but having a preexisting mood disorder, including bipolar disorder. Some nonpharmacological approaches, like taking Ginko biloba or deep brain stimulation, may be helpful in managing tardive dyskinesia symptoms; nevertheless, the FDA has already approved deutetrabenazine and valbenazine, two VMAT2 inhibitors that work by controlling dopamine release, for specifically treating tardive dyskinesia.

Myriad other medication side effects have been reported by individuals with bipolar disorder depending upon the specific medication prescribed and its dosage. These side effects can include things such as confusion, diarrhea, dizziness, dry mouth, elevated cholesterol and blood sugar levels, increased urination, loss of appetite, sedation, sleepiness, and vomiting. It is important to recognize that for many individuals who are taking bipolar medications, some of these side effects, like dizziness or sedation, are usually transient. Ultimately, it is vitally important to remember that there is considerable variability in how any one particular individual may respond to respective bipolar disorder medications.

32. Are there ways to monitor and determine if treatments for bipolar disorder are working?

There are several different techniques available to monitor an individual with bipolar disorder in order to determine if the treatments selected are working and if they are being adhered to, or not. First of all, health care providers should be talking with and listening to the individuals they are treating. Simply asking an individual how they are doing can open up the channels of communication and can often reveal much about their treatment progress, or lack thereof. Unfortunately, lack of treatment compliance, particularly adherence to the taking of medication(s) as prescribed, is typically the reason that most treatment regimens do not work.

There are many, relatively non-invasive, self-report psychosocial assessment instruments that can be utilized to monitor progress, or lack thereof, of treatment. For instance, the Bipolar Spectrum Diagnostic Scale (BSDS), the Mood Disorders Questionnaire (MDQ), the Mood Swings Survey (MSS), the Mood Swings Questionnaire (MSQ), and the Rapid Mood Screener (RMS) are some widely used screening instruments that have been validated for bipolar disorder. The BSDS consists of nineteen yes/no items and one multiple choice item, with a cutoff score of greater than 13. The BSDS has good sensitivity (*c.* 75 percent) and high specificity (93 percent). The MDQ consists of thirteen yes/no questions to screen for a lifetime history of mania or hypomania, followed by one yes/no question about timing of symptoms, and a final question assessing the level of impairment associated with the symptoms. Changes in the response to the last item, in particular, can be helpful in monitoring treatment response. The MDQ has fairly good sensitivity (*c.* 70 percent) and high specificity (90 percent). The MSQ consists of forty-six items and has a cutoff score of greater than 36. The MSQ has very good sensitivity (84 percent) and high specificity (93 percent). The MSS consists of twenty-seven items with a cutoff score of greater than 22. The MSQ has good sensitivity (81 percent) and very high specificity (98 percent). The RMS is composed of six items to help differentiate between bipolar disorder and major depressive disorder (MDD). The RMS can be administered in less than two minutes and if four or more test items are responded to with "Yes," it suggests that the individual is experiencing bipolar disorder rather than MDD. The RMS has high sensitivity (*c.* 88 percent) and its specificity is good at 80 percent. Many other psychosocial assessment instruments are available to screen for signs of bipolar disorder; these include tools such as the Center for Epidemiologic Studies Depression Scale (CES-D), the Beck Depression Inventory (BDI), the Hypomania Checklist (HCL-32), the Patient Health Questionnaire (PHQ), and the Young Mania Rating Scale (YMRS). These sorts of psychosocial assessment instruments, most of which are self-report, self-administered (or easily administered by staff in a short period of time) questionnaires, in most cases, can readily and cost-effectively be used to monitor treatment changes.

Many standard medical tests, including most commonly, but not exclusively, blood tests, are probably the most frequently used methods of monitoring, assessing, and determining if bipolar disorder treatments, particularly medication-based approaches, are working or not; other than, of course, asking the individual and listening to their responses, which should normally, of course, be the first strategy. Blood testing can closely monitor drug levels to assess medication compliance, as well as other types of substance use and diverse biomarkers. For instance, it is known that a drop in glucose available in the blood can trigger release of stress hormones that have overlap with not only hunger, but also with feelings of anger and irritability, two accepted signs of bipolar disorder. Research into the identification and examination of potential biomarkers for bipolar disorder is ongoing and, hopefully, offers considerable promise for the development of more individualized treatment regimens in the future.

33. What if someone does not respond to a prescribed bipolar medication?

Bipolar medications do not work the same way for all as individuals can respond differently. A medication that effectively resolves certain bipolar symptoms in one individual may not necessarily do so for another individual. Genetic, metabolic, physiological, and other idiosyncratic differences can alter how a respective medication may work effectively in one person but not so in another. In addition, the same individual may respond differently to different preparations and formulations of the same respective medication. Finding the right medication and its dosage that functions optimally, if at all, in an individual is essential to discovering the appropriate bipolar medication.

If individuals feel that the medication prescribed for their bipolar disorder is not working properly, then they should contact their health care provider immediately in order to discuss these concerns and establish a new treatment plan. It is often necessary to explore adjustments to a particular bipolar disorder medication, such as its dosage, timing, or even to consider switching to another medication. However, it is important to not abruptly stop taking the medication. Some medications take time to reach a therapeutic level; until then some may work partially, or even not at all. Some medications must be taken with regard to timing of meals or other special concerns. If unclear as to what a specific bipolar disorder medication is supposed to do, individuals should ask questions of their healthcare providers.

Medications can also interact with other substances we are exposed to, directly or indirectly, such as herbs, vitamins, dietary supplements, alcohol, tobacco, and other drugs, prescribed or not, including over-the-counter products. Air pollution, for instance, has been suggested as a factor that may trigger episodes of bipolar disorder as well as alter the pharmacodynamics of respective medications. Food-drug interactions are possible as well; for instance, MAOIs can interact with pickled, cured, and fermented foods.

Some individuals for whom prescribed bipolar medication(s) appears to be ineffective have been referred to as non-responders. However, by targeted efforts, such as optimizing dosages, managing side effects, breaking down denial, and improving treatment adherence, many cases of individuals suspected as being a non-responder can be converted into that of a responder.

34. What non-drug approaches are used to treat and prevent recurrence of bipolar disorder?

There are myriad non-drug measures that can be used to treat and prevent bipolar disorder and related conditions. These efforts significantly contribute to reduced disease burden and better overall health. Perhaps the most commonly used non-drug approach to treat and prevent bipolar disorder is that of the various psychotherapeutic strategies, some of which were discussed earlier.

Good self-care, including getting regular good medical care, is extremely helpful in preventing and treating most health conditions, including bipolar disorder. Getting regular medical screenings and check-ups is a sound general practice. There is considerable evidence supporting these and the other diverse initiatives and interventions discussed below.

Getting regular physical activity can go a long way in helping prevent and treat many disorders, including bipolar disorder. Regular physical exercise strengthens muscles and immune response; increases flexibility, balance, and most other health parameters; promotes blood flow; and reduces impacts that stress can cause. Moderate levels of exercise have also been shown to be associated with improved circulatory levels of the biomarker BDNF, as well as of levels of kynurenine. It can improve both physical and mental health and is one of the simplest ways to combat many diseases and promote overall health. Furthermore, regular exercise stimulates release of BDNF, which helps keep the brain healthy. Staying physically active typically means getting at least 150 minutes of moderate or 75 minutes of vigorous activity per week, usually by being active at least three days per week, incorporating cardiovascular and strength-building activities. Moderate physical activity in combination with proper diet has been shown to significantly improve depressive symptoms and functioning in individuals with bipolar disorder. On the other hand, over exercising can be unhealthy. Working-out too hard can impair sleep, weaken immune function, cause irritability and anhedonia, and even lead to depression. Proper rest can help mitigate these symptoms, as can reduce the intensity of work-outs.

Not abusing substances including alcohol, tobacco, and other drugs of abuse is also a recommended general approach to treat and prevent recurrence of bipolar disorder. Those who abuse substances generally have a younger age of bipolar disorder onset. It is known that bipolar disorder has the highest comorbidity of any psychiatric condition with alcohol or other drug abuse. For example, one study reported 60.7 percent of individuals with bipolar I had a substance use disorder comorbidity; 46 percent also had alcohol use disorder, and 40.7 percent had another drug abuse/dependence diagnosis. Studies report that individuals who are comorbid for bipolar disorder and a substance use disorder have a greater number of lifetime psychiatric hospitalizations. Increased consumption of alcohol in individuals with bipolar disorder results in heightened mood symptoms. Rather than serving as a form of self-medication, as is commonly asserted, alcohol use is associated with greater symptom severity. However, there is no evidence that increased mood symptoms predict lasting changes to alcohol use, which would be expected if self-medication was occurring. It is well established that over 50 percent of individuals with a bipolar diagnosis will experience alcohol use disorder at some point in their lives. The adverse effects of alcohol use appear to be more pronounced in those with bipolar II disorder. These effects are speculated to stem from alcohol's disruption of an individual's circadian rhythms and their brain reward circuits, rather than from its psychoactive effects.

Metabolism and brain health are intimately related; while the brain only accounts for about 2 percent of body weight, it utilizes around 20–30 percent of the calories consumed. Getting the brain appropriate nutrients daily is critical to mental health. Eating a healthy balanced diet including at least seven of the twelve eligible food items daily, namely fruits, vegetables, cereals, dairy products, eggs, fish, meat, legumes, nuts, oils, salt, and teas, is recommended for preventing and treating bipolar disorder. Healthy diets directly impact our brains, and thereby brain-based conditions like bipolar disorder, in many significant ways. Our brains consist of a high proportion of fat; neurons are insulated by myelin sheaths composed of fat cells that modulate neurotransmission. Furthermore, neurotransmission relies on several micronutrients, including iron, sodium, vitamin D, and zinc; if we are deficient in, or have an excess of, these varied nutrients, which has been reported in studies of those with bipolar disorder, then attention, focus, impulse control, and mood regulation will suffer.

Accordingly, healthy comprehensive diets are critically important. For example, eating more nuts and seeds can be beneficial as they are generally not only high in things like protein, good fats, magnesium, and selenium, but also can boost levels of serotonin, which helps regulate, among other things, mood, aggression, anxiety, and feelings of contentment and happiness. Nutritional supplements may be considered, but with some cautions. In fact, broad-spectrum micronutrients (BSMs) are increasingly being recommended for treating and preventing bipolar disorder and other psychiatric disorders. It is known that vitamin B6 levels enhance neuronal function, but that simple intake of it as a dietary supplement, on its own, is insufficient to prevent or treat bipolar disorder as it does not raise levels to a therapeutic range. However, 7,8-dihydroxyflavone is a molecule that can be taken as a supplement to improve brain health, as it inhibits the enzyme that metabolizes vitamin B6. Maintaining a healthy gastrointestinal microbiome is critical for brain health; many neurotransmitter precursors and substances are produced in our guts, imbalances there are implicated in the genesis of bipolar disorder. Hydrating adequately is likewise essential. Dehydration affects all body systems; when the brain is deprived of water, we can become confused and irritable, which are also signs suggestive of bipolar disorder.

Quality sleep is essential for attaining and maintaining optimal physical and mental health. Adequate, restful sleep can be a restorative factor in helping regulate mood. Brain imaging studies demonstrate that the brain is very active during sleep, allowing us to replay and consolidate information exposed to during waking hours. Sleep patterns, particularly as related to insomnia, have polygenic links to associated psychiatric conditions, specifically bipolar disorder, ADHD, and schizophrenia. These phenotypic expressions appear related to circadian rhythm disruptions, perhaps springing from a shared genetic underpinning. Poor sleep can lead to impaired coping with stress, which can result in associated impairments, including bipolar disorder and associated conditions. Daylight savings time can disrupt sleep patterns, which can cascade for some individuals into a bipolar episode. Disrupted sleep, or too little sleep, puts one at greater risk for having bipolar disorder and related conditions. In this regard, it is important to recognize that acute sleep deprivation is believed to potentially induce mania in about 30 percent of individuals with bipolar disorder. Interestingly, insufficient sleep duration and late onset sleep, either separately or in combination, are associated with greater glycemic variability. Furthermore, sleep deprivation can elevate levels of cortisol, the stress hormone, and too much cortisol can cause sleep deprivation.

Time management, planning intentional allocation of the amount of time allotted for specific activities, is an oft-overlooked tool that can support good mental health. With proper time execution, many activities can be performed more effectively, reducing stressful challenges that can trigger bipolar episodes. Furthermore, chronotherapy, assessing individual circadian rhythms to individualize the temporal administration of bipolar medication, increases probabilities of achieving optimal therapeutic results and to having fewer recurrences.

Basic lifestyle choices help determine the degree to which anyone may, or may not live with health challenges, including bipolar disorder and related psychiatric conditions. The prevention and treatment of bipolar disorder and the goal of striving for optimal health are all augmented by comprehensive, positive lifestyles. Socializing with others, for instance, can enhance cognitive function and help regulate moods, just some of the benefits from human interaction and intellectual stimulation when interacting positively with others. Lifestyles are the summation of decisions made throughout a life, incorporating more healthier lifestyle choices decreases, but does not necessarily eliminate, the likelihood that the choices others may have made that ultimately led to their becoming bipolar, will do so for you. Healthy lifestyle dimensions, like sleep, exercise, and diet, interact and overlap. For instance, there are synergistic benefits such as when good nutrition generates sufficient energy for intense physical activity, and such activity helps prepare one for restful sleep. These sorts of lifestyle modifications not only can reduce, or even possibly eliminate, the need for medications and psychotherapeutic counseling for bipolar disorder, they can prevent its occurrence.

Reducing the number and severity of risk factors provides safe, feasible, and highly cost-effective results that go a long way to promoting overall health, such that bipolar disorder treatments will ultimately be less necessary. Initiatives supporting better parenting and more stable households, for instance, could reap immense dividends in decreasing subsequent bipolar prevalence. The precise causes of bipolar disorder are not fully understood, but there are many risk factors that have been identified and are potentially modifiable. Genetics, certainly, plays a role, and may, in the future, be somewhat modifiable; other causes relate to differences in the brain, both structural and functional; as well as myriad environmental factors, including childhood traumas, stressful major life events, and misuse of psychoactive substances; and, even the epigenetic interaction between these two dimensions. Universal prevention strategies would contribute to lower incidences of bipolar disorder and of a plethora of other conditions.

Other non-drug therapeutic techniques can be called upon, particularly for addressing treatment resistant bipolar disorder, such as varied forms of electrotherapy, like electroconvulsive therapy (ECT), deep brain stimulation (DBS), vagus nerve stimulation (VNS), and transcranial electromagnetic stimulation (TMS). ECT, a non-invasive treatment administered under anesthesia using weak electric currents to trigger a minor, controlled seizure that appears to change brain function, is particularly effective for severe or treatment-resistant depression; up to 80 percent of individuals report at least a 50 percent reduction in symptom severity. DBS utilizes small surgically implanted electrodes connected to a small pulse generator. VNS usually uses a pulse generator implanted in the chest to change brain function, but a non-invasive version known as transcutaneous auricular VNS (taVNS) is being investigated. TMS is a non-invasive technique using magnetic fields to stimulate brain neurons, particularly those that have been associated with mood regulation; 30–64 percent of individuals administered TMS report improvements in depression symptoms; TMS is especially useful in treating individuals who did not respond adequately to medication-based treatment. Phototherapy, such as with the use of lightboxes, is often used with individuals who are bipolar. Similarly, sunlight exposure, as usually increases in the Spring, helps enhance moods, partially explained by the understanding that a byproduct of increased sunlight exposure is increased levels of vitamin D, which plays a role in serotonin production. Numerous other diverse alternative techniques are also potentially available to help prevent, manage, and treat bipolar disorder, such as acupuncture, aromatherapy, autogenic training, biofeedback, hypnosis, massage, meditation, and yoga; these will be collectively discussed next.

It must be remembered that although bipolar medications work for most individuals most of the time, they sometimes do not work for some individuals. Even for those individuals for whom bipolar medications do readily work, the sorts of non-drug approaches discussed here can also be beneficial, and at least will generally cause no harm. Nor, if someone takes bipolar medications for a period of time, does that necessarily mean that they will need to take them for the rest of their lives; this possibility offers hope to many individuals.

35. What are some complementary health approaches used to treat and prevent bipolar disorder?

A broad host of complementary health approaches is regularly drawn upon to treat and prevent bipolar disorder. The use of complementary, integrative medical approaches to prevent, manage, and treat bipolar disorder is increasing. If these diverse techniques, such as acupuncture, aromatherapy, chiropractic, herbal remedies, hypnosis, massage, meditation, and yoga, are consistently used in combination with traditional medical regimens, we can expect prevalence declines. Many of these alternative approaches could hopefully promote better health and wellness, not only for individuals with bipolar disorder, but for the general population as well. Traditional medical and other therapeutic methods have not completely eliminated bipolar disorder and related conditions. Therefore, even if the research support for application of such complementary approaches to bipolar disorder is not terribly strong, as long as traditional medical approaches are not avoided, they generally cause no harm and potentially enhance prevention and treatment efforts. Many individuals believe these techniques aid in their recovery. Integrative strategies that combine both traditional and complementary methods as part of a comprehensive treatment plan seem to be most adhered to and, accordingly, most successful.

Unfortunately, however, some advocates of complementary approaches have made quixotic, unsubstantiated claims for some approaches that are ultimately untenable.

Recognition of bipolar disorder as a metabolic disorder, which it at least partially is, suggests that nutrition should be considered as a complementary therapy. Bipolar disorder may result, at least in part, from varied metabolic issues, like mitochondrial dysfunction and associated processes, such as how the brain processes things like glucose or insulin, or that the brain may be overly inflamed as a consequence of poor dietary choices, or from numerous other related factors, each of which may stimulate trials of novel treatment and prevention methods.

What we eat, drink, inhale, and otherwise absorb impacts how our brain and the rest of our body works. Nutritional deficiencies or excesses can affect many behavioral aspects, such as those of executive function. Insufficient amounts of certain amino acids used as precursor substances could result in deficient levels of respective neurotransmitters, whereas excessive precursor levels could potentially produce excessively high neurotransmitter levels.

Taking of dietary supplements, such as omega-3 fatty acids which have been found to decrease risks for developing severe variants of schizophrenia, may be helpful. Other dietary supplements might prove efficacious as well. Folate supplementation, for example, which has been shown to support healthy neurons, has been shown to have mental health benefits for certain forms of mental illness; in fact, the FDA has approved a specific form of folate, l-methylfolate, for an adjunctive treatment for depression and schizophrenia. Many substances have been suggested for supplementation; however, conclusive research supporting their safety and efficacy is not generally available. Overconsumption of some dietary supplements as well as of certain herbal remedies can, in fact, be harmful and even toxic. Caution should be observed and, at any rate, we must discourage self-diagnosing and self-prescribing, not only as potentially harmful in themselves, but more so if possibly resulting in delaying or preventing use of treatments with demonstrated medical efficacy.

Mindfulness mediation helps individuals to stay in the present moment, offering relief from the uncertainties of the future. This sort of approach has been found to improve both physical and mental health. Meditation, for instance, has been shown to reduce levels of interluken-6, a biomarker for inflammation associated with stress. Various forms of yoga, particularly those employing breath control, mindful movements, and meditation, have been demonstrated to enhance neuroplasticity.

36. What are some of the most common negative consequences of untreated bipolar disorder?

Bipolar disorder if untreated can result in many adverse outcomes, including death. Untreated bipolar disorder is highly correlated with both poor self-care and decreased lifespan. Accordingly, it is critical to initiate treatments for bipolar disorder, even its milder variants, promptly and consistently.

Neuroimaging profiles have identified substantial structural and functional damage to the brains of individuals with bipolar disorder. Immune dysregulation, including that indicated by chemokines, low-grade inflammatory cytokines, abnormal cell populations, genetic expression, and indicator biomarkers, can wield immense havoc on the brains and the rest of the bodies of individuals with untreated bipolar disorder, even to the extent of causing irreversible organ damage and facilitation of numerous secondary diseases commonly associated with the disorder.

Bipolar disorder during childhood and early adolescence, particularly if untreated, can produce dynamic changes to T-cells resulting in differentiation defects. Implicated processes include disturbances in cellular metabolic pathways, inflammatory homeostasis, mitochondrial function, monoaminergic signaling, and neuronal-glial plasticity.

If left untreated, bipolar disorder can cause major problems in many life areas. If appropriate treatment is not provided in a timely fashion, untreated bipolar disorder can lead to many adverse results, such as poor performance at school or work, damaged and strained personal and professional relationships, and financial problems. The abuse of alcohol and other drugs of abuse is a very common feature of untreated or undertreated bipolar disorder. Untreated or undertreated bipolar disorder is also associated with suicidal thoughts, or ideations, and suicidal attempts, which, ultimately, can be fatal. As evidence of the potential for disability arising from untreated bipolar disorder, it should be recognized that it has, at 39 percent, the highest hospitalization rate of any mental health condition. A serious concern is that an individual with bipolar disorder is fifteen times more likely to attempt suicide than those in the general population.

The consequences of untreated bipolar disorder cut across many categories and often surfaces when there is obvious impairment in performance at school and/or at work. Substance abuse can be a predisposing condition increasing the likelihood of transitioning to bipolar disorder, but it is also a common response to someone attempting to cope with the throws of emerging bipolar disorder, as in the inevitability unsuccessful strategy of self-medicating, and resulting in the unintentional exacerbation of negative symptoms. If left untreated long enough, a startling finding is that individuals with untreated bipolar disorder have a decrease of more than nine years of life expectancy. Fortunately, bipolar disorder is a highly treatable medical condition, typically with a combination of medication-based and psychotherapeutic approaches, such that remission and recovery are quite possible.

37. What sorts of approaches may be available in the future to address bipolar disorder?

No one, of course, fully knows what prevention, management, and treatment approaches unavailable now, may, in fact, become available in the future, both short term and long term, for addressing bipolar disorder and its associated complications. Nevertheless, awareness of the breadth and depth of research efforts, including numerous clinical trials, into varied ways to potentially deal with the genesis, development, and persistence of conditions like bipolar disorder, provides realistic hope that forthcoming approaches may significantly advance the effectiveness of such techniques.

Various upstream approaches implemented before specific problems arise could no doubt dramatically reduce the incidence of bipolar disorder and related conditions. In this regard, it has been recognized that adults who had four or more adverse clinical experiences as children are three times more likely to have clinical depression; however, adults who had more positive childhood experiences as children and adolescents are 72 percent less likely to have adult depression, even if they had some adverse clinical experiences, early positive experiences can still help promote resilience later in life.

Myriad new technologies can be assimilated into our arsenal of prevention, screening, diagnosing, interventional, management, treatment, and relapse prevention tools that can be directed at bipolar disorder. For example, technologies such as artificial intelligence (AI) and virtual environments (VE) offer exciting new applications. Magnetic seizure therapy (MST) has, for another possibility, been suggested as an alternative to electroconvulsive therapy (ECT). Statistical modeling, aided by AI, is being employed to analyze neural pathways to help restore functional impairments, such as those that occur in bipolar disorder. Social media, although implicated as a possible risk factor for bipolar disorder, also has potential beneficial applications; similarly, self-management, smartphone-based, intervention apps are being developed to reduce episodic recurrence of bipolar disorder and related conditions.

Novel kinds of neurotechnology, such as tools for deep brain stimulation, may prove helpful not only in reducing symptom severity, but in potentially curing bipolar disorder and related conditions. Neural interfaces may be of use in recording electrical signals in the brain, such as is being tried optogenetic trials which can be employed to estimate genetically modified neurons. Different stimulation parameters using these techniques offer possibilities to direct neural connections to better predict behavioral changes, which perhaps can be achieved by individuals tailoring the strengths, frequency, and location of neurostimulation. This sort of approach could substantially advance new treatments and therapies for bipolar disorder and related psychiatric conditions.

New neuroimaging techniques may be developed to monitor brain activity in less invasive, real-time modalities than current approaches. Specific brain activity may be a potential biomarker for bipolar disorder. For example, increased theta wave activity in the basolateral amygdala has been found to be associated with depressive behaviors, like persistent sadness, fatigue, and anhedonia, all symptomatic of depressive episodes in bipolar disorder. This sort of activation monitoring of brain functional and structural changes could prove helpful on both developing diagnostic and treatment and prevention approaches for better addressing bipolar disorder. Similarly, actigraphy and accelerometry can be used to measure circadian activity rhythms, which perhaps could be monitored to predict emerging critical episodic transitions.

Psychiatric conditions, like bipolar disorder, appear to produce common changes to the functional connectivity in neural pathways between three central brain networks related to cognition, specifically the frontoparietal network, the default mode network, and the salience network. For instance, the salience network, which is involved in reward and attention processing, is nearly twice as large in depressed individuals. Brain imaging studies indicate a reduction of gray matter in these three critical brain networks; therefore, these structural alterations can directly be matched to functional alterations. In addition, distinct brain networks linked to the left amygdala have been linked to internalizing behaviors, which are characteristic of several subtypes of bipolar disorder. These sorts of studies suggest that in the future there may be brain-based diagnostic biomarkers that are beyond the scope of current traditional diagnostic categories.

There appears to be developmental timing for the formation of some neural circuits, such as those associated with bipolar disorder and other psychiatric conditions. This is because maturation of human neurons in the brain appears to take longer than that for most other cells, modulated by transcriptional, metabolic, and physiological processes; this lasts about two decades for some neurons allowing for epigenetic modification. It appears that the genes regulating neuronal excitability and connectivity, as well as the associated immunologic and metabolic processes, including chromatin organization, become activated in a progressive manner, permitting epigenetic pathways with increased electrical activity to facilitate stem cell differentiation to direct brain development. Better understanding of these cellular processes could help generate models to study these disorders and to develop more effective prevention and treatment interventions.

Proper diagnosis of bipolar disorder and possible comorbid conditions is absolutely critical to effectively address it and its associated complications. For example, use of electrocardiogram (EKG) screening is indicated for treating elderly individuals before prescribing antidepressant medications. An EKG is a non-invasive, easy-to-administer technique that can assess heart rate variability to differentiate between bipolar disorder and major depressive disorder. Individuals with bipolar II disorder exhibit cardiac sympathetic excitation with vagal impairment, while those with major depressive disorder only show vagal impairment. Furthermore, reduced heart rate variability has been suggested as a potential biomarker for bipolar disorder as lower heart rate variability has been found to be correlated to greater bipolar severity, including disorder duration, duration of most severe mania or hypomanic episodes, and family history of suicide. Blood and other biomarkers to better differentiate bipolar disorder from depression and other related conditions could also be tremendously helpful. For example, multiplex blood diagnostic testing, such as that combining B-cell and T-cell data, is under development which could help simplify and shorten differential diagnosis. Likewise, genetic risk scores for bipolar disorder, in the future, may enable earlier intervention and diagnosis.

Routine blood screening should include broad assessments of individuals suspected of being bipolar, such as serum parathyroid hormone, vitamin D, and calcium levels. For example, serum vitamin D levels are positively correlated to age of first psychiatric contact and inversely related to both total number of depressive episodes and to cyclothymic temperament. Similarly, studies suggest calcium imbalance may influence long-term outcomes of bipolar disorder.

Furthermore, increased levels of parathyroid hormone have been correlated with worse clinical outcomes. Depending upon an individual's presentation, other exclusionary laboratory testing indicated could include things like antinuclear antibody testing, HIV testing, urinary copper levels, and VDRL testing.

The development and administration of new medications and medication protocols offer great promise in better addressing bipolar disorder. For example, an orally dissolving film formulation for dexmed-etomidine is being evaluated as a treatment for rapid relief of acute agitation associated with bipolar disorder. Novel therapeutic strategies are being explored to improve efficacy of pharmacotherapeutic agents. For example, nanoparticle-based drug delivery systems, particularly those that can readily cross the blood-brain barrier, such as that recently tried with a brain-targeting peptide (KS-487), or that using a low-density lipoprotein receptor-related protein (e.g., LRP1), may facilitate enhanced drug delivery approaches. Medications being evaluated as potential new antidepressants include drugs like adiphenine, ciprofibrate, pindolol, and pioglitazone, as well as neutral compounds like asiaticoside and chlorogenic acid.

Considerable research is being conducted on both pharmacological and non-pharmacological approaches to treating bipolar disorder. For instance, $150 million has been awarded to Breakthrough Discoveries for Thriving with Bipolar Disorder (BD2), an organization being operated by the Center for Strategic Philanthropy; it is looking for genetic markers for bipolar disorder in order to find more effective treatments. Several pharmaceutical companies are running clinical trials to evaluate the safety and efficacy of new bipolar disorder medications.

Novel paradigms to differentially understand bipolar disorder and ways to address it may offer revolutionary advancements. For instance, dynamic systems theory, which allows viewing conditions like bipolar disorder on a spectrum that can vary considerably between individuals, and need not assume that possible psychiatric states can be clearly separated, offers potential promises for diagnosing and thus differently treating psychiatric conditions like bipolar disorder, particularly by its ability to incorporate the dynamic potential of resilience and for consideration of spontaneous recovery and other variables. Unfortunately, there is often a lag between when a new treatment becomes available and when it is routinely prescribed. Lithium, for instance, the original magic bullet for treating bipolar disorder, was available for twenty years before physicians in the United States started regularly using it to treat bipolar disorder.

38. What are clinical trials and how do they relate to developing new treatments for bipolar disorder?

Clinical trials evaluate how effective medical prevention, management, and treatment approaches are for bipolar disorder or any other health problem. Every clinical trial has its protocol, a plan of action to conduct a specific test. This plan describes what will be done, steps implemented, along with justification why each step is needed. Every clinical trial has a set of specific rules of who can, and who cannot, participate. Clinical trials provide information about which pharmaceutical products, or other interventions, should be investigated further.

Clinical trials are typically divided into four phases. Phase 1 studies generally involve a small test group, maybe 20–100 subjects who are usually normal, healthy young adults, like college students, and these trials generally take up to one year to conduct. Baseline data, particularly demographic data, like age, gender, racial background, and so forth, are typically collected. The main purpose of Phase 1 trials is to evaluate safety, like dosage ranges, route of administration, rate of absorption, and drug distribution in the body, as well as potential toxicities. A major goal of Phase 1 trials is determination of safe dosages before minor side effects, such as headaches or nausea, are experienced. Phase 1 subjects are typically compensated financially, due to likelihood of experiencing undesired side effects. Phase 1 clinical trials for a bipolar medication are primarily concerned with estimation of maximally tolerated dosage, as well as assessing pharmacodynamic and pharmacokinetic properties.

Phase 2 clinical trials for bipolar medications are concerned with safety and efficacy issues for particular kinds of subjects. These are relatively small studies having around 100 or up to several hundred subjects who have the disorder. Phase 2 trials usually take between one and three years to conduct. Requirements for participation are stricter for Phase 2 than Phase 1 trials and subjects are usually randomly assigned to a control or treatment group. Control groups may get placebo or the standard treatment. There may be several different treatment groups used in a trial. Usually neither subjects nor investigators know who gets the new medication and who doesn't; this is referred to as a double-blind study, intended to eliminate as much bias as possible. Different dosages are typically examined in Phase 2 trials. Primary purpose of a Phase 2 clinical trial is to determine if the new bipolar medication has sufficient biological activity or efficacy for the disorder to warrant more extensive research. About one-third of all drugs under development that begin clinical trials pass Phase 2.

Phase 3 clinical trials are generally larger and more expensive than Phase 1 or 2 studies. Phase 3 trials usually involve hundreds and up to thousands of subjects and typically last two to four or even five years. Phase 3 trials are sometimes conducted in doctor's offices and may involve a more diverse group of subjects beyond those who are only bipolar. Investigators typically examine safety and efficacy, as well as cost-benefits for different demographic groups, like younger and older, female and male, different racial and ethnic groups, and those with mild, moderate, and more severe forms of the disorder. Usually, different dosage levels are explored to find maximum effectiveness while having fewer side effects.

Once clearing Phase 3 trials, researchers can submit a New Drug Application (NDA) to the FDA. This application takes a review period of about one year, and of all NDAs about 60 percent are eventually approved. At that point, an acceptable package insert must be prepared through a joint effort between manufacturer and the FDA; it includes precautions, warnings, approved indications, contraindications, negative reactions, and so forth. The medication can then finally be produced and marketed, but only under conditional approval.

Phase 4 clinical trials are conducted post-marketing after FDA approval for the new bipolar medication. It is understood there may be unanticipated adverse, as well as perhaps beneficial effects, that might be detected after the medication has been more widely administered, which is why the FDA often urges Phase 4 trials. For example, it has been found, after widespread administration, that lithium appears to have a dose-dependent relationship to reduced cancer risk. Similarly, as over half of individuals with bipolar disorder also have insulin resistance, it has been noted that administration of metformin, a medication used to treat type 2 diabetes by lower glucose production in the liver and increasing sensitivity to insulin, also appears to result in improvement and sometimes even remission of mood dysregulation for individuals with bipolar disorder. In addition, release of new medications is closely monitored by the FDA and individuals taking such medications are under specified supervision. Phase 4 trials usually involve several hundred to several thousand subjects, and are usually conducted at selected medical centers, administered by qualified physicians, and can take two and up to ten years to conduct. There is also an accelerated approval process for medications used for conditions that lack other satisfactory treatments.

Research and development into new medications and other therapies for preventing and treating bipolar disorder and related conditions continues unabated. No doubt novel substances will be created, as well as others already used for other purposes, and some will eventually garner FDA approval for preventing and treating bipolar disorder. For instance, in 2024 iloperidone, a second-generation antipsychotic medication initially approved for treating schizophrenia in adults, gained recognition in use for those individuals with bipolar disorder. Similarly, deep repetitive transcranial magnetic stimulation appears in preliminary studies to not have many of the undesired effects of ECT for treating bipolar disorder.

It is estimated it may take twenty years and around $800 million to bring one new bipolar disorder medication from discovery to get it to the market. It often takes roughly ten years of testing in test-tubes and on animals before one might be ready for initial human testing. It is recognized that only about 1-out-of-50 drugs that undergoes preclinical testing will ever be considered safe and effective for testing on humans. Preclinical investigations are usually conducted before Phase 1 trials can begin and they are generally done as *in vitro* and/or as animal studies. Results of lab and animal testing, along with detailed protocols, must be submitted in an Investigational New Drug (IND) application to the FDA. If the application is not rejected, then clinical trials can commence.

Of all new drugs that begin clinical trials, it estimated only about 1-in-5 will eventually be determined to be safe and effective enough for FDA approval. Approximately 120 new medical interventions get FDA approval each year. Many entities, including pharmaceutical companies, medical institutions, and governmental agencies, such as the National Institute of Mental Health (NIMH), are currently conducting clinical trials to better understand ways to address bipolar disorder. Clinical trials will ultimately discover new treatments for bipolar disorder; hopefully, they will be even more effective than those currently available and provide hope and relief for those struggling with it.

Living with Bipolar Disorder

39. How can having bipolar disorder impact an individual's daily life, including school, work, and relationships?

Understanding how bipolar disorder affects an individual's daily life, including school, work, and relationships, is not easy. It becomes even more complex when individuals who have experienced complications typically associated with bipolar disorder, such as family trauma, academic failure, relational disruptions, or cultural factors, require and deserve a more individualized, nuanced, sensitive, and informed approach. In summary, appreciating and addressing how bipolar disorder affects the brain, emotions, actions, and relationships is not simple or easy.

School, work, and relationships can all take a major hit from bipolar disorder, particularly during a severe manic or depressive episode. An individual having a moderate phase of mania may become a "super" student or employee going well above and beyond the norm, but they may also be too restless or impulsive to show up to school or work. A comprehensive bipolar treatment plan should include addressing impacts of the disorder on school, work, and relationships.

It is not uncommon for individuals with bipolar disorder to have considerable difficulties in maintaining meaningful interpersonal relationships. Those individuals experiencing a manic episode, in particular, often engage in behaviors that can easily destroy relationships, such as romantic delusions of those they are not actually involved with, excessive promiscuity, infidelities, cheating, or simply ignoring their actual partners. After successful treatment and recovery, it can be rather awkward to disclose that one has been diagnosed with bipolar disorder, let alone to admit to indiscretions; the stigma surrounding bipolar disorder is prevalent and further complicates honest disclosure. It is important to recognize that individuals with strong, supportive long-term relationships are far more likely to experience successful recovery.

Increased severe mood swings, along with other indicators associated with adverse consequences of having bipolar disorder, such as increased use of alcohol and other drugs of abuse, unexplained increases in absenteeism, noticeable lack of attention to appearance and hygiene, depression, social withdrawal, and overreaction to changes in procedures and policy, are some of the sorts of things usually associated with many other risky behaviors, including potentially becoming violent in school or at the workplace. There is also an increased likelihood of negative behaviors like self-harm and/or suicidality.

It is important to recognize that bipolar disorder lies on an immense spectrum of other psychiatric conditions, some appearing to, generally-speaking, be rather closely related, such as the various depressive conditions, like major depression, while others, at first glance, may not be so obviously related, such as schizoaffective disorder and schizophrenia. The deeper one fully understands these varied conditions, the clearer their relations become. In terms of genetic similarities, typically the more proximate respective disorders are along the spectrum, the greater the degree of genetic overlap shared. Nevertheless, it is critical to recognize that even psychiatric disorders not so apparently related, in fact, share many identical genes and, therefore, genetic predispositions. Likewise, the commonalities in symptoms tend to be greater the closer the conditions are on the spectrum. Accordingly, individuals with bipolar disorder can readily transition from one disorder to another on the spectrum, and, often, can go back and forth, with episodes where they may meet diagnostic criteria for more than one condition.

40. What approaches do people use to cope with bipolar disorder?

There are many different approaches that people use to cope with bipolar disorder. There are the traditional medical approaches for specifically addressing bipolar disorder, particularly medication-based and psychotherapeutic ones, and there are also the arsenals of other healthy decisions and activities that enhance one's overall health and wellbeing and also make it somewhat easier to cope with the challenges of living with bipolar disorder.

Living with bipolar disorder can indeed be very challenging, but, fortunately, there are many things that can help make it better and lessen the chances that it will cause major life disruptions. First, taking good care of yourself and your health helps to prevent and makes dealing with bipolar disorder and related conditions easier. Accordingly, practicing engaging in regular, physically low or moderate activities, such as exercising like walking, swimming, or yoga, helps to promote all around physical and mental health, such that your brain, heart, lungs, etc. all work better; strength, endurance, balance, and flexibility are improved; body weight is healthier; regular physical activity also helps to alleviate depression and anxiety. Keeping to a daily routine, structuring your eating, sleeping, and other daily activities also tend to help lead to healthy adjustment.

Seeing your health care provider regularly, collaboratively developing treatment plans, if needed, and sticking to them, including taking bipolar and other medications if indicated, help us all feel better. Seeking support from your friends and family members aids in developing our resource arsenal.

Optimistic thinking, believing that things will work out eventually, is also helpful. Ultimately, living in the moment, mindfully, being patient, and appreciating the truth that improving things takes time are good recipes for achieving optimal health and happiness. Diverse wellness approaches can be incorporated into ways to cope with bipolar disorder. Individuals who do not find and follow healthy ways to cope with bipolar disorder are, not surprisingly, far more likely to have to struggle with it.

Multiple strategies are potentially available to help manage stress, which has many health benefits, including helping to cope with bipolar disorder. Doing things that you enjoy, such as a hobby or other activity, perhaps things like dancing, gardening, or even cleaning, can bring joy as well as lower levels of cortisol, the stress hormone. Spending time with a pet can help reduce stress and anxiety. Laughter, even a forced giggle and even smile, can help lower cortisol levels to support stress reduction, and positively alters neurotransmitter levels.

The brain, and the rest of the central nervous system, mediates our actions, behaviors, emotions, functions, and perceptions. Understanding this neurobiology is crucial for successfully making changes that impact every aspect of our health and daily life, from emotions to behaviors. Any impairment, imbalance, or other alteration to this delicate system can derail normal functioning. The complex interactions between neurotransmitters and neural signals regulate all aspects, physical and mental, of human functioning. Myriad physiological and psychological processes direct all outcomes, including bipolar disorder. Reaching out to others for support, whether family, friends, and associates, self-help peers, or therapists and other health care specialists when starting to feel mood shifts can be highly preventative and therapeutic.

Diet can also help one cope with bipolar disorder, as well as assist with stress management, which can produce positive results, including lowering cortisol levels and improving hormone balance. Consuming certain kinds of foods, such as those foods high in polyphenols, like dark chocolate and berries; foods with high dietary fiber, like vegetables, beans, lentils, nuts, and whole grains; and foods rich in Omega-3 fatty acids, like salmon, tuna, chia seeds, and flax seeds, or taking the dietary supplement Ashwagadha can all help reduce stress and anxiety, which helps to lower cortisol levels.

Regular low or moderate physical activities like walking or swimming can help one cope with bipolar disorder. Exercise also promotes production of BDNF, which is critical for the differentiation, growth, and survival of neurons to keep the brain healthy, but if deficient it is also involved in the pathophysiology of bipolar disorder and related mood disorders, and also influences the mechanism of action of respective bipolar disorder medications. However, engaging in high-intensity exercising, like cycling, running, or weightlifting, can actually raise cortisol levels and make one more stressed. Sometimes just getting up, walking outside, breathing fresh air, getting a change of scenery can serve as a positive mood adjustment.

The profound connections between the mind and body have helped to make us aware of the benefits of mindfulness. Bringing our awareness to the present moment, whether by focusing on breathing, sitting quietly, walking, doing household chores, or whatever, can have immense physical and mental health benefits. Silence provides the opportunity to develop mindfulness, particularly if we learn how to listen. Being conscious of the experience at hand contributes to controlled, relaxed emotional states, reducing the likelihood of an individual transitioning to a bipolar disorder episode. Practicing gratitude by recognizing and being appreciative of positive things can also help maintain balance. A related beneficial practice is setting realistic expectations and working toward achieving them; those who set themselves up with unrealistic expectations are prone to beat themselves up over things done or left undone; this typically leads to episodes of depression. Focusing on accomplishing simpler, reachable tasks can generally promote a more positive outlook. These sorts of coping mechanisms can help one ward off mood swings that can precede the full-blown manic, hypomanic, mixed, or depressive episodes that characterize bipolar disorder. Maintaining a calm, balanced emotional state of equilibrium has many potential health benefits to aid one coping with bipolar disorder.

41. Are bipolar disorder and its medications linked to suicide?

Unfortunately, bipolar disorder itself and its medications are both significantly linked to suicide. There is a real risk that an individual with bipolar disorder could harm or even kill themselves. Suicide is the second leading cause of death among individuals aged 15–34, and the third leading cause of death among those 10–14 years old; each day approximately 3,500 Americans attempt suicide and about 110 Americans take their own lives every day. Since 2008, preteen (8–12 years old) suicide rates have increased by 8 percent every year. Increases are highest among females, American Indian-Alaska Native and Asian-Pacific Islanders, while Black preteens had the overall highest suicide rate. Hanging and suffocation were the most common suicide methods among these preteens, with firearm use rapidly rising. This suggests the need for age-appropriate and culturally responsive prevention efforts, including lethal means safety screening, and more suicide risk screening.

Suicide is not a uniquely American problem. A study of suicidal behavior among South African youth reported a prevalence of 19.0 percent for suicidal ideation and 21.8 percent for a suicide attempt at least once in the last six months. A study of adolescent girls in northern Ethiopia reported a prevalence of 11.2 percent for suicidal ideation and 2.3 percent for suicide attempts in the last three months. Another study of adolescents from an HIV-endemic region of western Kenya reported a suicidal ideation prevalence of 16.0 percent. While a study of adolescents from sixteen sub-Saharan countries reported a prevalence of 20.8 percent for suicidal thoughts. In fact, suicide accounts for about 1.5 percent of all deaths every year around the world.

Suicide risk is higher among those who are bipolar compared to those who are not. About 4 percent of individuals with bipolar disorder attempt suicide annually, which is between ten and twenty times that of the general population. One out of every two individuals with bipolar disorder attempt suicide at least once in their lifetime. Individuals with bipolar disorder die by suicide at least fifteen times the rate of the general population. Research suggests post-adolescence lifetime risk of completing suicide increases more than three-fold for those with bipolar disorder and related conditions, like depression, epilepsy, schizophrenia, substance use disorders, and traumatic brain injury (TBI). Thus, someone with bipolar disorder has an extraordinarily high risk of suicidal ideation and of suicide.

An individual with bipolar disorder has more than ten times the risk of attempting suicide compared to the general population. Up to 50 percent of individuals with bipolar disorder will attempt suicide at some point in their life and about 1-out-of-12 will successfully commit suicide. Today, suicide is the second leading cause of death among youth 10–24 years old; approximately 11-out-of-every-100,000 youth now die by suicide every year. If not dying by suicide, youth with bipolar disorder are more likely to engage in self-harm, such as cutting or burning themselves, as well as being more likely to abuse alcohol, tobacco, or other drugs of abuse.

Individuals with bipolar disorder and other comorbid conditions and risk factors are at even greater risk for suicide. For example, individuals with bipolar disorder comorbid with PTSD, or who have a genetic predisposition to PTSD, are at greater risk for suicide. Tobacco-related deaths account for 48 percent of deaths among individuals with bipolar disorder. Polysubstance use complicates most adverse issues. The odds of suicide are twice as high for individuals with tobacco use disorder, 5.3 times higher for individuals with drug use disorders, 5.8 times higher for individuals with alcohol use disorder, and 11.2 times higher for individuals with comorbid tobacco, alcohol, and other drug use disorders. Certain substance comorbidities, of course, carry more risk than others, such as, for instance, use of methamphetamines and opioids, particularly fentanyl and carfentanil, that have both substantially increased overdose death rates, including suicides. Other factors, however, can offer some protection in terms of a reduction in suicide risk; for example, LGBTQIA+ youth with families that are accepting are four times less likely to attempt suicide than those with unsupportive families; perhaps demonstrating resilience.

Research suggests that use of antidepressant medications, as commonly prescribed for those with bipolar disorder, may be associated with increased suicidality, particularly among individuals younger than twenty-four years soon after starting treatment. These findings prompted the FDA some time ago to add black box warnings of this danger; unfortunately, numerous studies subsequently found that these warning notices actually resulted in a decline in mental health treatment and an increase in both suicide attempts and deaths by suicide among young people. Several studies reported substantial declines in antidepressant medication treatment and use, even among adults, after the addition of these warning labels which ultimately caused more harms than benefits.

If you, or someone you know, are struggling with or are having thoughts (ideations) of suicide, call or text the 988 Suicide and Crisis Lifeline at 988, or chat 988lifeline.org. If in a near life-threatening situation, call 911.

42. What are some ways family, friends, and others can help someone with bipolar disorder?

Family, friends, and others can help someone with bipolar disorder in many ways. Perhaps one of the fundamental things that needs to be addressed is for family, friends, and others to gain a better understanding of what bipolar disorder is, and, also, what it is not. Education on the nature of bipolar disorder, its characteristics, its management and treatment, and the hope that remission and recovery are possible are of paramount value to family, friends, and others, and this will also have immense impact in helping individuals with bipolar disorder.

It is not uncommon for family, friends, and others to sabotage treatment for individuals with bipolar disorder. Those individuals with the condition who are offered support are more likely to experience positive results, including greater likelihood of treatment compliance and recovery. Family, friends, and others can help develop action plans for treatment and recovery. They can also be invaluable aids in monitoring changes in moods and gauging treatment progress, or lack thereof.

Family, friends, and others do not always have to have the right answers or advice to be of help to individuals with bipolar disorder. For those with the condition, often just having someone who will simply listen to them can be highly therapeutic. To talk about the challenges that they are facing and to be able to bounce off possible ways to respond to them can be extremely beneficial for individuals struggling with bipolar disorder. Having someone who will just listen, non-judgmentally, and maybe even express acceptance can be very empowering. Being able to be an active listener is a skill that generally needs to be learned and practiced as most people are actually poor listeners. Family, friends, and others who learn how to avoid arguments and to shy away from topics that might easily irritate or frustrate the individual with bipolar disorder are going to have far more success in helping those they know deal positively with the disorder.

Individuals with bipolar disorder typically feel that everyone is against them and judging them harshly. Family, friends, and others who genuinely convey the understanding that they are on the same side as the individual with bipolar disorder can enhance chances of achieving and maintaining emotional stability. However, they need not necessarily endorse all the attitudes, decisions, actions, and behaviors of the individual with bipolar disorder, but letting them know that they will always have their back can be very powerful and truly supportive.

Just as there are therapists and support groups for individuals with bipolar disorder, there are trained therapists and specialized groups for families and associates of those with bipolar disorder. Family members of individuals with bipolar disorder, particularly parents and caregivers, need support, as well as education, and a safe place to process the emotional toll the condition may have on them and other family members, particularly siblings. For children and adolescents with bipolar disorder, in particular, family therapy is generally warranted.

For family, friends, and others to really be able to help someone with bipolar disorder, they first need to take care of themselves. Having the emotional maturity and stability and the time to devote to assisting the individual with the disorder can be very challenging. Just as the individual with the condition needs to keep healthy, to sleep, eat, and exercise properly, so to do the family, friends, and others around them in order to really be able to help.

Helping an individual with bipolar disorder can indeed be challenging. Their moods and behaviors may be unpredictable, which makes dealing with them even more difficult. Nevertheless, it is incredibly more likely that the individual with bipolar disorder and those around them will recover and be restored to healthy functioning if all are on the same team working for the same goal.

43. What can be done about the social stigma attached to bipolar disorder?

The concept of being "bipolar" is casually cast about to describe any sorts of seemingly irrational or unpredictable behaviors. Media depictions of someone experiencing episodes of bipolar disorder, particularly mania, are usually exaggerated and inaccurate. Reports tend to suggest these individuals are unpredictable and possibly dangerous; while, in fact, the impaired decision-making which is characteristic of bipolar disorder makes it far more likely that individuals with bipolar disorder will harm themselves before they hurt others. Regrettably, there is a consistent societal tendency to stigmatize individuals with mental health challenges, in particular those with bipolar disorder, which was formerly referred to as manic depression. Many other names have been used for bipolar disorder, such as agitated depression, depressive mania, manic stupor, and mixed states.

Stigma typically discredits and damages the reputations and status of persons perceived as different or deviant, often isolating and distancing them from mainstream society; perhaps most clearly indicated by the operation of asylums and other sorts of mental health hospitals and treatment centers, as well as jails and prisons. One of the most salient features of stigmatization is its inherent devaluation of individuals regarded as being "others," particularly those experiencing episodic bipolar disorder and related psychiatric conditions.

Stigma is also a form of negative stereotyping which casts mental health patients as dangerous, particularly those experiencing a manic episode. They are typically physically restrained and sedated with potent medications.

For millennia, members of dominant social groups in most societies have generally perceived mentally ill individuals as members of less powerful groups but within the collective "others," which is not at all where most actual mentally ill persons come from. This orientation generates conditions of widespread discrimination, which can make things like finding gainful employment, avoiding incarceration, and getting access to needed services, including mental health treatment and related services, more difficult and problematic.

Ironically, stigma makes it more difficult for individuals to get treatment for bipolar disorder and related conditions. The prevalence of stigmatizing attitudes toward individuals who are bipolar is not conducive to getting access to therapeutic interventions and interactions; it also conversely contributes to the chances of treatment failure. In fact, stigmatized individuals, like those who experience bipolar disorder, commonly internalize the perspectives and prejudices of others who regard them in a contemptible frame. This routinely manifests in individuals being afraid of getting labeled as mentally ill which, of course, further blocks efforts to pursue access to appropriate treatment. Unfortunately, we have a long way to go in this area. Nonetheless, public health efforts that endeavor to counter the prevailing bias and fear of being around someone who is mentally ill may hopefully help to ease some of the social stigma placed on those individuals with this condition. Furthermore, efforts supporting issues of treatment effectiveness for such conditions can be very helpful. Perhaps even more effective, but certainly more difficult to achieve, is getting people to accept the premise emphasizing that the commonalities we share between us, rather than the divergences, are greater and more meaningful.

The mentally ill are particularly stigmatized by this society. This reality is underscored by the fact that some of the common signs that one is experiencing bipolar disorder only serve to reinforce the notion that they are really different, such as the characteristic lack of attention to personal hygiene and appearance, frequently being disheveled, hair uncombed, and so forth. The mentally ill, particularly during depressive episodes, tend to withdraw from interaction with others and from situations that they once enjoyed; thus, they are often accurately characterized by their personal and social behaviors as being disconnected, which serves as a self-fulling prophecy reinforcing their isolation and aiding illness progression. Their readily observed behaviors further help to identify them as being of the "others;" these include traits such as paranoia, either excessive or insufficient sleeping, lack of appetite and lack of interest in much of anything, and, sometimes, even erupting with acts of aggression and hostility. These sorts of processes, unfortunately, only serve to further confirm assumptions of differentness and thereby reinforce stigmatization.

Understanding more accurately about what bipolar disorder is actually like, as presented throughout this book, can go a long way toward educating the public, as well as those either directly or indirectly experiencing it. This tactic is widely recognized as being one of the best ways to overcome stigma about bipolar disorder. More people listening to individuals who are living and successfully coping with bipolar disorder telling their story can be very humanizing and powerful. Media announcements heralding stories of successful treatment, rather than sensationalizing behavioral aberrations, could serve to encourage more help-seeking behaviors, improving the lot of all with this disorder.

Recognition that bipolar disorder is a relatively common condition and that many individuals with bipolar disorder are capable of being active, contributing members of their communities, schools, and workplaces is a potential potent counter to stigma. Acceptance of the fact that most individuals with bipolar disorder, in fact, live healthy, productive, functional lives could seriously help shatter the prevailing societal misconceptions and dramatically reduce stigma.

Case Studies

Case 1. Clay Engages in Risky Behaviors

Clay is a twenty-year-old Native American male who was arrested for assaulting a fellow male student at the community college he is enrolled in, and, consequently after some additional incidents, he was admitted to a locked-down psychiatric ward at one of the hospitals in his local city. When Clay was eighteen years old, he had a severe depressive episode that lasted for a little over two weeks, which resulted in him then withdrawing from the classes he was registered in that Fall semester, his first attempt at college. He waited two years after that episode before returning to school.

Five days before his arrest, Clay was observed pacing repeatedly back and forth in the lounge of the Student Center at his community college. He had, immediately before that, walked out of the English class that he was taking as he felt unable to sit still and was having difficulty communicating with his English instructor. Clay had not slept the night before and appeared to be very confused, irritable, and anxious; in fact, he was verbally aggressive toward fellow students when a couple of them were concerned, seeing him pacing, and asked if he was alright. While pacing, Clay would intermittently wave his arms up and down exhibiting excessive gross motor activity. He later said the "flapping" helped alleviate some of the internal tensions that he was feeling. When a Campus Security Officer approached Clay and asked him to sit down and relax, he refused and soon wandered out of the building and left campus.

Clay somehow made his way to the outskirts of the city and engaged in conversation with a group of prostitutes. He, apparently, had a similar extensive history of such sexual activities. Clay hired two prostitutes and they rented an hourly room at a nearby motel he had frequented often. After completing several sexual acts with them, he informed them he only had $20 left after paying for the room. They became irate and loudly accosted him for not paying them for their services and one of them threw a lamp at his head, which missed but went through breaking a window. He then jumped on top of the bed and, again, began "flapping" his arms and panting. The hotel manager became alarmed and called the police who quickly came, but they could not calm Clay down, so they called an ambulance to take him to the city hospital for a psychiatric exam. He was admitted for a psychiatric hold as he appeared to be a danger to himself and to others.

Analysis

Clay experienced several episodes both of depression and mania, and of exhibiting anger and sexually risky behaviors; all characteristic signs of bipolar disorder. Hypersexuality, as exhibited by Clay, is a common feature of manic episodes in bipolar disorder. These intensely frequent sexual urges often consist of indiscretions or escalated sexual activities that frequently result in risky sexual behaviors and, not uncommonly, jeopardize existing relationships. Hypersexuality during mania is typically contrasted by low sexual interest during depressive episodes. It is estimated that about 25 percent of individuals with bipolar disorder also have borderline personality disorder; Clay's impulsive actions, extreme mood swings, and severe emotional outbursts are characteristics that overlap with both bipolar disorder and borderline personality disorder.

Case 2. Maria's Troubled Family

Maria is a fourteen-year-old Hispanic female. Her mother, who had just had her fourth baby four months earlier, had chronic melancholia and was severely depressed, and when Maria was seven years old, she awoke one morning to find that her mother was unexplainably gone and so her father put the children into the family car and drove them all to their uncle's house, where they stayed for a couple of weeks, but without knowing why. Her father was manic, drank heavily, and was often physically violent and abusive, while her mother generally had a rather flat affect and was somewhat unapproachable. Her brother, who was four years older, was always very "troubled." He had severe mood swings; he was very impetuous, and could even be menacing; he eventually became psychotic, had hallucinations and delusions; and progressively declined from there. He had been differentially diagnosed as schizophrenic, and at other times as having schizoaffective disorder. At times he was hilarious and brilliant, but as he got sicker and sicker, he and his troubles dominated the family dynamic even more. He had attempted suicide many times, some were more public than others; and, then finally, when Maria was eleven years old, he successfully committed suicide. The morning after he died, her father called the family together and told them all to tell everyone that it had been an accident. This only added to the stigma and the notion that mental illness was a choice that could have been avoided. Her family was Roman Catholic and the Church teaching was that suicide was an unforgivable mortal sin. He died on a Friday night and the funeral, actually a memorial service since a full mass was not an actual option, was on the next Monday morning; but his body was not allowed into the church; and then afterward Maria went to school that Tuesday. She told everyone that it had been an accident, which only led to further feelings of shame and confusion.

Analysis

Family therapy ultimately would have helped and was warranted, but it was not available at the time for Maria and her family. Since the time after the first appearance of symptoms to diagnosis is typically about ten years for bipolar I and about twelve years for bipolar II, we might expect that it will yet be some time before Maria is actually diagnosed with bipolar disorder. Due to Maria's experiences at an early age, she is a likely candidate for a PTSD diagnosis also, which is recognized to be far more common in individuals with bipolar disorder relative to the general population. At any rate, it is recognized that impacts to developing brains stemming from early life adversity can foster epigenetic changes that affect later mental health, including the development of bipolar disorder and related conditions.

Mood disorders have always been a part of the human condition. Advances in diagnosis and treatment might mean that fewer individuals will have to struggle with the disabling episodes of depression or uncontrolled mania. With better diagnosis and treatment, partly accomplished by means of more refined disorder definitions and more fine-tuned diagnostic criteria, as well as more targeted treatments and therapeutic monitoring, mood swings are frequently being prevented, or at least diminished in intensity if they occur. Advances have yielded better understandings of recurrent mood disorders such that available approaches to prevent, treat, and manage have dramatically improved the quality of numerous lives.

Case 3. Leslie Has Bipolar II

Leslie is a 21-year-old White non-binary individual who was designated female at birth and uses they/them pronouns. Leslie experienced some subthreshold depressive symptoms in mid-adolescence at sixteen years of age, when she was identified as having gender dysphoria. At that time, they received gender informed counseling, which was very helpful. They had their first major depressive episode the following year; they were then treated with low-dose sertraline, which was moderately effective. They continued to receive gender informed counseling, were administered testosterone injections, and improved sufficiently, soon felt better, but then stopped taking the prescribed psychiatric medications. About a year later, Leslie presented with a major depressive episode with typical symptoms, including low mood, low energy, anhedonia, weight gain, poor concentration, passive death wish, not sleeping that much, and with diminished self-esteem. They were diagnosed with MDD and placed on citalopram starting at 10 mg daily, which was subsequently titrated to 20 mg daily. They continued to receive testosterone cypionate injections at 200 mg/mL every two weeks and they were prescribed medical cannabis. A toxicology screen indicated positive for cannabis, which was used consistently. Thyroid functioning was fine, and there were no metabolic panel abnormalities. Leslie liked the citalopram and felt invincible, talking a lot, and purchasing many things, particularly online, staying up late and ordering items throughout the night. A family history was taken and it was found that the father had alcohol use disorder and the mother had reported repeated emotional ups and downs, but had not been formally diagnosed with bipolar disorder.

Leslie was skeptical of the MDD diagnosis, but was willing to enter psychotherapy. Leslie was, however, initially unwilling to cease medical cannabis, which was strongly recommended, as such use impacts bipolar medication effectiveness, but she was willing to cease taking citalopram. Initially Leslie was doing fine, but three months later presented with a major depressive episode and then, finally, agreed to taking the medications as prescribed. Use of cannabis is contraindicated by individuals with bipolar disorder, particularly in younger individuals due to the substantially elevated risk of psychosis. Cannabis use also interferes with the pharmacodynamics and effectiveness of bipolar and other medications. Polysubstance use generally should be avoided by individuals with bipolar disorder, particularly younger individuals whose brains are not fully developed.

Analysis

The early onset of symptoms, abrupt onset, high levels of recurrence, family history, response to antidepressant medications, irritability, and substance abuse comorbidity are all supportive signs of a bipolar disorder diagnosis for Leslie. Additional medical history elicited a probable hypomanic episode. Leslie was never hospitalized, had recurrent major depressive episodes, but no psychotic symptoms, and no specific trauma, all indicative of bipolar II disorder, a highly chronic illness. The economic burden is estimated to be about four times greater in bipolar II compared to bipolar I, probably due to the high levels of cycling, which typically cause major life disruptions, particularly for continued employment and/or education.

Case 4. Anxiety Accompanies Rami's Bipolar Disorder

Rami is a nineteen-year-old university sophomore at a private, prestigious liberal arts college. He appears to be a Southeast Asian/Indian male and expresses that his preferred pronouns are he/him. He says that he has a poignant feeling of being "trapped;" his parents have intense expectations for him, to follow their paths, which he says is "crushing," both are successful professors at an elite university. Rami really wants to pursue his dream of becoming a journalist.

Rami's grades in school have been excellent; he is majoring in biology/pre-medicine and serves as Vice-President of the Biology Club. He has an intimate circle of close friends in his fraternity. He has been selected to do an internship at a major pharmaceutical company over the next summer. However, he says that all of his academic accomplishments feel more like a gilded cage, holding him back from his true pursuits. He reports that he feels that he is only "going through the motions" at school and with his friends and family. He holds little hope for the future and feels a growing sense of emptiness inside. Most of his friends are Asian American, predominantly from India, and they assume he is also. However, he was adopted by White parents and raised in a Midwestern city with few Indians or Indian cultural organizations. He wakes up in the mornings frustrated and feeling hollow inside. Worse, he feels that he is just going through the motions, particularly with his friends. They mostly assume that he understands the cultural references they use, which he usually doesn't. Being an Indian American adoptee, he feels fraudulent, looking Indian on the outside but

White on the inside. He does not like Indian food, which his friends do, nor does he enjoy watching Bollywood movies, which they want to watch constantly in the fraternity house. He also does not speak Hindi or any other Indian language. He says this makes him uncomfortable and that he really doesn't "measure up."

He has tried to set aside his "shortcomings" with his lack of Indian heritage, and, instead, focus on school. However, while walking to campus last week he was harassed by a man who screamed "terrorist" at him and told him to go back to Afghanistan with the Taliban. He felt so disturbed that he turned around and went back to the fraternity missing his classes that day. He has since been compulsively scrolling online about anti-Indian hate crimes. He became exceptionally distraught when reading about an older Indian man in New York City who was pushed onto the subway tracks and killed. He wonders if that sort of thing could happen to him.

He wonders why this is all happening to him, and admits that he has pretty much been running from his Indian identity his whole life. He says that he thought that if he kept quiet and ignored the feelings of being stuck between his adoptive family and the expectations of others because he looks Indian, that he could just laugh it off; but that has increasingly become harder for him to do.

Analysis

Depression has been reported at higher levels among Asian Americans during and after the Covid-19 epidemic. A few studies have also suggested that Asian Americans taking bipolar disorder medications may be at more risk of adverse effects like tremor or constipation, but that overall differences in efficacy and tolerability of psychiatric medications are similar to non-Asian Americans. Asian Americans, generally, have a cultural bias that regards depression as a personal weakness or moral failing, which reinforces stigma. On the other hand, Rami also demonstrated many anxiety symptoms. Anxiety disorders are the most common comorbidity among individuals with bipolar disorder, reportedly 3–4 times more common than in the general population. It is estimated that at least half of individuals with bipolar disorder will develop an anxiety disorder during their lifetime. Furthermore, as Rami was adopted at the age of five years and had several pronounced scars on his torso at that time, it was understood that he must have had a traumatic early childhood. In this regard, Rami has been battling "demons" his whole life and is likely to need professional help, particularly psychotherapy for some time. Rami has been encouraged to seek family counseling, but his parents have been resistant.

Case 5. Sarah Jane Seeks Help

Sarah Jane is an eighteen-year-oldbiracial female. She immigrated to the United States at the age of sixteen years from Jamaica, where she grew up with her maternal grandmother; she rarely saw her mother and did not even know who her father, reputedly a White man, was. After she arrived in the United States, Sarah Jane started working as a Nursing Aide at a Senior Citizen's health care facility. It was long hours at low pay there, but she really enjoyed getting to know the patients and building relationships with them; some of the seniors reminded her of her grandmother, whom she missed intensely. However, the challenges of losing patients, as routinely happened there, soon became overwhelming, and she became somewhat depressed.

Sarah Jane then sought a fresh start somewhere that she could make a meaningful impact, but with better pay, and opportunities to advance, without the constant specter of death among her patients. Eventually, perhaps somewhat impulsively, she quit her job at the Senior Citizen health care facility, but did so before she had found another job, which actually took considerably longer than she thought it would. It was very difficult keeping up with her rent and other bills in the interim. However, she eventually found employment with a group home for developmentally disabled adults that was open twenty-four hours a day. Sarah Jane found the work there deeply meaningful by being able to help the clients meet their immediate needs, but also forming long-term plans and goals, instilling them with hope and vision. The clients there expressed gratitude for simple things, like a brief outing or for having a good meal.

Sarah Jane was not happy with her life and went to see a psychiatric mental health nurse practitioner who administered the Patient Health Questionnaire (PHQ-9) to her. Sarah Jane scored 12 on the PHQ-9, which along with her clinical interview indicated that she was having a moderate depressive episode. The psychiatric mental health nurse practitioner decided that the most appropriate tool to next administer to Sarah Jane, to further clarify whether it was unipolar or bipolar depression, was the Rapid Mood Screener (RMS), results of which indicated bipolar disorder. Sarah Jane was then given a prescription for lithium, which she has been taking regularly and seems, in fact, to be doing rather well. She also attends a once-a-week group counseling session, which is part of a local mental health program; she has established rapport with the group facilitator, whom she trusts, and has also bonded with some of the other participants who have a similar diagnosis to her. Her prognosis is good and Sarah Jane remains optimistic about her recovery and her future.

Analysis

Behavioral deficits, as observed with Sarah Jane and other individuals with bipolar disorder and related conditions, such as addiction, anxiety disorder, ADHD, Parkinson's disease, PTSD, and schizophrenia, appear to be a result of diminished levels of dopamine released from the ventromedial prefrontal cortex, which impairs cognitive flexibility, a component of executive functions. This recognition may lead to researchers developing more targeted prevention and treatment approaches.

Glossary

Abuse Intentional continued consumption of any substance despite recognition of harmful consequences of such problems.

Acetylcholine Cholinergic neurotransmitter to control memory and movement in the central nervous system; in general, it has effects opposite dopamine and norepinephrine, such that it causes dilation of blood vessels, lowering of blood pressure, and slowing of heart rate.

Action potential Rapid change in electrical potential between inside and outside of a neuron, which, when attained, results in depolarization with electrical impulse transmitted down the axon; it is an all-or-nothing process resulting in activation, or not firing at all.

Acute onset Sudden, as opposed to gradual, occurrence of a disorder.

Adrenergic Related to activation of neurons and organs controlled by catecholamine neurotransmitters, like epinephrine, dopamine, and norepinephrine.

Affect Observable behavioral expression of emotional state, like anger, elation, or sadness; also referred to as mood.

Agonist Substance that binds to receptor site and activates it by mimicking action of other substances, like neurotransmitters, that also bind there.

Alternative therapies Various modalities of promoting health, also referred to as complementary, integrative, or holistic medicine.

Amygdala Almond-shaped part of brain's limbic system, located in temporal lobe of cerebral hemisphere, functions in receiving emotional information, forming emotionally relevant memories, and generating feelings of pleasure, pain, or fear.

Anhedonia Loss of interest in and pleasure from previously pleasurable things.

Antagonist Substance that binds to receptor site and blocks its action preventing medications or neurotransmitters from occupying receptor and activating neurons.

Anticholinergic Medication that blocks action of acetylcholine; individual administered typically experiences dry mouth and skin, accelerated heart rate, blurry vision, and difficulty urinating; severe side effects include delirium and clouded thinking.

Anticonvulsant Medication used to prevent convulsions or seizures, as in epilepsy, but also can be effective in bipolar disorder.

Antidepressant Medication that relieves depressive symptoms.

Antipsychotic Medication, also called major tranquilizer, used primarily to treat psychotic symptoms, as in schizophrenia; as well as treating related mental disorders, including bipolar disorder since it can serve as an antimanic medication by antagonizing action of dopamine.

Aromatherapy Use of essential oils employing sense of smell to promote relaxation and heighten concentration.

Art therapy Alternative therapeutic modality using nonverbal self-expression to enhance self-awareness; also used to treat anxiety.

Attention Directing and focusing psychological resources to enhance mental faculties, such as information processing, mental experience, and performance.

Autogenic training Alternative therapeutic modality in which individual gives conscious messages to respective parts of their body.

Autonomic nervous system Part of peripheral nervous system that regulates internal organs and glands.

Axon Fibrous structure that transmits neuronal impulses away from cell body to neurons or other structures, like glands or muscles.

Basal ganglia Groups of neurons located at base of cerebrum to control complex learned movements, mainly motor activities like walking or riding a bike.

Behavioral therapy Therapeutic approach based on principles of classical and operant conditioning to help individuals change problematic or self-defeating behaviors.

Biofeedback Alternative therapeutic modality using equipment to monitor and amplify body signals so someone can alter their intensity, often learning to control physiological processes.

Biotransformation Processes by which the body, usually the liver, alters chemical structure of a substance so that it can be eliminated, typically by excretion through urine.

Bipolar Describes spectrum of illnesses with mood disturbance consisting of both depression and mania, opposite poles of affect; formerly called manic depression.

Brain stem Part of brain connecting spinal cord to cerebrum through which signals are transmitted; most basic natural functions are controlled here, like respiration and heart rate; consists of medulla, pons, and midbrain, serving as neural relay station.

Catecholamines Group of biogenic amines derived from phenylalanine that contain a catechol nucleus, like dopamine, epinephrine, and norepinephrine.

Caudate nucleus Part of corpus striatum shaped with long extension, like a tail.

Central nervous system (CNS) The brain, ganglia along the spinal cord, and nerves to peripheral organs, like the heart, glands, and blood vessels, controls physiological changes associated with expression of emotions.

Cerebellum Part of human hindbrain located below posterior part of cerebrum; responsible for balance, posture, movement, and muscular coordination, including storing learned associations involving movement, such as in sports and dance.

Cerebral cortex Outer surface of cerebral hemispheres, consisting of frontal, parietal, occipital, and temporal lobes to comprise brain's gray matter.

Cerebrum Largest and most complex part of human forebrain, divided into right and left hemispheres; responsible for control of higher cognitive processes, like thought and learning, including imagining, thinking, planning, and remembering, as well as coordinating sensory and motor activities; also called the telencephalon.

Ch'i Asian concept of universal life force said to surround and permeate everything.

Cholinergic Neurons and neural pathways related to activation controlled by acetylcholine, particularly parasympathetic nerve fibers.

Chromosome Threadlike structure in cell nucleus containing genetic code; human cells, other than sperm and egg, consist of twenty-three pairs.

Circadian rhythm Physiologically controlled cycle that repeats once per day, like sleeping and waking.

Clinical trial Experimental study designed to determine if a medicine or other medical intervention is safe and effective.

Cognition Act of knowing or perceiving; a conglomerate of different domains including attention, emotions, intelligence, all thinking, reasoning, judging, planning, memories, and other executive functions of the mind.

Cognitive behavioral therapy (CBT) Psychotherapeutic treatment that helps individuals change the ways they think and behave to correct ingrained patterns which may contribute to symptoms.

Comorbid Having two or more disorders at the same time.

Corpus striatum Part of human brain situated at base of each cerebral hemisphere.

Cortisol Hormone released by adrenal glands to help prepare response to stressful events by increasing release of glucose and lipids into circulatory system for rapid energy metabolism.

Cyclothymia Mood disorder characterized by extreme swings between depression and elation, but less severe than full bipolar disorder.

Delirium Mental disorder, usually organic in nature, involving distorted state of consciousness and emotional lability, typically appearing confused, disoriented, excited, and unable to focus attention.

Delusion Any false idea or belief firmly held that seems contrary to reality and that is not widely accepted in the respective culture or subculture.

Dendrite Fibrous structure that transmits neuronal impulses toward cell bodies; one neuron can have up to several thousand dendrites, each of which can potentially receive signals from adjacent neurons and transmit them to cell body.

Depolarization Increase in action potential across neuronal membrane, accompanied by build-up of positive charges inside cell reversing its charge or polarity.

Depression Chronic mood disorder beyond extreme sadness, with feelings of apprehension, hopelessness, and worthlessness; it disrupts an individual's daily functioning. Sadness is a natural reaction to difficulties which may be accompanied by effects like low mood and lack of sleep, while depression is a serious and common mental health condition.

Distress Negative interpretation of real or imagined event as being unfavorable or threatening and prompting feelings of anger or fear.

Dizygotic twins Twins developed from two separate fertilized eggs; only 50 percent genetically alike; also called fraternal twins.

Dopamine Catecholamine neurotransmitter that helps regulate emotions and movement, including feelings of arousal and pleasure; associated with types of psychosis and certain forms of abnormal movement disorders.

Dopaminergic Related to cells stimulated by the neurotransmitter dopamine.

Downregulation Process by which number of receptor sites on neuron is reduced decreasing sensitivity to stimulation.

Dysthymia Pattern of depressed mood less severe than major depressive disorder, typically of shorter duration, characterized by sadness, lack of interest, and lack of pleasure; previously referred to as depressive neurosis.

Elation Abnormally elevated or expansive mood, often associated with mania.

Electroconvulsive therapy (ECT) Commonly referred to as "shock" therapy, uses electricity; administered to patients under general anesthesia and a neuromuscular blocker to prevent musculoskeletal harm, in order to induce mild seizures to treat psychotic symptoms, as sometimes occur with mania; particularly used if medications ineffective.

Emotion Internalized sense of what is happening to an individual, associated with both learned and reflexive responses to environmental challenges and problems.

Endorphins Class of neurotransmitters that bind to same receptors as opioids such that they produce same behavioral effects, such as euphoria, pain relief, and even sleep; commonly referred to as "runners high."

Enzyme Protein that affects a specific molecule to accelerate rate of chemical reaction in the body, either through degradation or synthesis.

Epinephrine Catecholamine neurotransmitter that elevates blood pressure and heart rate, among other physical consequences of fear and anxiety; also known as adrenaline.

Eustress Term introduced by Hans Selye to designate positive, life-enhancing form of stress.

Executive functioning Cognitive abilities to plan and devise strategies, as well as to self-monitor performance.

Forebrain Most developed part of human brain, responsible for most complex aspects of cognition and behavior.

Frontal lobe Anterior part of cerebral hemispheres, responsible for reasoning, planning, and other higher mental processes.

Gamma-aminobutyric acid (GABA) Inhibitory neurotransmitter that reduces likelihood postsynaptic neurons will acquire an action potential; involved in anxiety disorders, as well as bipolar disorder and other related conditions.

Gene Chromosomal structure encoding hereditary instructions for physical development.

Gray matter Tissue consisting primarily of neuronal cell bodies covering brain, spinal cord, and nerves.

Hippocampus Long, tube-like structure in brain's limbic system stretching from septal area into temporal lobe, responsible for emotion, learning, memory formation.

Hypersexuality State of increased sexual behavior, typically engaging in risky sexual behaviors, such as multiple partners, unprotected sex, impulsive and random sexual acts.

Hypomania State of elated mood, typically producing increased energy, confidence, happiness, or irritability, and decreased need for sleep, but without significant functional impairment of daily life activities.

Hypothalamus Structure in forebrain responsible for regulation of many visceral processes, like hunger, metabolism, temperature, thirst, and sex drive, also involved in generation of behaviors including emotions and motivation; regulator of all endocrine glands.

Immune system Body's defensive network against infection by invading microorganisms, like viruses, and against foreign substances, like drugs and toxins.

Impulsivity Tendency to act without thinking through about consequences.

Indolamines Biogenic amines that have both an indole ring and an amine group chemical structure, like serotonin and tryptophan.

Interpersonal therapy (IPT) Psychotherapeutic treatment to modulate interpersonal triggers for emotional, behavioral, or mental symptoms.

Irritability Emotional state in which one is easily aggressive or angered; in those with bipolar disorder may manifest as hostility, rage, or sarcasm, typically out of proportion to stimuli.

Limbic system Interconnected brain structures controlling emotions, memories, and motivation; includes amygdala, hypothalamus, and septum.

Lithium A mineral salt used to medicate symptoms of depression and mania associated with bipolar disorder.

Locus coeruleus Region in brain stem associated with fear and anxiety.

Maintenance therapy Any treatment intended to prevent symptom recurrence.

Major depressive disorder (MDD) Mental condition characterized by persistent symptoms of low mood, feelings of guilt, hopelessness, sadness, loss of interest and of pleasure, often accompanied by loss of appetite, sleep, and weight.

Mania Very active, elated, or irritable emotional state, contextually inappropriate, often accompanied by excessive talking, racing thoughts, grandiosity, and lack of concern for negative consequences; typically resulting in impaired personal and social functioning, sometimes associated with psychotic symptoms.

Massage Alternative therapeutic modality based on manipulation of skin, muscles, and soft tissues.

Meditation Alternative therapeutic modality based on focused concentration of internal stimuli to attain state of greater focused attention and awareness.

Medulla Hindbrain region controlling blood pressure, breathing, heart rate, and other vital functions.

Mental illness Any psychiatric disorder characterized by abnormal emotions, moods, thoughts, or behaviors.

Meridians Pathways of subtle energy said to flow throughout the body with hundreds of points along them used in techniques like acupuncture and shiatsu.

Mesolimbic system Interconnected brain system controlled by dopamine and running from ventral tegmental to nucleus accumbens and responsible for reward.

Misuse Consumption of any drug in any manner or for any purpose other than recommended or prescribed by a health care professional.

Mixed mood Emotional state characterized by coexisting symptoms of depression and mania.

Monoamine oxidase inhibitors (MAOIs) Medications that inhibit enzymes that break down neurotransmitters, like dopamine and serotonin, thereby increasing their levels.

Monozygotic twins Genetically identical twins developed from one fertilized egg.

Mood Pervasive and sustained emotional state that dominates an individual's perception of reality, such as anger, anxiety, depression, or elation; also referred to as affect.

Mood disorder Condition in which individual experiences extremes of mood for extended periods of time, can switch from one extreme mood to another as in bipolar disorder.

Myelin sheath Fatty, white lipid and protein protective covering around some axons; provides white matter for brain and spinal cord and helps accelerate transmission of neural impulses.

Neural pathway Axons that travel together in bundles, also called fiber tracts or nerves.

Neuron Nerve cell in brain and rest of nervous system that transmits chemical and electrical impulses.

Neurotransmitter Chemical substance that enables signal transmission of messages between neurons and related structures, for example, GABA, norepinephrine, dopamine, and serotonin.

Norepinephrine Catecholamine adrenergic neurotransmitter, also referred to as noradrenalin, that among other things prepares for fight-or-flight during stress response, and helps regulate mood, learning, and sleep.

Omega-3s Substances found in foods like salmon, tuna, flaxseed, pecans, and walnuts, that have anti-inflammatory properties.

Oppositional defiant disorder Psychiatric condition characterized by persistent pattern of defiance, hostility, or uncooperation.

Phenotype Totality of physical characteristics and behaviors of an individual, based on interaction of genetics and environment.

Physical dependence Physiological state of adaptation resulting from chronic use of a substance, where tolerance is generally developed, and in which withdrawal symptoms typically manifest when use is dramatically reduced or ceased. It can occur with any type of chronic use, either appropriate or inappropriate use, of a substance.

Polydrug abuse Abuse of two or more drugs at the same general time.

Polygenetic hereditary Inheritance of a trait influenced by many genes, as opposed to a single gene.

Pons Part of brain stem situated between medulla and midbrain serving as bridge between right and left halves of cerebellum.

Postsynaptic potential Change in potential of a neuron's membrane that received transmission signal from another neuron.

Posttraumatic stress disorder (PTSD) Condition of disruptive and dysfunctional reactions after experiencing a traumatic event, sometimes including reliving experience through nightmare or with vivid memories.

Prefrontal cortex Brain region in frontal lobe; acts as controller for all cognitive functions, including focusing emotions, attention, problem-solving, and planning responses to threats and rewards.

Prescription abuse Use of a drug without a prescription, or use in any way other than prescribed; used interchangeably with non-medical use.

Psychoactive drug Any substance, licit or illicit, that acts on brain to produce a psychological effect.

Psychosis Mental state characterized by delusions and/or hallucinations, typically resulting in loss of contact with reality or inability to perform daily activities; individual may exhibit dangerous or vulnerable behaviors.

Psychostimulant Any substance which when administered increases arousal, blood pressure, heart rate, respiration, and so forth.

Putamen Large, lateral part of lenticular nucleus of corpus striatum.

Rapid cycling Aspect of bipolar disorder where individual has at least four mood episodes within a year.

Rational emotive therapy Psychotherapeutic approach developed by Albert Ellis as a way to help individuals to change their perceptions of stressors by identifying self-defeating, problem-causing thoughts.

Receptor Structure on surface of neuron (or on related structures that receive neural impulses like organs or muscles) allowing specific neurotransmitters or other substances, such as psychoactive drugs, to bind to it and thereby inhibit or activate it to create action potential.

Resilience Ability to overcome possible risk factors, in order to function adaptively despite potential negative circumstances.

Reuptake Processes that absorb neurotransmitters back into neurons after release.

Schizoaffective disorder Severe psychiatric disorder where manic or depressive episodes occur simultaneously as schizophrenic symptoms.

Schizophrenia Severe psychiatric disorder characterized by disturbed thinking, delusions, emotions, and perceptions not supported by reality, often accompanied by psychosis and psychological withdrawal.

Serotonin Indolamine neurotransmitter that serves as vasoconstrictor and also important in neurotransmission, sensory perception, moods, pain sensation, and sleep; actively involved in depression, as well as gastrointestinal activity.

Stress Nonspecific physiological response to a real or imagined threat or challenge.

Striatum Part of corpus striatum consisting of caudate nucleus and putamen.

Substantia nigra Large nucleus located in midbrain containing dark melanin pigmented cells and responsible for motor functions.

Substitution Practice of administering any substance with intent of replacing it for misuse or abuse of any drug.

Synapse Minute space at junction between two or more adjacent neurons where neurotransmission or inhibition of chemical signals occurs.

Thalamus Major relay station consisting of two egg-shaped lobes in inner part of cerebrum, responsible for integrative and sensory functions, except olfaction, and transmission of impulses to cerebrum for higher processing.

Tolerance Situation of adaptation where increasingly greater amounts of a substance are required to produce a similar effect experienced during earlier use with lower dose.

Transcranial magnetic stimulation (TMS) Therapeutic technique using electromagnet inserted near the scalp to deliver short energy bursts to stimulate neurons in the brain.

Twin study Research investigation that examines effects of hereditary and environmental variables.

Unipolar disorder Severe mood disorder of persistent low affect, also called major depressive disorder.

Use Consumption of any drug whether by legal or illegal means.

Vesicle Small sac-like structure of neuron containing a neurotransmitter or precursor substances.

White matter Tissue of brain, spinal cord, and nerves composed of neural tracts, essentially bundles of myelinated nerve fibers.

Withdrawal Unpleasant physical and psychological effects appearing when chronic use of substance one was habituated to is abruptly reduced or stopped; symptoms might include abdominal pain, convulsions, delirium, tremors, and vomiting; also emotional, intellectual, or physical retreat.

Yoga Alternative therapeutic systems from India intended to unite mind, body, and soul; the term "yoga" is derived from Sanskrit meaning union.

Directory of Resources

General Books

Aiken, C., & Phelps, J. (2017). *Bipolar, Not So Much: Understanding Your Mood Swings and Depression*. New York, NY: W. W. Norton & Company.

Atkins, C. (2007). *The Bipolar Disorder Answer Book: Answers to More than 275 of Your Most Pressing Questions*. Naperville, IL: Sourcebooks, Inc.

Austrian, S. G. (2005). *Mental Disorders, Medications, and Clinical Social Work*. New York, NY: Columbia University Press.

Birmaher, B. (2004). *New Hope for Children and Teens with Bipolar Disorder: Your Friendly, Authoritative Guide to Traditional and Complementary Solutions*. New York, NY: Three Rivers Press/Random House, Inc.

Bullmore, E. (2018). *The Inflamed Mind: A Radical New Approach to Depression*. New York, NY: Picador.

Burgess, W. (2006). *The Bipolar Handbook: Real-Life Questions with Up-to-Date Answers*. New York, NY: Avery/Penguin Group Inc.

Brynie, F. H. (2009). *Brain Sense: The Science of the Senses and How We Process the World around Us*. New York, NY: AMACOM/American Management Association.

Caponigro, J. M., Lee, F. H., Johnson, S. I., & Kring, A. M. (2012). *Bipolar Disorder: A Guide for the Newly Diagnosed*. Oakland, CA: New Harbinger Publications.

Diler, R. S. (2007). *Pediatric Bipolar Disorder: A Global Perspective*. New York, NY: Nova Science Publishers.

Duckworth, K. (2022). *You Are Not Alone: The NAMI Guide to Navigating Mental Health*. New York, NY: Zando.

Fieve, R. R. (2006). *Bipolar II: Enhance Your Highs, Boost Your Creativity and Escape the Cycles of Recurrent Depression*. New York, NY: Rodale.

Fieve, R. R. (2009). *Bipolar Breakthrough: The Essential Guide to Going beyond Moodswings to Harness Your Highs, Escape the Cycles of Recurrent Depression and Thrive with Bipolar II*. New York, NY: Rodale.

Findling, R. L., Kowatch, R. A., & Post, R. M. (2003). *Pediatric Bipolar: A Handbook for Clinicians*. London: Martin Dunitz Ltd./Taylor & Francis Group.

Fink, C., & Kraynak, J. (2005). *Bipolar Disorders for Dummies*. Hoboken, NJ: Wiley Publishing, Inc.

Fristad, M. A., Arnold, J. S. G., & Leffler, J. M. (2011). *Psychotherapy for Children with Bipolar and Depressive Disorders*. New York, NY: Guilford Press.

Geller, B., & DelBello, M. P. (Eds.) (2003). *Bipolar Disorder in Childhood and Early Adolescence*. New York, NY: The Guilford Press.

Gold, M. S. (1987). *The Good News about Depression: Cures and Treatments in the New Age of Psychiatry*. New York, NY: Villard Books.

Gold, P. W. (2023). *Breaking through Depression: A Guide to the Next Generation of Promising Research and Revolutionary New Treatments*. New York, NY: Twelve/Hatchette Book Group.

Goodwin, G., & Sachs, G. S. (2010). *Fast Facts-Bipolar Disorder*. Basel, CH: S. Karger AG.

Kowatch, R. A., Fristad, M. A., Findling, R. L., & Post, R. M. (2009). *Clinical Manual for Management of Bipolar Disorder in Children and Adolescents*. Arlington, VA: American Psychiatric Publishing, Inc.

Kraepelin, E. (1921). *Manic-Depressive Insanity and Paranoia*. Edinburgh: Livingstone.

Marohn, S. (2011). *The Natural Medicine Guide to Bipolar Disorder*. Newburyport, MA: Hampton Roads Publishing.

Miklowitz, D. J. (2008). *Bipolar Disorder: A Family-Focused Treatment Approach*. New York, NY: Guilford Press.

Mondimore, F. M. (1995). *Depression: The Mood Disorder*. Baltimore, MD: Johns Hopkins University Press.

O'Connor, R. (1999). *Undoing Depression: What Therapy Doesn't Teach You and Medication Can't Give You*. New York, NY: Berkley Books.

Palolos, D., & Papolos, J. (2006). *The Bipolar Child: The Definitive and Reassuring Guide to Childhood's Most Misunderstood Disorder*. New York, NY: Broadway Books.

Papolos, D. F., & Papolos, J. (1988). *Overcoming Depression*. Mount Vernon, NY: Consumers Union.

Shatkin, J. P. (2024). *Child and Adolescent Mental Health*. New York, NY: W. W. Norton & Company.

White, R. C. (2014). *Preventing Bipolar Relapse: A Lifestyle Program to Help You Maintain a Balanced Mood and Live Well*. Oakland, CA: New Harbinger Publications.

White, R. C., & Preston, J. D. (2009). *Bipolar 101: A Practical Guide to Identifying Triggers, Managing Medications, Coping with Symptoms, and More*. Oakland, CA: New Harbinger Publications.

Guides for Families and Friends

Burgess, W. (2008). *The Bipolar Handbook for Children, Teens, and Families: Real-Life Questions with Up-to-Date Answers*. New York, NY: Avery/ Penguin Group Inc.

Evans, D. L., Benton, T. D., & Ellison, K. (2023). *If Your Adolescent Has Bipolar Disorder: An Essential Resource for Parents*. Oxford: Oxford University Press.

Fast, J. A., & Preston, J. (2012). *Loving Someone with Bipolar Disorder: Understanding and Helping Your Partner*. Oakland, CA: New Harbinger Publications.

Fast, J. A., & Preston, J. (2023). *Take Charge of Bipolar Disorder: A 4-Step Plan for You and Your Loved Ones to Manage the Illness and Create Lasting Stability*. New York, NY: Balance/Hachette Book Group.

Last, C. G. (2009). *When Someone You Love Is Bipolar: Help and Support for You and Your Partner*. New York, NY: Guilford Press.

Lowe, C., & Cohen, B. M. (2010). *Living with Someone Who's Living with Bipolar Disorder: A Practical Guide for Family, Friends and Coworkers*. San Francisco, CA: Jossey-Bass/John Wiley & Sons.

Lynn, G. T. (2000). *Survival Strategies for Parenting Children with Bipolar Disorder: Innovative Parenting and Counseling Techniques for Helping Children with Bipolar Disorder and the Conditions That May Occur with It*. Philadelphia, PA: Jessica Kingsley Publishers.

Miklowitz, D. J. (2019). *The Bipolar Disorder Survival Guide: What You and Your Family Need to Know*. New York, NY: The Guilford Press.

Miklowitz, D. J., & George, E. L. (2008). *The Bipolar Teen: What You Can Do to Help Your Child and Your Family*. New York, NY: Guilford Press.

Mondimore, F. M. (2014). *Bipolar Disorder: A Guide for Patients and Families*. Baltimore, MD: Johns Hopkins University Press.

Mondimore, F. M., & Kelly, P. (2015). *Adolescent Depression: A Guide for Parents*. Baltimore, MD: Johns Hopkins University Press.

Pavuluri, M. (2008). *What Works for Bipolar Kids: Help and Hope for Parents*. New York, NY: The Guilford Press.

Personal Accounts

Chang, D. (2020). *Eat a Peach: A Memoir*. New York, NY: Clarkson Potter/Crown Publishing.

Cheney, T. (2009). *Manic: A Memoir*. New York, NY: William Morrow.

Dougherty, K. (2008). *Less Than Crazy: Living with Bipolar II*. Cambridge, MA: Da Capo Lifelong Books.

Duke, P., & Hochman, G. (2010). *A Brilliant Madness: Living with Manic-Depressive Illness*. New York, NY: Bantam Books.

Dunn, A. (2022). *Burn Rate: Launching a Startup and Losing My Mind*. Sydney, AU: Currency.

Fisher, C. (2009). *Wishful Drinking*. New York, NY: Simon and Schuster.

Forney, E. (2018). *Rock Steady: Brilliant Advice from My Bipolar Life*. Seattle, WA: Fantagraphics Books.

George, H., J. (2019). *Yellow Tulips: One Woman's Quest for Hope and Healing in the Darkness of Bipolar Disorder*. Hendersonville, NC: Cheerful Word.

Hamilton, C. (2004). *Broken Open*. New York, NY: Bantam/Penguin Random House.

Hamilton, C. (2012). *A Better Life*. New York, NY: Allen and Unwin.

Hamilton, S. (2015). *All the Things We Ever Knew*. New York, NY: Seal Press/Hachette Book Group.

Hines, K. (2023). *The Art of Being Broken: How Story Telling Saves Lives*. Nashville, TN: Post Hill Press.

Hornbacher, M. (2008). *Madness: A Bipolar Life*. New York, NY: Houghton Mifflin.

Ikpi, B. (2019). *I'm Telling the Truth; but I'm Lying: Essays*. New York, NY: Harper Perennial/HarperCollins Publishers.

Jamison, K.R. (1995). *An Unquiet Mind: A Memoir of Moods and Madness*. New York, NY: Vintage/Penguin Random House.

Jones, P. E. (2008). *The Up and Down Life: The Truth about Bipolar Disorder—The Good, the Bad, and the Funny*. New York, NY: TarcherPerigee/Penguin Group Inc.

Lowe, J. (2017). *Mental: Lithium, Love and Losing My Mind*. New York, NY: Blue Ridge Press/Penguin Random House.

Lyden, J. (1997). *Daughter of the Queen of Sheba: A Memoir*. Boston, MA: Houghton Mifflin.

Martin, G. F. (2023). *Bipolar General: My Forever War with Mental Illness*. Annapolis, MD: Naval Institute Press.

McDermott, Z. (2017). *Gorilla and the Bird: A Memoir of Madness and a Mother's Love*. Boston, MA: Little, Brown and Company.

Miller, B. (2021). *Dining in the Dark: A Famed Restaurant Critic's Struggle with and Triumph Over Depression*. New York, NY: Skyhorse.

Moezzi, M. (2014). *Haldol and Hyacinths: A Bipolar Life*. New York, NY: Avery/Penguin Random House.

Nielsen, E. (2018). *Sound Mind: My Bipolar Journey from Chaos to Composure*. Tampa, FL: Trigger.

Peck, J. (2016). *Bulletproof*. Cupertino, CA: iBooks.

Steadman, K. A. (2008). *The Bipolar Expeditionist*. Bloomington, IN: iUniverse/Writer's Club Press.

Articles

Abe, C., Liberg, B., Klahn, A. L., Petrovic, P., & Landen, M. (2023). Mania-Related Effects on Structural Brain Changes in Bipolar Disorder: A Narrative Review of the Evidence. *Molecular Psychiatry 28*(7), 2674–82.

Akiskal, H. S., Azorin, J. M., & Hantouche, E. G. (2003). Proposed Multidimensional Structure of Mania: Beyond the Euphoric-Dysphoric Dichotomy. *Journal of Affective Disorders 73*, 7–18.

Angst, J., Gasmma, A., Benazzi F., Ajdacic, V., Eich, D., & Rossler, W. (2003). Toward a Re-definition of Subthreshold Bipolarity: Epidemiology and Proposed Criteria for Bipolar-II, Minor Bipolar Disorders and Hypomania. *Journal of Affective Disorders 73*, 133–46.

Baldessarini, R. J. (2000). A Plea for Integrity of the Bipolar Disorder Concept. *Bipolar Disorders 2*, 3–7.

Biederman, J., Faraone, S. V., Woznoiak, J., et al. (2005). Clinical Correlates of Bipolar Disorder in a Large, Referred Sample of Children and Adolescents. *Journal of Psychiatric Research 39*, 611–22.

Biederman, J., Faraone, S. V., Woznoiak, J., Mick, E., Kwon, A., & Aleardi, M. (2005). Further Evidence of Unique Developmental Phenotypic Correlates of Pediatric Bipolar Disorder: Findings from a Large Sample of Clinically Referred Preadolescent Children Assessed Over the Last 7 Years. *Journal of Affective Disorders 82*, S45–S58.

Cardno, A. G., & Owen, M. J. (2014). Genetic Relationships between Schizophrenia, Bipolar Disorder, and Schizoaffective Disorder. *Schizophrenia Bulletin 40*(3), 504–15.

Carlson, G. A. (2011). Will the Child with Mania Please Stand Up? *British Journal of Psychiatry 198*, 171–2.

Carlson, G. A., & Youngstrom, E. A. (2003). Clinical Implications of Pervasive Manic Symptoms in Children. *Biological Psychiatry 53*, 1050–8.

Casarez, R. L., Johnson, C. M., Soares, J. C., & Meyer, T. D. (2024). Use of a Virtual Environment to Promote Self-Management as Lifestyle Changes in Persons with Bipolar Disorder. *Archives of Psychiatric Nursing 49*, 73–82.

Chang, K., Saxena, K., & Howe, M. (2006). An Open-Label Study of Lamotrigine Adjunct or Monotherapy for the Treatment of Adolescents with Bipolar Depression. *Journal of the American Academy of Child and Adolescent Psychiatry 45*, 298–304.

Chiu, C. D., Li, D. J., Hsieh, Y. C., Chou, L. S., Au, J., et al. (2024). Linking Childhood Trauma and Dissociation to Psychotic Symptoms in Major Depressive Disorder, Bipolar Disorder, and Schizophrenia: A Transdiagnostic Examination Using Patient and Clinician Ratings. *Psychological Trauma: Theory, Research, Practice, and Policy 16*(S.1), S242–S249.

Cordeiro, R. C., Lima, C. N. C., Fries, G. R., Zunta-Suares, G., Soares, J. C., Quevedo, J., & Scaini, G. (2023). Mitrochondrial Health Index Correlates with Plasma Circulating Cell-Free Mitrochondrial DNA in Bipolar Disorder. *Molecular Psychiatry 28*(11), 4622–31.

Craney, J. L., & Geller, B. (2003). A Prepubertal and Early Adolescent Bipolar Disorder-I Phenotype: Review of Phenomenology and Longitudinal Course. *Bipolar Disorders 5*, 243–56.

Dilsaver, S. C., & Akiskal, H. S. (2004). Preschool-Onset Mania: Incidence, Phenomenology and Family History. *Journal of Affective Disorders 82*, S35–S43.

Faedda, G. L., Baldessarini, R. J., Glovinsky, I. P., & Austin, N. B. (2004). Treatment-Emergent Mania in Pediatric Bipolar Disorder: A Retrospective Case Review. *Journal of Affective Disorders 82*, 149–58.

Fang, M., Fan, Z., Liu, S., Zhu H., Yin, D., Jia, H., & Wang, G. (2023). Preventive Interventions for Individuals and Risk of Developing Bipolar Disorder: A Systematic Review and Meta-Analysis. *Journal of Affective Disorders 340*, 53–63.

Faraone, S. V., Glatt, S. J., & Tsuang, M. T. (2003). The Genetics of Pediatric-Onset Bipolar Disorder. *Biological Psychiatry 53*, 970–7.

Findling, R. L., Youngstrom, E. A., Fristad, M. A., Birmaher, B., Kowatch, R. A., Arnold, L. E., et al. (2010). Characteristics of Children with Elevated Symptoms of Mania: The Longitudinal Assessment of Manic Symptoms (LAMS) Study. *Journal of Clinical Psychiatry 71*, 1664–72.

Gee, D.G. (2022). Neurodevelopmental Mechanisms Linking Early Experiences and Mental health: Translating Science to Promote Well-Being among Youth. *American Psychologist 77*(9), 1033–45.

Geller, B., Tillman, R., Craney, J., L., & Bolhofner, K. (2004). Four-Year Prospective Outcome and Natural History of Mania in Children with a Prepubertal and Early Adolescent Bipolar Disorder Phenotype. *Archives of General Psychiatry 61*, 459–67.

Goldstein, B. I., Shamseddeen, W., Axelson, D. A., Kalas, C., Monk, K., Brent, D. A., et al. (2010). Clinical, Demographic, and Familial Correlates of Bipolar Spectrum Disorders among Offspring of Parents with Bipolar Disorder. *Journal of the American Academy of Child and Adolescent Psychiatry 49*, 388–96.

Gram, L. F., & Rafaelsen, O. J. (1972). Lithium Treatment of Psychotic Children and Adolescents. *Acta Psychiatria Scandinavia 48*, 253–260.

Harrington, R., & Myatt, T. (2003). Is Preadolescent Mania the Same Condition as Adult Mania? A British Perspective. *Biological Psychiatry 53*, 961–9.

Jairam, R., Srinath, S., Girimaji, S. C., & Seshadri, S. P. (2004). A Prospective 4-5 Year Follow-Up of Juvenile Onset of Bipolar Disorder. *Bipolar Disorders 6*, 386–94.

Kafantaris, V., Coletti, D. J., Dicker, R., Padula, G., & Kane, J. M. (2003). Lithium Treatment of Acute Mania in Adolescents: A Large Open Trial. *Journal of the American Academy of Child and Adolescent Psychiatry 42*, 1038–45.

Kendley, K. S., Ohlsson, H., Sundquist, S., & Sundquist, K. (2024). The Relationship Between Familial-genetic Risk in a Swedish National Sample of Patients with Major Depression, Bipolar Depression, and Schizophrenia. *Molecular Psychiatry 29*(3), 742–9.

Kim, H., McInnis, M. G., & Sperry, S. H. (2024). Longitudinal Dynamics Between Anxiety and Depression in Bipolar Spectrum Disorders. *Journal of Psychopathology and Clinical Science 133*(2), 129–39.

Kowatch, R. A., Fristad, M. A., Birmaher, B., Wagner, K. D., Findling, R. L., & Hellander, M. (2005). Treatment Guidelines for Children and Adolescents with Bipolar Disorder. *Journal of the American Academy of Child and Adolescent Psychiatry 44*, 213–35.

Kozloff, N., Cheung, A. H., Schaffer, A., Cairney, J., Dewa, C. S., Veldhuizen, S., et al. (2010). Bipolar Disorder Among Adolescents and Young Adults: Results from an Epidemiological Sample. *Journal of Affective Disorders 125*, 350–4.

Leibenluft, E. (2011). Severe Mood Dysregulation, Irritability, and the Diagnostic Boundaries of Bipolar Disorder in Youths. *American Journal of Psychiatry 168*, 129–42.

Leibenluft, E., Charney, D. S., Towbin, K. E., Bhangoo, R. K., & Pine, D. S. (2003). Defining Clinical Phenotypes of Juvenile Mania. *American Journal of Psychiatry 160*, 430–7.

Li, M., Wu, Y., Zheng, N., Liu, X., Cai, A., Zheng, D., et al. (2024). In Vivo Imaging of Astrocytes in the Whole Brain with Engineered AAVs and Diffusion-Weighted, Magnetic Resonance Imaging. *Molecular Psychiatry 29*(3), 545–52.

McClellan, J. (2005). Commentary: Treatment Guidelines for Child and Adolescent Bipolar Disorder. *Journal of the American Academy of Child and Adolescent Psychiatry 44*, 236–9.

Merikangas, K. R., Cui, L., Kattan, G., Carlson, G. A., Youngstrom, E. A., & Angst, J. (2012). Mania with and without Depression in a Community Sample of US Adolescents. *Archives of General Psychiatry 69*, 943–51.

Mulder, D., & Aarts, E. (2023). A Systematic Review Exploring the Association Between the Human Gut Microbiota and Brain Connectivity in Health and Disease. *Molecular Psychiatry 29*(12), 5037–61.

Muscatewll, K. A., Alvarez, G. M., Bonar, A. S., Cardenas, M. N., Galvan, M. J., Merritt, C. C., & Starks, M. D. (2022). Brain-body Pathways Linking Racism and Health. *American Psychologist 77*(9), 1049–60.

Numberger, J. L., Jr., & Foroud, T. (2000). Genetics of Bipolar Affective Disorder. *Current Psychiatry Reports 2*, 147–57.

Parker, N., Cheng, W., Hindley, G. F. L., Parekh, P., Shadrin, A. A., Maximov, I. I., et al. (2023). Psychiatric Disorders and Brain White Matter Exhibit Genetic Overlap Implicating Developmental and Nerve Cell Biology. *Molecular Psychiatry 29*(11), 4924–32.

Pavuluri, M. N, Herbener, E. S., & Sweeney, J. A. (2004). Psychotic Symptoms in Pediatric Bipolar Disorder. *Journal of Affective Disorders 80*, 19–28.

Picardi, A. (2009). Rating Scales in Bipolar Disorder. *Current Opinion in Psychiatry 22*(1), 42–9.

Sigurdsson, E., Fombonne, E., Sayal, K., & Checkley, S. (1999). Neurodevelopmental Antecedents of Early-Onset Bipolar Affective Disorder. *British Journal of Psychiatry 174*, 121–7.

Singh, M. K., Gorelik, A. J., Stave, C., & Gotlib, I. H. (2024). Genetics, Epigenetics, and Neurobiology of Childhood-Onset Depression: An Umbrella Review. *Molecular Psychiatry 29*(3), 553–65.

Soutullo, C. A., Chang, K. D., Diez-Suarez, A., Figueroa-Quintana, A., Escamilla-Canales, I., Rapado-Castro, M., & Ortuno, F. (2005). Bipolar Disorder in Children and Adolescents: International Perspective on Epidemiology and Phenomenology. *Bipolar Disorders 7*(6), 497–506.

Stolberg, V. B. (1995). Awareness of Mental Illness as a Disability. *ECC Observer 27*(6), 4.

Stolberg, V. B. (1999). Mental Health Matters. *ECC Observer 30*(5), 12.

Stolberg, V. B. (2000). Serving Students with Disability in a Higher Education Setting. *National Social Science Perspectives Journal 16*(2), 146–54.

Stolberg, V. B. (2005). Issues of Mental Health. *ECC Observer 38*, 21.

Stolberg, V. B. (2014a). Delirium (Cultural Comparisons). In A. Scull (Ed.), *Cultural Sociology of Mental Illness* (Vol. *1*, pp. 179–81). Thousand Oaks, CA: SAGE Publications

Stolberg, V. B. (2014b). Melancholia (Cultural Comparisons). In A. Scull (Ed.), *Cultural Sociology of Mental Illness* (Vol. *1*, pp. 507–8). Thousand Oaks, CA: SAGE Publications.

Stolberg, V. B. (2022). Mood Disorders. In J.M. Duquaine-Watson (Ed.), *Women's Health: Understanding Issues and Influences* (Vol. *2*, pp. 447–51). Santa Barbara, CA: Greenwood/ ABC-CLIO, LLC.

Tartt, A., Mariani, M., Hen, R., Mann, J. J., & Boldrini, M. (2024). Electroconvulsive Therapy- A Shocking Inducer of Neuroplasticity. *Molecular Psychiatry 29*(1), 35–7.

Taylor, L., Faraone, S. V., & Tsuang, M. T. (2002). Family, Twin, and Adoption Studies of Bipolar Disease. *Current Psychiatry Reports 4*, 130–3.

Van Meter, A. R., Moreira, A. L., & Youngstrom, E. A. (2011). Meta-Analysis of Epidemiologic Studies of Pediatric Bipolar Disorder. *Journal of Clinical Psychiatry 72*, 1250–6.

Vieta, E., & Suppes, T. (2008). Bipolar II Disorder: Arguments for and against a Distinct Entity. *Bipolar Disorders 10*, 163–78.

Wagner, K. D. (2004). Diagnosis and Treatment of Bipolar Disorder in Children and Adolescents. *Journal of Clinical Psychiatry 65*(Sup. 15), 30–4.

Wei, W., Deng, L., Qiao, C., Yin, Y., Zhang, Y., Li, X., et al. (2023). Neural Variability in Three Major Psychiatric Disorders. *Molecular Psychiatry 29*(12), 5217–27.

Yolken, R. (2023). Infections and Neuropsychiatric Disorders: New Studies Document Pathways to Prevention and Treatment. *Molecular Psychiatry 28*(7), 2624–6.

Youngstrom, E. A., Birmaher, B., & Findling, R. L. (2008). Pediatric Bipolar Disorder: Validity, Phenomenology, and Recommendations for Diagnosis. *Bipolar Disorders 10*, 194–214.

Youngstrom, E. A., Freeman, A. J., & Jenkins, M. M. (2008). The Assessment of Children and Adolescents with Bipolar Disorder. *Child & Adolescent Psychiatric Clinics 18*(2), 353–90.

Youngstrom, E. A., Youngstrom, J. K., & Starr, M. (2005). Bipolar Diagnoses in Community Mental Health: Achenbach Child Behavior Checklist Profiles and Patterns of Comorbidity. *Biological Psychiatry 58*, 569–75.

Organizations

American Academy of Child & Adolescent Psychiatry (AACAP)
36125 Wisconsin Avenue, N.W.
Washington, DC 20016-3007
(202) 966-7300
https://aacap.org/

AACAP is a professional association of child and adolescent psychiatrists devoted to improving mental health treatment.

American Foundation for Suicide Prevention (AFSP)
AFSP National Office
199 Water Street- 11th floor
New York, NY 10038
(888) 333-AFSP (2377)
https://afsp.org/

AFSP is a voluntary health organization advocating for education and research on suicide.

American Psychiatric Association
800 Maine Avenue SW- Suite 900
Washington, DC 20024
(202) 559-3900
https://www.psychiatry.org/

Publishes the DSM-5 and other professional clinical resources.

American Psychological Association (APA)
750 First Street NE
Washington, DC 20002-4242
(800) 374-2721
https://www.apa.org/

APA is a leading authority on psychotherapeutic approaches to mental health.

Centers for Disease Control and Prevention (CDC)
1600 Clifton Road
Atlanta, GA 30329
(800) CDV-INFO [800-233-4636]
https://www.cdc.gov/

US government agency charged with protecting America from health, safety, and security threats. To do this, CDC conducts research and provides health information, including that related to bipolar disorder.

Depressives Anonymous
329 East 62nd Street
New York, NY 10021
(212) 689-2600

Self-help groups for those with depressive illnesses.

Food and Drug Administration
10903 New Hampshire Avenue
Silver Spring, MD 20993
(888) INFO-FDA [888-463-6332]
https://www.fda.gov/

US federal agency responsible for review and approval of medications and other medical devices, including those for managing and treating bipolar disorder, in order to protect public health by assuring drugs and foods are properly labeled and sanitary. For drugs and medical devices, the FDA is responsible for ensuring they are safe and effective.

International Bipolar Foundation
1050 Rosecrans Street- Suite M
San Diego, CA 92106
(888) 598-5967
https://www.ibpf.org/

International organization devoted to supporting individuals with bipolar disorder and their families; concerned with reducing stigma.

International Foundation for Research and Education on Depression (iFred)
P. O. Box 17598
Baltimore, MD
http://www.iFred.org/

International organization devoted to preventing mood disorders and reducing stigma.

National Alliance on Mental Illness (NAMI)
3803 N Fairfax Drive- Suite 100
Arlington, VA 22203
(800)950-NAMI [800-950-6264]
https://www.nami.org/

NAMI offers information and sources of support for those affected by bipolar disorder and related conditions.

National Institute of Mental Health (NIMH)
6001 Executive Blvd- Rm. 6200, MSC 9663
Bethesda, MD 20892-9663
(866) 615-6464
https://www.nimh.nih.gov/

NIMH is a US government agency that publishes current information on symptoms, causes, and treatments for mental illnesses, including bipolar disorder.

Substance Abuse and Mental Health Services Administration (SAMHSA)
5600 Fishers Lane
Rockville, MD 20857
(877) SAMHSA-7 [877-726-4727]
https://www.samhsa.gov/

Federal agency under the US Dept. of Health & Human Services charged to improve availability and quality of substance abuse prevention, treatment, and mental health services, including for bipolar disorder.

Websites

American Public Health Association
https://www.apha.org/publications/Published-Books
Major website that presents information on public health policies from all levels of government.

Black Mental Wellness
https://www.blackmentalwellness.com/
Promotes initiatives for culturally responsive mental health care.

Child & Adolescent Bipolar Foundation
https://www.bpkids.org/
Global resources for families with children with bipolar disorder, including referrals and support groups.

Depression and Bipolar Support Alliance
https://www.dbsalliance.org/
Major resource for consumers and their families dealing with manic and other depressive illnesses.

International Society for Bipolar Disorders
https://www.isbd.org
Offers scientific information to foster international collaboration for education and research to advance treatment for bipolar disorder.

Juvenile Bipolar Research Foundation
https://jbrf.org/
Promotes professional discussion between clinical experts to advocate for families with children with bipolar disorder; focuses on educational concerns.

MedlinePlus
https://medlineplus.gov/bipolardisorder.html
Important government website to access medical research, including about bipolar disorder.

National Library of Medicine: PubMed
https://www.ncbi.nlm.nih.gov/ebtrez/query.fcgi
Comprehensive medical database to access medical research, including that related to bipolar disorder.

National Suicide Prevention Lifeline
(888) 628-9454 Text: 988 TTY Users: Dial 711 then 988
https://suicidepreventionlifeline.org/
Free and confidential emotional support for those in crisis.

Index

About the Author

Victor B. Stolberg, PhD, is Associate Professor/Counselor at Essex County College in Newark, New Jersey, where he previously directed the Office of Disability Support Services and the Office of the Substance Abuse Coordinator. He has delivered hundreds of professional papers, workshops, and other presentations in over twenty states across the country on myriad subjects, as well as a few internationally. He has authored 50 scholarly articles, 163 encyclopedia articles, 6 chapters and contributed papers, 13 technical reports, and 65 other miscellaneous publications, as well as several books including *Painkillers: History, Science, and Issues*; *ADHD Medications: History, Science, and Issues*; and *What You Need to Know about ADHD*. This amounts to a total of over 300 publications. Recent (2024) articles written by Dr. Stolberg include "Biomarkers for High Metabolic Burden in Neurologic Disease," "Issues Between Addiction and Gender," and "Stroke as a Lifestyle Disease." He holds three bachelor's degrees; nine master's degrees from Montclair State University, New Jersey Institute of Technology, Rutgers University, the State University of New York at Cortland, and the University of Buffalo; and, a Ph.D.; he has studied abroad in Germany, Greece, and Israel. Research interests include historical and cross-cultural studies of substance use and abuse, disabilities, ethnic patterns, and college student issues. He is actively involved in faculty governance and serves in a leadership role in the Faculty Association, as well as on many professional and civic organizations. He lives in Bloomfield, New Jersey with his wife and two sons, with whom he regularly travels to Europe and Africa.